How English Works

A grammar practice book

How English Works

A grammar practice book

Michael Swan & Catherine Walter

With answers

Oxford University Press

OXFORD
UNIVERSITY PRESS

Great Clarendon Street, Oxford OX2 6DP

Oxford University Press is a department of the University of Oxford.
It furthers the University's objective of excellence in research, scholarship,
and education by publishing worldwide in

Oxford New York

Auckland Cape Town Dar es Salaam Hong Kong Karachi
Kuala Lumpur Madrid Melbourne Mexico City Nairobi
New Delhi Shanghai Taipei Toronto

With offices in

Argentina Austria Brazil Chile Czech Republic France Greece
Guatemala Hungary Italy Japan Poland Portugal Singapore
South Korea Switzerland Thailand Turkey Ukraine Vietnam

OXFORD and OXFORD ENGLISH are registered trade marks of
Oxford University Press in the UK and in certain other countries

ISBN-13: 978 0 19 431456 5 (with answers)

ISBN-13: 978 0 19 431457 2 (without answers)

Typeset by Tradespools Ltd, Frome, Somerset
in Monotype Photina and Franklin Gothic

Printed in China

ACKNOWLEDGEMENTS

Designed by Richard Morris, Stonesfield Design, Oxfordshire

Paintings by David Downton
Drawings on page 129 by pupils in Year 1 of Stonesfield School, Oxfordshire
Map on page 145 by Neil Gower, Allez Studios, Brighton

In writing this book the authors obtained information from the British
National Corpus. The British National Corpus is a collaborative initiative
carried out by Oxford University Press as a Lead Partner, Longman,
Chambers Harrap, Oxford University Computing Services, Lancaster
University's Unit for Computer Research in the English Language, and the
British Library.

Contents

Authors' acknowledgements

We could not have produced this book without several kinds of help. In particular, we would like to express our gratitude to:

- Keith Brown, Brian Graver and Diann Gruber, for their care in reading the original typescript: their comments and suggestions have resulted in many important improvements

- Inge Bullock and Barbara Hately-Broad, for organising our personal and professional lives while we were doing the writing

- our children Mark and Helen, for putting up with us while it was going on

- Stewart Melluish of Oxford University Press and Richard Morris, our editor and designer, for the expertise, creativity, patience and good humour with which they handled us and the typescript.

Publisher's acknowledgements

The Publisher thanks the following for their kind permission to reproduce cartoons:

André Deutsch Ltd: p. 224, from *Modern Times* by Mel Calman (© Mel Calman 1988); S and C Calman: pp. 30, 137 (© S and C Calman); Encyclopaedia Britannica International Ltd: p. 111, *Britannica Yearbook of Science and the Future 1995* (© 1996 by Sidney Harris); Mirror Syndication International: pp. 55, 142, 210, 252 (© Mirror Group Newspapers); The New Yorker Magazine Inc.: pp. 24 (Dana Fradon), 78 (Vietor), 82 (Gahan Wilson), 115 (Drucker), 116 (Mankoff), 138 (M Stevens), 143 (Gahan Wilson), 226 (Barsotti), 250 (Joseph Farris); *Private Eye*: pp. 39 (Nick Newman), 175 (Michael Heath), 187 (Michael Heath), 244 (Ken Pyne); Punch Cartoon Library: pp. 27, 29, 34, 37, 47, 49, 55, 57, 60, 67, 75, 87, 88, 89, 94, 96, 98, 101, 105, 107, 108, 110, 117, 123, 125, 131, 135, 136, 151, 153, 155, 171, 174, 175, 177, 193, 203, 216, 218, 223, 232, 234, 235, 245, 253, 254, 255, 256, 261, 263, 266, 273, 274, 282, 286, 291, 295; Solo Syndication Ltd: pp. 49, 55, 146, 158, 215 (© Associated Newspapers Ltd); *The Spectator*: pp. 27, 33, 37, 65, 67, 73, 125, 132, 134, 143, 146, 148, 158, 192, 199, 213, 219, 221; The Tessa Sayle Agency: pp. 47, 96, 183, 195 (© R Searle 1948, 1951, 1944, 1944).

The Publisher thanks the following for their kind permission to use extracts and adaptations from copyright material:

Clarks and McCann Erikson (Manchester) Ltd: p. 71, Springers advertisement 'Feel like you're in Paradise', from *Life* magazine, *The Observer*, 7 May 1995; *Didcot Herald*: pp. 64, headline 'Football club burglars cut home phones', 29 September 1994, 73, advertisements 'Wonderful, tall energetic guy, ...', 2 June 1994 and 'Wood Street', 2 June 1994, 178, extract 'A driver has been sent to jail ...', 27 January 1994; Dorling Kindersley Ltd: p. 173, extract from *Chronicle of the 20th Century* (Longman, © Jacques Legrand S A International Publishing, Paris); David Higham Associates: p. 112, abridged extract from *Under Milk Wood* by Dylan Thomas (J M Dent, 1954, 1955, © Dylan Thomas Trustees); *The Independent*: p. 64, headlines 'Channel ferry safety drill' (James Cusick), 26 September 1994, and 'Decision day in rail dispute' (Barrie Clement), 27 September 1994; International Music Publications Ltd: p. 121, extract from the lyric 'What shall I say?' by Peter Tinturin (© 1973 Chappell & Co. Inc., USA, Warner/Chappell Music Ltd, London W1Y 3FA); Penguin Books: p. 218, Potato Pancake recipe from *Father in the Kitchen* by Bruce Beeby (Michael Joseph, 1977, © Bruce Beeby 1977); Peters Fraser & Dunlop: pp. 141, extracts from *The General* by C S Forester (Penguin, 1936, © C S Forester Estate), 225, *Modern Humour* by E M Delafield (Everyman's Library Ltd, © E M Delafield's estate), 241, *The Two Brothers* by V S Pritchett from *The Complete Short Stories* (Chatto & Windus, © V S Pritchett 1990), 297, *Three Rusty Nails* by Roger McGough from *In the Glassroom* (Jonathan Cape Ltd, © Roger McGough 1976); James Thurber Literary Estate: p. 173, adapted extract from 'The Little Girl and the Wolf', *Fables For Our Time* (HarperCollins, © 1940 James Thurber, © 1968 Rosemary A Thurber); Ed Victor Ltd: p. 165, adapted extract from *Playback* by Raymond Chandler (Hamish Hamilton, 1958, © Raymond Chandler 1958, Estate of Raymond Chandler); Witt, Thomas Productions: p. 210, transcription from an episode of the American TV serial *Soap* (© Witt, Thomas Productions); Writer's Digest Books: p. 269, extract from *Who wrote that song?* by Dick and Harriet Jacobs (Writer's Digest Books, Cincinnati, Ohio, © Harriet Jacobs 1994).

Every effort has been made to trace the owners of copyright material used in this book, but we should be pleased to hear from any copyright holder whom we have been unable to contact.

Introduction

The purpose of the book

How English Works is for learners of English who want to speak and write more correctly. It contains:

- short clear explanations of the rules of English grammar
- examples of correct use
- exercises.

How to use the book

If you are studying with a teacher, he or she will help you to use the book effectively. If you are studying at home, the following suggestions may be useful:

- Don't go through the whole book from beginning to end. *How English Works* contains explanations of basic rules (e.g. how to make questions), intermediate points (e.g. the use of passives) and more advanced problems (e.g. difficult structures with *who, whom* and *which*). Different learners will need to study different parts of the book.

- Start by trying the tests on pages 4–9. These will help you to decide what you need to learn – what are the most important problems in English grammar *for you*.

- Use the list of sections (at the beginning) and the Index (at the end) to help you find the sections that you want. Read the explanations and do the exercises. If you still have problems with a point, work through the section again.

- You will sometimes need to know some of the words that we use when we talk about grammar in English (e.g. *verb, preposition, tense, plural, countable*). These words are explained on pages 298–302.

The explanations

We have tried to make these as clear and simple as possible. You can find more complete explanations of some points in Michael Swan's book *Practical English Usage* (Oxford University Press).

Sometimes we ask you to try to work out a rule for yourself. When you have tried these 'Do It Yourself' activities, you can look at the blue pages (303–305) at the back of the book to see if you were right.

The exercises

Most of the exercises are simple in structure. More difficult exercises are marked with the sign ▲.

A few exercises are designed for group work in class.

What kind of English does the book teach?

We teach the grammar of everyday spoken and written British English. We have used the British National Corpus – a collection of 100 million words of modern spoken and written English – to help us make sure that our rules and examples give a true picture of the present-day language.

For information about differences between British and American English, see *Practical English Usage*.

How important is grammar?

Grammar is not the most important thing in the world, but if you make a lot of mistakes you may be more difficult to understand, and some kinds of people may look down on you or not take you seriously. Hardly anybody speaks or writes a foreign language perfectly, but you will communicate more successfully if you can make your English reasonably correct. We hope this book will help.

Test yourself

These tests will help you to decide what you need to learn. First of all, try the 'basic points' test on pages 4–5 and check your answers on page 11. If you have problems with any of the points, go to the sections where these are explained and do the exercises; then try the test again. The tests on pages 6–9 are suitable for intermediate and advanced students, and can be done in the same way.

Test yourself: basic points

Here are some of the basic grammar points from *How English Works*. Do you
know them all? Check your answers on page 11.

Choose the correct answer(s). One or more answers may be correct.

1 She's ... university teacher.
A a   B an   C the   D one

2 I like ... small animals.
A the   B — (= *nothing*)   C every   D all

3 Is this coat ... ?
A yours   B your   C the yours

4 Is Diana ... ?
A a friend of yours   B a your friend   C your friend

5 Who are ... people over there?
A that   B the   C these   D those

6 ... is your phone number?
A Which   B What   C How

7 Could I have ... drink?
A other   B an other   C another

8 There aren't ... for everybody.
A chairs enough   B enough chairs   C enough of chairs

9 They're ... young to get married.
A too much   B too   C very too

10 Most ... like travelling.
A of people   B of the people   C people

11 Ann and Peter phone ... every day.
A them   B themself   C themselves   D each other

12 It's ... weather.
A terrible   B a terrible   C the terrible

13 *The plural of* car *is* cars. *Which of these are correct plurals?*
A journeys   B ladys   C minuts   D sandwichs   E babies

14 *Which of these is/are correct?*
A happier   B more happier   C unhappier   D beautifuller

15 This is ... winter for 20 years.
A the more bad   B worse   C the worse   D worst
E the worst

16 She's much taller ... me.
A than   B as   C that

17 He lives in the same street ... me.
A that   B like   C as   D than

18 Her eyes ... a very light blue.
A are   B have   C has

19 ... help me?
A Can you to   B Do you can   C Can you

20 You ... worry about it.
A not must   B don't must   C must not   D mustn't

21 It ... again. It ... all the time here in the winter.
A 's raining, 's raining   B rains, rains
C rains, 's raining   D 's raining, rains

22 I ... she ... you.
A think, likes   B am thinking, is liking
C think, is liking   D am thinking, likes

23 Who ... the window?
A open   B opened   C did opened

24 Why ... ?
A those men are laughing
B are laughing those men
C are those men laughing

25 What ... ?
A does she want   B does she wants   C she wants

26 I didn't ... he was at home.
A to think   B think   C thinking   D thought

27 ... a hole in my sock.
A There's   B There is   C It's   D It is   E Is

28 I'll see you ... Tuesday afternoon.
A at   B on   C in

29 What time did you arrive ... the station?
A at   B to   C —

30 We're going ... the opera tomorrow night.
A at   B —   C in   D to

Test yourself: intermediate points

Here are some of the intermediate grammar points from *How English Works*.
Do you know them all? Check your answers on page 11.

Choose the correct answer(s). One or more answers may be correct.

31   I went out without ... money.
     A some   B any

32   He's got ... money.
     A much   B many   C a lot of   D lots of

33   'Who's there?' '... .'
     A It's me   B It is I   C Me   D I

34   Although he felt very ..., he smiled ... .
     A angrily, friendly   B angry, friendly   C angry, in a friendly way

35   I ... to America.
     A have often been   B often have been   C have been often

36   My mother ... my birthday.
     A always forgets   B always is forgetting   C forgets always

37   You look ... a teacher.
     A like   B as   C the same like

38   How many brothers and sisters ... ?
     A have you got   B do you have   C are you having

39   Good! I ... work tomorrow.
     A mustn't   B don't have to   C haven't got to

40   I ... smoke.
     A — (= *nothing*)   B use to   C used to

41   Andrew ... to see us this evening.
     A will come   B comes   C is coming

42   Alice ... have a baby.
     A will   B shall   C is going to

43   I knew that he ... waiting for somebody.
     A is   B was   C would

44   ... Gloria last week?
     A Have you seen   B Did you see   C Were you seeing

45   She's an old friend — I ... her ... years.
     A 've known, for   B know, for   C 've known, since
     D know, since

46　We met when we ... in France.
　　A studied　　　B were studying　　　C had studied

47　As soon as she came in I knew I ... her before.
　　A have seen　　　B saw　　　C had seen

48　This picture ... by a friend of my mother's.
　　A is painting　　B is painted　　C was painting　　D was painted

49　Can you ... ?
　　A make me some tea　　　B make some tea for me
　　C make for me some tea

50　Try ... be late.
　　A not to　　　B to not

51　I went to London ... clothes.
　　A for buy　　B for to buy　　C for buying　　D to buy

52　You can't live very long without ... .
　　A to eat　　B eat　　C eating　　D you eat

53　I enjoy ... , but I wouldn't like ... it all my life.
　　A to teach, to do　　B teaching, doing　　C to teach, doing
　　D teaching, to do

54　Her parents don't want ... married.
　　A her to get　　B her get　　C that she get　　D that she gets

55　I'm not sure what ...
　　A do they want?　　B do they want.　　C they want.

56　The policeman ... me not to park there.
　　A asked　　B said　　C told　　D advised

57　I ... you if you ... that again.
　　A hit, say　　B 'll hit, 'll say　　C hit, 'll say　　D 'll hit, say

58　It would be nice if we ... a bit more room.
　　A would have　　B had　　C have

59　If you ... me, I ... in real trouble last year.
　　A didn't help, would have been
　　B hadn't helped, would have been
　　C hadn't helped, would be
　　D didn't help, would be

60　There's the man ... took your coat.
　　A which　　B who　　C that　　D —

Test yourself: advanced points

Here are some of the more advanced grammar points from *How English Works*.
Do you know them all? Check your answers on page 11.

Choose the correct answer(s). One or more answers may be correct.

61 My family ... thinking of moving to Birmingham.
     A is   B are

62 We watched a ... on TV last night.
     A war film   B war's film   C film of war

63 He was wearing ... riding boots.
     A red old Spanish leather   B old leather red Spanish
     C old red Spanish leather   D Spanish red old leather

64 ... he gets, ...
     A The richer, the more friends he has
     B Richer, more he has friends
     C Richer, more friends he has
     D The richer, the more he has friends

65 It's ... if you take the train.
     A quicker   B the quicker   C quickest   D the quickest

66 He ... very annoying.
     A 's   B 's being

67 That ... be Roger at the door – it's too early.
     A can't   B mustn't   C couldn't

68 At last, after three days, they ... get to the top of the mountain.
     A could   B managed to   C succeeded to   D were able to

69 It was crazy to drive like that. You ... killed somebody.
     A may have   B might have   C could have   D can have

70 I wonder if John ... this evening.
     A will phone   B phones

71 Who ... you that ring?
     A 's given   B gave

72 He ... quite different since he ... married.
     A is, has got   B has been, has got   C is, got   D has been, got

73 This is the first time I ... a sports car.
     A 've driven   B 'm driving   C drive

74 On her birthday ... .
     A she was given a new car   B a new car was given to her

75 We can't use the sports hall yet because it ... .
     A is still built   B is still building   C is still being built

76 I look forward ... you soon.
A seeing   B to seeing   C to see

77 If you have trouble going to sleep, try ... a glass of milk before bedtime.
A drinking   B to drink   C drink

78 This is my friend Joe. I ... met, have you?
A don't think you've   B think you haven't

79 How ... !
A he works hard   B hard he works

80 *Which of these sentences are correct in spoken English?*
A Car's running badly.   B Seen Peter?
C Can't come in here, sorry.   D Careful what you say.
E Lost my glasses.   F Have heard of her.

81 Nobody phoned, did ... ?
A he   B she   C they   D it   E he or she   F anybody

82 If you were ever in trouble, I would give you all the help you ... .
A will need   B would need   C need   D needed

83 My wife will be upset ... .
A if I don't get back tomorrow   B unless I get back tomorrow

84 Tell me at once ... Margaret arrives.
A if   B when   C in case

85 It's time you ... home, but I'd rather you ... here.
A go, stay   B went, stayed   C go, stayed   D went, stay

86 I wish I ... more time.
A had   B have   C would have   D will have

87 John Hastings, ... , has just come to live in our street.
A that I was at school with   B I was at school with
C with who I was at school   D with whom I was at school

88 She keeps tapping her fingers, ... gets on my nerves.
A which   B what   C that which

89 Can you finish the job ... Friday?
A till   B until   C by   D for

90 There's a supermarket ... our house.
A in front of   B opposite   C facing

Test yourself: answers

basic points			intermediate points			advanced points		
		see page			*see page*			*see page*
1	A	18	31	B	32	61	A,B	60
2	B, D	22	32	C, D	40	62	A	63
3	A	28	33	A, C	48	63	C	73
4	A, C	28	34	C	68, 70	64	A	84
5	B, D	30	35	A	74	65	A, C	86
6	B	31	36	A	74	66	A, B	94
7	C	43	37	A	90	67	A, C	108
8	B	44	38	A, B	102	68	B, D	114
9	B	44	39	B, C	113	69	B, C	122
10	C	47	40	A, C	128	70	A	137
11	D	51	41	A, C	130, 134	71	B	153
12	A	56	42	C	132–3	72	C, D	162
13	A, E	58	43	B	141	73	A	170
14	A, C	79	44	B	154	74	A	180
15	E	80	45	A	156	75	C	181
16	A	87	46	B	164	76	B	198
17	C	88	47	C	166	77	A	205
18	A	95	48	D	176	78	A	217
19	C	106	49	A, B	183	79	B	221
20	C, D	106	50	A	188	80	A, B, C, D, E	224
21	D	142	51	D	192	81	C	227
22	A	148	52	C	196	82	D	245
23	B	210	53	D	199, 204	83	A	264
24	C	210	54	A	202	84	A, B	265
25	A	210	55	C	251	85	B	267
26	B	213	56	A, C, D	252	86	A	269
27	A, B	222	57	D	256	87	D	276
28	B	284	58	B	258	88	A	277
29	A	284	59	B	262	89	C, D	286
30	D	285	60	B, C	270	90	B, C	287

Explanations and exercises:
list of sections

(**Note:** for explanations of the words that we use for talking about grammar, see pages 298–302.)

Phonetic alphabet

It is necessary to use a special alphabet to show the pronunciation of English words, because the ordinary English alphabet does not have enough letters to represent all the sounds of the language. The following list contains all the letters of the phonetic alphabet used in this book, with examples of the words in which the sounds that they refer to are found.

Vowels and diphthongs (double vowels)

iː seat /siːt/, feel /fiːl/
ɪ sit /sɪt/, in /ɪn/
e set /set/, any /'eniː/
æ sat /sæt/, match /mætʃ/
ɑː march /mɑːtʃ/, after /'ɑːftə(r)/
ɒ pot /pɒt/, gone /gɒn/
ɔː port /pɔːt/, law /lɔː/
ʊ good /gʊd/, could /kʊd/
uː food /fuːd/, group /gruːp/
ʌ much /mʌtʃ/, front /frʌnt/
ɜː turn /tɜːn/, word /wɜːd/
ə away /ə'weɪ/, collect /kə'lekt/, until /ən'tɪl/

eɪ take /teɪk/, wait /weɪt/
aɪ mine /maɪn/, light /laɪt/
ɔɪ oil /ɔɪl/, boy /bɔɪ/
əʊ no /nəʊ/, open /'əʊpən/
aʊ house /haʊs/, now /naʊ/
ɪə hear /hɪə(r)/, deer /dɪə(r)/
eə air /eə(r)/, where /weə(r)/
ʊə tour /tʊə(r)/, endure /ɪn'djʊə(r)/

Consonants

p pull /pʊl/, cup /kʌp/
b bull /bʊl/, rob /rɒb/
f ferry /'feriː/, life /laɪf/
v very /'veriː/, live /lɪv/
θ think /θɪŋk/, bath /bɑːθ/
ð then /ðen/, with /wɪð/
t take /teɪk/, set /set/
d day /deɪ/, red /red/
s sing /sɪŋ/, rice /raɪs/
z zoo /zuː/, days /deɪz/
ʃ show /ʃəʊ/, wish /wɪʃ/
ʒ pleasure /'pleʒə(r)/, occasion /ə'keɪʒn/

tʃ cheap /tʃiːp/, catch /kætʃ/
dʒ jail /dʒeɪl/, bridge /brɪdʒ/
k case /keɪs/, take /teɪk/
g go /gəʊ/, rug /rʌg/
m my /maɪ/, come /kʌm/
n no /nəʊ/, on /ɒn/
ŋ sing /sɪŋ/, finger /'fɪŋgə(r)/
l love /lʌv/, hole /həʊl/
r round /raʊnd/, carry /'kæriː/
w well /wel/
j young /jʌŋ/
h house /haʊs/

The sign (') shows stress.

a and **an**

We use ***a* before a consonant** and ***an* before a vowel**.
But it depends on the **pronunciation** of the following word, not the spelling.

a dog	*a hat*	*a one-pound coin (/ə wʌn .../)*	*a union (/ə ˈjuːnɪən/)*
an orange	*an uncle*	*an hour (/ən aʊə/)*	*an MP (/ən em ˈpiː/)*

1 *A* or *an*?

1 ___ elephant	7 ___ half-hour lesson	13 ___ hand
2 ___ university	8 ___ one-hour lesson	14 ___ underpass
3 ___ umbrella	9 ___ useful book	15 ___ unit
4 ___ ticket	10 ___ SOS	16 ___ CD
5 ___ VIP	11 ___ X-ray	17 ___ exam
6 ___ honest man	12 ___ European	18 ___ school

a/an and **one**

We use ***one***, not *a/an*:
- in contrast with ***another*** or ***other(s)***
- in the expression ***one day***
- with *hundred* and *thousand* when we want to sound **precise** (see page 294)
- in expressions like ***only one*** and ***just one***.

One girl wanted to go out, but *the others* wanted to stay at home.
One day I'll take you to meet my family.
'How many are there? About a hundred?' 'Exactly *one* hundred and three.'
We've got plenty of sausages, but *only one* egg.

1 *A* or *one*?

___1___ day last year – it was ___2___ very hot afternoon in June – I was hurrying to get home. I was about ___3___ hour late – well, to be precise, exactly ___4___ hour and ten minutes: I had taken the train that arrived at the station at 6.15. Anyway, there was ___5___ woman standing under the trees, and there were several children with her. I saw ___6___ child clearly – she was ___7___ lovely dark-haired girl – but I only heard the others. Suddenly ___8___ strange thing happened. The girl took some stones and leaves out of her pocket, and threw ___9___ stone after another into the air.

a/an: main uses

We use **a/an** to say **what kind of thing** somebody or something is, **what job** a person does, or **what** something is **used as**. *A/an* has no plural.

She's **a farmer**.	They're **farmers**.
He worked as **a taxi-driver**.	They worked as **taxi-drivers**.
Don't use the plate as **an ashtray**.	Don't use the plates as **ashtrays**.

1 **Say what these people's jobs are, using the words in the box.**
  Example:

A is a conductor.

> builder   butcher   conductor   cook   doctor   electrician
> gardener   hairdresser   lorry driver   mechanic   musician
> painter   photographer   scientist   secretary   teacher

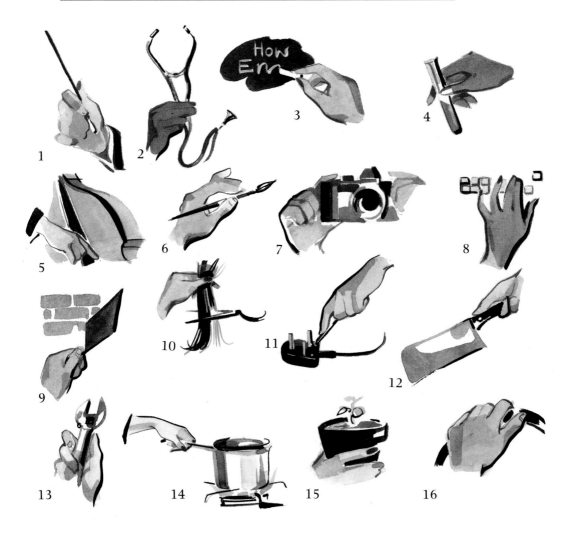

A/an can mean **'any example of something'**.
In the **plural**, we use **no article** or *some* (see page 34 for the difference).

*A **spider** has eight legs.*	***Spiders** have eight legs.*
*A **CD** costs more than a **cassette**.*	***CDs** cost more than **cassettes**.*
*I'd like **a cup of coffee**.*	*I'd like **some chips**.*

2   Say what these people and things are. Then make some similar sentences of your own. Examples:

A doctor is a person who helps people who are ill.
A pen is a thing used for writing.

curtain	person	that water comes out of
dictionary	thing	who helps people to learn things
dentist		who services and repairs cars
lawyer		used for finding the meanings of words
mechanic		who helps people to keep their teeth healthy
tap		that you put across a window
teacher		who helps people with legal problems
telephone		used for talking to people who are far away

A/an can mean **'a particular one'**, if you don't say exactly who or which.
In the **plural**, we use *some* or **no article**.

*A **man** called while you were out.*	***Some men** called.*
*James married **a doctor**.*	*They both married **doctors**.*

3   Complete these sentences in any way you like.

1   There's a/an _____ in my pocket/handbag.
2   In my town, there's a big _____.
3   If you see a/an _____ you'll have good/bad luck.
4   I recently bought a/an _____.
5   I've got a beautiful _____.

We don't use *a/an* with **uncountable** nouns. (NOT ~~a rain~~)
We don't use *a/an* with **possessives**. (NOT ~~a my friend~~)
After **kind of** or **sort of**, *a/an* is usually **dropped**.   *a kind of tree* (NOT ~~a kind of a tree~~)
In **exclamations** with **what**, *a/an* is **not dropped**.   *What a pity!* (NOT ~~What pity!~~)
A/an usually comes **after quite, rather** and **such**.   *quite/rather/such a nice day*

a/an in descriptions

Descriptions: *He's got **a** long nose.* (NOT ... ~~the long nose.~~)
*She's got **an** interesting face.* (NOT ... ~~the interesting face.~~)

1   **Make sentences like those above to describe the people in the
pictures, using some of the words from the box.**

long/small nose	long neck	round/square/oval face
big/small mouth	big/small moustache	long/short beard
nice smile/laugh	quiet/loud voice	bad temper
good sense of humour		

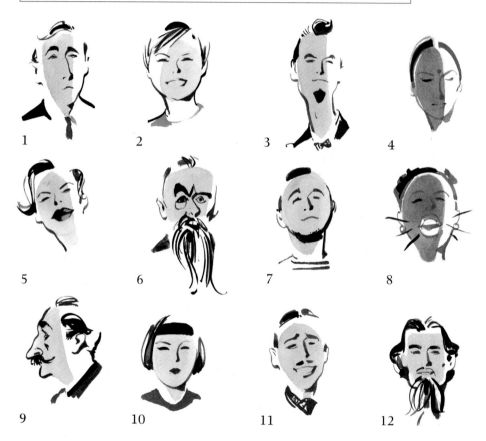

2   **Describe people you know, using *a/an* + singular as much as
possible. If you can work with a partner, describe another person
without giving their name. Your partner must try to guess who it is.**

Note that **hair** is **singular**, and has **no article**.

*She's got **dark hair**.* (NOT ... ~~a dark hair~~ OR ... ~~dark hairs.~~)

the = 'you know which one(s)'

The means 'you know **which (one/ones)** I mean'.

*I bought a radio and a CD player, but **the CD player** didn't work.*
  (= the CD player I just told you about – you know which one.)
***The women** over there work with my sister.*
  (= the women I'm pointing out to you – you know which ones.)
*Please close **the door**.* (You can see which one.)
*He's been to **the North Pole**.* (It's obvious which – there's only one.)

We often use **the** with **only** and with **superlatives.**
  *She's **the only** woman for me.*   *It's **the best** restaurant in town.*

---

1 **Put in *the* if the speaker and hearer probably know exactly which (one/ones). Put in *a/an* or – (= no article) if not.**

1   Who opened _____ window?
2   She lives in _____ centre of Glasgow.
3   I'd like _____ glass of water.
4   My sister is married to _____ farmer.
5   _____ man in _____ next flat is French.
6   He's _____ oldest child in _____ school.
7   Who's _____ girl by _____ piano?
8   They've got _____ boy and _____ girl. _____ boy's two years older than _____ girl.
9   Today is _____ only day that I'm free.
10 'Which coat is yours?' '_____ red one.'

2 **Put in *the, a/an* or – (= no article).**

'Do you see __1__ man standing near __2__ door? He works as __3__ assistant in __4__ same shop as I do. Well, I saw him the other day and he was driving __5__ big red Porsche. And do you see __6__ expensive clothes he's wearing? Where does he get __7__ money to pay for it all? __8__ month ago he hadn't got __9__ penny. I told you about __10__ burglary that we had at __11__ shop, didn't I? Do you think I should go to __12__ police?'

▲ **3** **Work with another student if you can. If you say the following expressions, will he/she know which one(s) you probably mean? If not, add some words so that he/she will know which one(s). Examples:**

the teacher *(OK)*   the window ➤ *the window on the right*

the teacher	the window	the light	the lights
the ceiling	the door	the light switch	the school
the lesson	the dictionary	the place	the car the bus
the house	the post office	the station	the President
the government	the restaurant		

generalisations without **the**

The does **not** mean '**all**'.
We **do not use** *the* in **generalisations** with plural and uncountable nouns. Compare:

I like **music**. (NOT ... ~~the music~~.)	*Can you turn off* **the music**?
She's very interested in **nature**.	*What is* **the nature** *of his illness?*
People have to live in **society**.	*I've joined* **the Poetry Society**.
Books *are expensive.*	*Put* **the books** *on the table.*

1 Put *the* or – (= no article) in each blank.

There must be something wrong with me. __1__ people usually think that __2__ babies are sweet and __3__ teenagers are annoying. Not me. I think __4__ babies are boring. For me, __5__ children are only interesting from about __6__ age of two, when you can understand __7__ things that they say. But __8__ time between ages thirteen and twenty are __9__ years that I like best. Oh, it's difficult at times, but I still prefer talking about __10__ money with a teenager to cleaning a baby's bottom.

We **do not** normally use *the* in **generalisations** with plural and uncountable nouns, even if there is an **adjective before the noun**.

She's studying **Chinese history**.   *He collects* **antique clocks**.

But we use *the* when a description with *of* follows the noun.
She's studying **the history of China**.

2 Use some adjectives from the box, or other adjectives, to write true (or false!) sentences about yourself. Don't use *the*. If you are in a group, pass the sentences round; see if everyone can guess who wrote what.

casual	classical	detective	foggy	formal	historical
Italian	really hot	pop	romantic	spicy	stormy

1 I like eating ____ food.
2 I can't stand listening to ____ music.
3 I (don't) like reading ____ novels.
4 I hate ____ weather.
5 I love ____ weather.
6 I like wearing ____ clothes.

We can use **the** in generalisations with **singular countable nouns**, to talk about a whole class of things. This is common in scientific and technical language.

*Who invented **the telescope**?*   ***The tiger** is in danger of dying out.*
*I can't play **the piano**.*   *I hate **the telephone**.*

Note also:
*I love **the sea**.*   *Do you like living in **the country**?*
*I never go to **the cinema** or **the theatre**.*

3   Complete the sentences with some of the expressions from the box.

> the aeroplane   the ballpoint pen   the Bible   the camera   the computer
> the dog   the fax machine   the novel   the personal stereo   the typewriter
> the violin   the whale   the wheel   the X-ray machine

1   Before people invented ____, they couldn't transport heavy loads easily.
2   In its early years, ____ wasn't thought to be good reading for young ladies.
3   Scientific calculations were much slower before the invention of ____.
4   ____ is one of the hardest instruments to play.
5   What did people write with before ____?
6   ____ is a much faster way of sending letters than the post.
7   What can we do to save ____ from dying out?
8   ____ is a valuable tool for doctors, but it has its dangers as well.

Never lend books, for no one ever returns them; the only books I have in my library are the books that other people have lent me.
Anatole France

Without music, life would be a mistake.
Nietzsche

I would give anything to hear and to love music, but do the best I can, it is just noise and nothing more.
Catherine the Great of Russia

I don't know anything about music – in my line you don't have to.
Elvis Presley

Classical music is the kind we keep thinking will turn into a tune.
Kin Hubbard

Give me books, fruit, French wine and fine weather and a little music out of doors, played by somebody I do not know.
John Keats

This, books can do – nor this alone: they give New views to life, and teach us how to live.
George Crabbe

I quite admit that modern novels have many good points. All that I insist on is that, as a class, they are quite unreadable.
Oscar Wilde

Nature is usually wrong.
The painter James McNeill Whistler

For expressions like *the blind, the old*, see page 72.

the and **no article**: special cases

Some common expressions with **no article** after a **preposition**:
to/at/from school, university, college, church, work   *at/from home*
to / in(to) / out of hospital, prison, bed   *to/in(to)/from town*   *on holiday*
by car/bus/plane etc (BUT **on** *foot*)   *to/at/after breakfast, lunch etc*
at night (BUT **in the** *morning/afternoon/evening*)   *on Monday etc*
in spring, summer etc (OR **in the** *spring etc*)   *at Easter, Christmas etc*
Compare:

> *She's **in prison**. (* = She's a prisoner.)   *She works as a cook **in the prison**.*
> *You should be **in bed**. (* = resting)   *I found chewing gum **in the bed** again.*

1   Choose a word or expression for each blank, and add a preposition.

bed	bus	car	Christmas	Easter	the evening	foot	home
hospital	night	school	summer	town	university	work	

1   'How do you usually get ____ to do your shopping?' 'Oh, I usually go there ____,
     but sometimes if I have a lot to carry I go ____.'
2   After a hard day ____ my mother used to come home and go ____ to rest for half an hour
     before making supper.
3   Children go ____ to learn to read and write.
4   Does your family usually go away ____ or do you stay ____?
5   Don't drink coffee ____ if you have trouble sleeping ____.
6   When Juliet was studying ____, she broke her leg and had to stay ____ for two weeks.

2   Which version of the cartoon caption do you think is correct?

'He's from *Texas / the Texas.*'

Place names with no article:

continents, most countries	*Africa, Germany, Peru* (BUT *The Netherlands*)
states, counties etc	*Texas, Oxfordshire, Normandy*
towns	*Ottawa, Prague, Sydney* (BUT *The Hague*)
most streets	*Fifth Avenue, Oxford Street*
lakes, most mountains	*Lake Superior, Everest, Mont Blanc*
town + buildings	*Oxford University, York Airport, Reading Station*

Place names with *the*:

name includes common noun	*the Czech Republic, the United States*
seas, rivers, deserts	*the Atlantic, the Thames, the Sahara Desert*
mountain and island groups	*the Alps, the Himalayas, the West Indies*
most geographical regions	*the Far East, the Ruhr, the Midwest*
hotels, cinemas, theatres	*the Ritz, the Playhouse*

▲ **3   Make sentences using words and expressions from the box.
Example:**

A 1/10/16: *Anna goes to work on foot.* OR *Anna often goes to work on foot if
the weather's fine.* OR *Everybody in the office except Anna comes to work
on foot.*

B 3/9/25/31   C 2/11/14   D 1/7/29/18   E 5/30/33
F 6/25/34/16   G 1/24/28/33   H 5/25/32/16   I 1/26/23
J 4/2/9/26   K 3/11/29   L 13/21/22   M 5/20
N 4/11/10/17   O 6/28/30/13   P 3/8/27

1 Anna	7 to college	13 by train	19 the Pacific	25 Oxford	31 Prison
2 Paul	8 in prison	14 by car	20 Everest	26 Stirling	32 Town
3 the King	9 at dinner	15 by plane	21 the Alps	27 Cardiff	Hall
4 I	10 to work	16 on foot	22 the North Sea	28 Ottawa	33 Airport
5 all of us	11 home	17 by bike	23 Lake Huron	29 Sydney	34 Station
6 it's easy	12 at work	18 by bus	24 the Hague	30 Boston	

**If you are in a group, write some 'number sentences' for other
students.**

**4   Write the English names of ten places you have been to, and ten
places you would like to go to.**

Other expressions with **no article**:
 *He was elected **President**.   She became **Queen**.   They made her **Manager**.
 What's **on TV**?   Let's **watch television**.
   (BUT **on the radio**, **listen to the radio**)
 This is **Alice's house**. (NOT ... ~~the *Alice's house.*~~ – see page 62)

articles: revision

1 *A, an, the* or – (nothing)?

1   ____ diplomat is ____ person who can tell you to go to hell in such a way
that you actually look forward to ____ trip. *Caskie Stinnett*

2   ____ dog is ____ only thing on earth that loves you more than you love
yourself. *Josh Billings*

3   ____ Americans like ____ fat books and ____ thin women. *Russell Baker*

4   ____ accountant is ____ man who is hired to explain that you didn't
make ____ money you did. *Anonymous*

5   ____ actor's ____ guy who, if you ain't talking about him, ain't listening.
Attributed to Marlon Brando

6   ____ optimist is someone who thinks ____ future is uncertain.
Anonymous

7   ____ death is ____ nature's way of telling you to slow down.
Anonymous

8   ____ diplomacy is the art of saying 'nice doggie!' until you can find ____
stone. *Wynn Catlin*

9   ____ equality is ____ lie – ____ women are better. *Anonymous*

10 ____ birds do it; ____ bees do it; even ____ educated fleas do it. Let's do it.
Let's fall in ____ love. *Cole Porter*

11 I always pass on ____ good advice. It is ____ only thing to do with it. It is
never any use to oneself. *Oscar Wilde*

12 I love acting. It is so much more real than ____ life. *Oscar Wilde*

13 Never put anything on ____ paper, my boy, and never trust ____ man
with ____ small black moustache. *P G Wodehouse*

14 Nothing's illegal if ____ hundred businessmen decide to do it, and that's
true anywhere in ____ world. *Andrew Young*

15 Remember that as ____ teenager you are at ____ last stage in your life
when you will be happy to hear that ____ phone is for you.
Fran Lebowitz

16 Save ____ water, shower with ____ friend. *Anonymous*

17 ____ happiest time of anyone's life is just after ____ first divorce.
John Kenneth Galbraith

18 Treat ____ work of art like ____ prince: let it speak to you first.
Attributed to Arthur Schopenhauer

19 When I was ____ boy of fourteen, my father was so ignorant I could
hardly stand to have ____ old man around. But when I got to be twenty-
one, I was astonished at how much he had learned in seven years.
Mark Twain

20 When I was born, I was so surprised that I couldn't talk for ____ year
and ____ half. *Gracie Allen*

21 A banker is ____ man who lends you ____ umbrella when ____ weather
is fair, and takes it away from you when it rains. *Anonymous*

22 California is ____ great place – if you happen to be ____ orange. *F Allen*

23 Writing about ____ art is like dancing about ____ architecture.
Anonymous

2 **Complete the captions with *a*, *an*, *the* or –, and say which cartoons they go with.**

1 'One night you'll get me out of ___ bed and it really will be ___ burglar.'
2 'I don't think much of ___ wedding photographer.'
3 'For heaven's sake, Harry! Can't you just relax and enjoy ___ art, ___ music, ___ religion, ___ literature, ___ drama and ___ history, without trying to tie it all together?'
4 'Good morning, Mr Dolby! It's 5.15 a.m., and this is radio station WJRM. If you name ___ next tune you will win ___ ride on ___ elephant and ___ two tickets to ___ rock concert!'

A

B   C

D

possessives (my and mine etc)

1 Complete the table and then check your answers in the key.

This belongs to **me**.	This is **my** coat.	This is **mine**.
This belongs to **you**.	This is ____ money.	This is ____.
This belongs to ____.	This is **his** car.	This is ____.
This belongs to **her**.	This is ____ office.	This is ____.
This belongs to ____.	This is **our** house.	This is ____.
This belongs to **them**.	This is ____ dog.	This is ____.
Who does this belong to?	____ bike is this?	____ is this bike?

Note also: *its* name (NOT ~~*it's name*~~); *its* value; *its* history.

2 Put in the right possessives.

1   'Is this Alice's book or *(your/yours)*, do you know?' 'It's *(her/hers)*.'
2   '*(Who/Whose)* car is that in the drive?' 'I don't know – not
    (our/ours).'
3   Take *(your/yours)* feet off the table. *(It/Its)* legs aren't very strong.
4   John's bringing ____ guitar and Catherine's bringing ____ drums.
5   Chris and Pat never cut the grass in ____ garden.
6   The Whartons are spending August in *(our/ours)* flat, and we're
    borrowing *(their/theirs)*.
7   That's *(my/mine)* coat, and the scarf is ____ too.

You can't put possessives immediately after articles or after *this/that* etc.

  She's **a friend of mine**. (NOT ~~She's a my friend.~~)
  How's **that brother of yours**? (NOT ~~How's that your brother?~~)

---

3 Join up the ideas to make expressions.

1   that + your smelly dog
    that smelly dog of yours
2   that + her unemployed brother
3   another + my good friend
4   a + my brilliant idea
5   these + his stupid plans
6   those + your old books

7   some + his distant relations
8   a + her beautiful cousin
9   this + your wonderful news
10 that + our lazy son
11 those + their impossible children
12 these + our silly cats

For explanations of the words that we use to talk about grammar, see pages 298–302.

We normally use **possessives** with **parts of the body** and **clothes**.

> *Anne broke **her** arm skiing.* (NOT *... broke **the arm** ...*)
> *He stood there, **his** eyes closed and **his** hands in **his** pockets.*

4 Put in one of the words from the box with a suitable possessive.

coats   foot   jacket   mouth   tail   raincoat

1 Martin stood up and put _____ on.
2 Helen hurt _____ very badly yesterday.
3 That dog's hurt _____.
4 They took off _____ and sat down.
5 Look at the weather – and I've forgotten _____ again.
6 I'll tell you everything if you promise to keep _____ shut.

5 Complete the cartoon caption with a suitable possessive.

'No, he's not _____! We thought you'd brought him.'

We often use ***the*** instead of a possessive in expressions with **prepositions**, especially when we talk about common kinds of **pain, illness** and **physical contact**, and when the possessor has already been mentioned.

> *He's got a pain **in the chest**.*   *Ann's got a cold **in the head**.*
> *She hit **me on the head**.*   *I looked **him in the eye**.*

We use **possessives** with ***own***.

> ***my own** room / a room of **my own*** (NOT ***an own room***)

this and **that**

1 Study the examples, and think about the difference between
this/these and _that/those_.

Come and look at this picture.
This isn't a very good party.
Do you like this music?
Listen – this will make you laugh.
(on the phone) This is Ann.
This is my friend Paula.
These shoes are hurting my feet.
These grapes are really sweet.

What's that on the roof?
He's ill. That's why he's away.
Stop that noise!
Thanks – that was a great meal.
(on the phone) Who's that?
I didn't like those stories he told.
Do you remember those people
  we met in Edinburgh?

2 Look at the examples again. Which words and expressions in the
box go with _this/these_, and which go with _that/those_? Check your
answers in the key.

finished	happening now	said before	just about to start
here	near	over there	distant	unwanted

3 Put in _this/that/these/those._

1 Why am I living in _____ country?
2 Get me _____ box from the table.
3 Ugh – _____ potatoes taste burnt!
4 What was _____ noise?
5 Who are _____ people over there?
6 Come _____ way, please.
7 Isn't _____ weather great?
8 Did you hear _____ rain in the night?
9 Tell her to stop _____ shouting.
10 _____ was a nice meal – thanks.
11 Who said _____?
12 Why did she marry _____ idiot?
13 Do it _____ way, not like _____.

4 _This_ or _that_?

'My wife told me to carry *this/that*.'

which? and what?

We ask **which?** when there is **a limited choice**.

We ask **what?** when there is **a wide choice**.

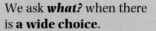

Which *size do you want –*
small, medium or large?

What *is your shoe size?*

Sometimes both are possible.

> **Which/What** *day next week can you come and see us?*

Before *of* and *one*, we can use *which* but not *what*.

> **Which of** *the countries in Europe have you visited?* (NOT ~~What of~~ *...?*)
> *Look at all those stars.* **Which one** *is the nearest?* (NOT ~~What one~~ *...?*)

1 *Which* or *what*?

1. We've got red wine and white – ____ will you have?
2. ____ books did you read for last year's English class?
3. ____ of the books on the list have you already read?
4. ____ French queen said, 'Let them eat cake'?
5. ____'s your name?
6. ____ hand do you write with?
7. ____ kind of car have you got?
8. ____ one is yours?
9. ____ party do you think will win the election?
10. ____ subject do you prefer, chemistry or physics?
11. ____ was your favourite subject at primary school?

When there is no noun, we use *who* for people, not *which*. Compare:

> **Which boxer** *won?*   **Who** *won?* (NOT ~~Which won?~~)

some and any

Some means **'a certain (not large) number or amount of'**.
Some is used mostly in **affirmative** sentences.
We also use *some* in questions when we expect people to say 'Yes'
(for example, in **requests** and **offers**).

✓✓✓✓✓
✓ SOME ✓
✓✓✓✓✓

> She's got **some** interesting ideas.   There's **some** mud on the carpet.
> **'Could I have some** coffee?' 'Sure. And **would you like some** biscuits?'

We use ***any*** instead of *some* in **negative** sentences, in most **questions**,
with *if*, and with words like *never, hardly, without, refuse, doubt* (which
have a **negative kind of meaning**).

✗ ✗ ✗ ✗ ✗
✗   ANY   ?
? ? ? ? ? ?

> **Do you know any** good jokes?   He has**n't** got **any** money.
> **If** you find **any** mistakes, please tell me.   She **never** has **any** fun.
> We got there **without any** difficulty.   I **refuse** to give him **any** help.

The difference between *somebody/anybody, someone/anyone, something/anything* etc is the
same as the difference between *some* and *any*.

> There's **somebody** outside.   Would you like **something** to drink?
> Does **anybody** understand this?   She didn't say **anything**.

1   Here are some sentences with *any*. Which word in each sentence
gives the 'negative kind of meaning'? Examples:

> He **never** listens to anyone.   We've **hardly** got any cat food.

1   The baby refuses to eat anything.
2   I doubt that you'll find any bread now.
3   There was hardly anybody in town.
4   You never get any sense out of her.
5   You seldom hear any birds here.
6   I left the house without any money.

2   **Affirmative/negative: choose the right word.**

1   I can't find *(some/any)* butter, but we've got *(some/any)* margarine.
2   Emma has got *(some/any)* old pictures of the house to show us.
3   I haven't got *(something/anything)* to wear to the party.
4   There aren't *(some/any)* buses on Sunday.
5   Helen brought me *(some/any)* beautiful roses from her garden.
6   There's *(somebody/anybody)* waiting for you at reception.

For explanations of the words that we use to talk about grammar, see pages 298–302.

3   Questions: Choose *some/any/somebody/anybody/something/anything*.

1   Did you meet ____ interesting at the party?   5   Is there ____ I can do?
2   Can I offer you ____ wine?   6   Would you like ____ to help you?
3   Shall we listen to ____ music?   7   Do you know ____ German?
4   Have you got ____ children?

4   Choose the right word.

1   Have you got (*some/any*) time free on Wednesday afternoon?
2   There's (*something/anything*) strange about the way Pete's acting today.
3   Nobody can find out (*something/anything*) about when the exams will be.
4   Is there (*something/anything*) we should bring to the meeting?
5   (*Some/Any*) of Laura's friends were at the party last night.
6   Shall I bring you (*something/anything*) to read while you wait?
7   I had three sets of house keys, and I can't find (*some/any*) of them now.
8   Hardly (*some/any*) of the smaller cars have enough leg room for Jill.
9   Do you know if (*some/any*) of the Morrises are coming on Sunday?
10   Can I get you (*some/any*) coffee? I've just made (*some/any*).
11   She refuses to have (*something/anything*) to do with her family now.
12   I haven't done (*some/any*) revision for the exam – I know I'll fail.
13   If there's (*some/any*) soup left, could you put it in the fridge, please?
14   I doubt that there's (*something/anything*) we can do now.
15   Never trust (*someone/anyone*) who has a perfectly tidy desk.
16   Helen can ride a bike without (*some/any*) help now.
17   Has Eve got (*some/any*) brothers or sisters, do you know?
18   Harriet has got (*some/any*) beautiful jewellery, but she never wears it.

5   Complete the cartoon caption.

'Oh, he's right here beside me making his "I don't want
to go ____where with ____body at ____ time" face.'

For *any* meaning 'it doesn't matter which', see page 36.

some/any and no article

We use *some/any* to talk about **indefinite, not very large numbers or amounts** – when we don't know, care or say exactly how much/many.
We use **no article** when we are thinking about **unlimited numbers or amounts**, or **not thinking about numbers/amounts** at all. Compare:

*I've planted **some roses**.* (A limited number; it isn't clear how many.)
*I like **roses**.* (No idea of number.)
*We got talking to **some students**.* (A limited number.)
*Our new neighbours are **students**.* (The idea is classification, not number.)
*Is there **any water** in the fridge?* (The speaker wants a limited amount.)
*Is there **water** on the moon?* (No idea of amount.)

1 Put *some*, *any*, or no article.

1 This car hardly uses ____ petrol.
2 This car doesn't use ____ petrol; it's battery-powered.
3 Would you like ____ beer?
4 In Belgium they make a stew with ____ beef and ____ beer.
5 Do you ever read ____ novels?
6 I read ____ wonderful novels by O'Brian when I was on holiday.
7 Are your sisters ____ doctors too?
8 We met ____ doctors at the party.
9 Could you lend me ____ money?
10 Is ____ money something you worry about?
11 Do you like ____ mushrooms?
12 Are there ____ mushrooms left?
13 We need ____ more milk.
14 Cheese is made from ____ milk.

2 Choose the correct version of the cartoon caption.

'Did we have *children* / *some children* that grew up and went away?'

We do **not** use *some/any* when it is clear **exactly how much/many**. Compare:

*You've got **some great books**.*
*You've got **pretty toes**.* (*You've got **some pretty toes*** would suggest that the speaker is not making it clear how many – perhaps six or seven.)

no = 'not a/any'

No is a more emphatic way of saying **'not a'** or **'not any'**.
At the beginning of a sentence, *no* is almost always used.

> *Sorry, I've got **no** time.*
> *There were **no** letters for you this morning.*
> ***No** cigarette is completely harmless.* (NOT ~~*Not any cigarette*~~ ...)
> ***No** tourists ever come to our village.*

Nobody, nothing etc are used in the same way.
> ***Nobody** loves me.*   *I've got absolutely **nothing** to say.*

Before *of*, we use *none*, not *no* (often with a singular verb).
> ***None of** his friends likes his wife.*

1   Put in *no/none/nobody*.

1   'Why can't I have toast for breakfast?' 'Because there's ＿＿ bread.'
2   'My students expect me to know everything.' '＿＿ knows everything.'
3   ＿＿ newspaper tells the whole truth.
4   'What were your photos like?' 'I'm afraid ＿＿ of them came out.'
5   'Do you think he's honest?' '＿＿ politician is completely honest.'
6   ＿＿ of the people there remembered seeing anything unusual.
7   I've got ＿＿ patience with people like her.
8   There's ＿＿ I can talk to in this place.
9   ＿＿ of you care what I think.
10 He had ＿＿ money, ＿＿ job and ＿＿ place to live.

▲ **2   Write answers. Use *no*, *none*, *nothing*, and *nobody*.**

1   'Why can't you take me to school in the car today?'
    Because I've got no time.
2   'Can you ask someone in your family to help you with your French?'
3   'Jeremy says his father speaks seventy-six languages.'
4   'Do we have to go out tonight? Can't we eat at home?'
5   'Do you think I could ask you for a cup of coffee?'
6   'Why don't you phone home to find out if your letter's arrived?'
7   'If you're bored, why don't you go to the cinema?'
8   'Why didn't you buy any flowers?'
9   'Why didn't you join in the conversation last night?'
10 'How many of your brothers are married?'

any = 'it doesn't matter which'

Any can mean **'it doesn't matter which'**.
With this meaning, *any* is common in affirmative sentences.
In negative sentences, we can use **just any** to make this meaning clear.

> **Any** *doctor will tell you that smoking is bad for you.*
> *He gets angry with **any** man who looks at his wife.*
> *Come **any** time you like.*
> *I don't do **just any** work: I choose jobs that interest me.*

Anybody, anything etc can be used in the same way.
> **Anybody** *can sing if they really want to.*
> *'Can I have something to eat?' 'Of course, take **anything** you like.'*

Any is **not negative** – it is the opposite of *no* or *not any*. Compare:

> *That's easy: **anybody** can do it.*
> *That's too hard: **nobody** can do it.*

> *I'm really hungry – I'll eat **anything**.*
> *I'm not hungry – I do**n't** want **anything**.*

1 Choose the best word or expression for each sentence.

1 *(Any/No)* doctor can tell you if you've got flu.
2 *(Any/No)* doctor can tell you exactly how long you're going to live.
3 Just say *(anything/nothing)*, so we can see if the microphone works.
4 If the police arrest you, say *(anything/nothing)* until your lawyer
   gets there.
5 What do you mean, music? I *(can't hear / can hear)* any music.
6 You can hear *(any/no)* kind of music you like at the Reading Festival.
7 Anna's very secretive: she talks to *(anybody/nobody)* about her problems.
8 Jim tells his problems to *(anybody/nobody)* who will listen.

▲ 2 Answer the questions using *any*.

1 Where can you get: a plane ticket? *any travel agent's*
   lead-free petrol? dog food? stamps? running shoes? a dictionary?
2 Who can give you advice on: English pronunciation? getting a divorce?
   paying your taxes? problems with your camera? milking cows?
3 Write advertisements for toothpaste, shampoo, a computer, an airline
   etc, using 'Don't buy/use/etc just any ..., buy/etc ...'
   Example: *Don't buy just any car, buy a Jaguar.*

For explanations of the words that we use to talk about grammar, see pages 298–302.

some, **any** and **no**: revision

1   **Fill in the blanks and put together the four sentences. Which goes with which cartoon?**

Cook ____ you want for supper   he's not seeing ____ today
I suppose you've brought me here   I'm sorry
in the church   There's ____ place for women
to tell me you haven't got ____ money   It's your birthday?

A

B

C

D

all, everybody and everything

All (*of*) can be used **with a noun** or pronoun.
All is **not** used without a noun or pronoun to mean **'everybody'**.
Compare:

> *All the people* were tired.
> *Everybody* was tired. (NOT *All were tired.*)

All can be used to mean **'everything'** or **'the only thing'**, but only with a
relative clause (*all that ...*). Compare:

> *She gave me **all/everything** (that) she had.*
> ***All** (that) I want* is a place of my own.
> *The thieves took **everything**.* (NOT *The thieves took all.*)

1 Put in *all* if possible; if not, put in *everything*.

1 ____ I need to make a comedy is a park, a policeman and a pretty girl.
   Charlie Chaplin
2 I hurry to laugh at ____, for fear of having to cry.   *Beaumarchais*
3 I can resist ____ except temptation.   *Oscar Wilde*
4 You can only have power over people so long as you don't take ____
   away from them.   *Solzhenitsyn*
5 'Beauty is truth, truth beauty,' – that is ____
   Ye know on earth, and all ye need to know.   *John Keats*
6 They say ____ in the world is good for something.   *John Dryden*
7 [A cynic] knows the price of ____ and the value of nothing.   *Oscar Wilde*
8 Life is like nothing, because it is ____.   *William Golding*
9 [We don't know] whether Laws be right,
   Or whether Laws be wrong;
   ____ that we know who lie in gaol
   Is that the wall is strong.   *Oscar Wilde*

2 Put in *all* or *everybody*.

1 ____ women become like their mothers. That is their tragedy. No man
   does. That's his.   *Oscar Wilde*
2 In the future, ____ will be famous for fifteen minutes.   *Andy Warhol*
3 ____ human beings are born free and equal in dignity and rights.
   Universal Declaration of Human Rights
4 I am free of ____ prejudices – I hate ____ equally.   *W C Fields*
5 He who praises ____ praises nobody.   *Samuel Johnson*
6 Justice is open to ____ people in the same way as the Ritz Hotel.
   Judge Sturgess

whole and **all**

We use **whole** most often with **singular countable nouns**.
We use **all** most often with **uncountable** and **plural** nouns.
Compare:

    a **whole** plate – **all** the food   the **whole** sweater – **all** the wool
    a **whole** concert – **all** the music   the **whole** orchestra – **all** the
                                                  musicians

Note the word order with *the*: **the whole ... / all the ...**
Before place names, we most often use *the whole of*.
    the whole of Europe

1   **Write an expression with *whole* or *all* for each item. Examples:**

    a football team ➜ *a whole football team*
    the flowers ➜ *all the flowers*

a family	the islands	the road system	South Africa	
the children	the country	the traffic	Asia	a week
the vegetables	the political party	the students		
the luggage	the meat	MPs	a class	

Note: In some common time expressions, both *whole* and *all* are possible.
    the whole afternoon/night/week – all (the) afternoon/night/week
    the whole day – all day; the whole time – all the time; my whole life – all my life

much, many, a lot (of), little, few

We use **much** with **singular** (uncountable) nouns and **many** with **plurals**.

> How **much time** have we got?   How **many tickets** do we need?

Much and **many** are most common in **questions** and **negatives**, and after **so**, **as**, **too** and **very**.

In other informal **affirmative** sentences, we generally prefer **a lot (of)**, **lots (of)** or **plenty (of)**. All three of these can be used with both uncountables and plurals.

> 'Do you have **much** trouble with English?' 'I don't have **much** trouble speaking, but I have **lots of** difficulty writing.' (NOT ... ~~much difficulty~~ ...)
>
> 'Are there **many** opera houses in London?' 'Not **many**, but **a lot of** theatres and **plenty of** cinemas.' (NOT '... ~~many theatres and many cinemas.~~')
>
> I love you **so much**.   Take **as much** as you like.
>
> There are **too many** people here.

1 **Write at least eight sentences about yourself. Have you got *not much*, *not many*, *a lot / lots of*, or *plenty of*...? Examples:**

I haven't got much ambition.   I've got lots of cousins.

ambition	cousins	problems	nice clothes	energy
books	confidence	work to do	old friends	free time

2 **Write *much/many* with *so*, *as*, *too* or *very* for each blank.**

1 Thank you ____ for your help.
2 Are there ____ chairs as people?
3 You can never have ____ love.
4 I like your hair ____.

5 Bob feels ____ better today.
6 I don't know ____ poems as you.
7 She's got ____ relatives!
8 Get ____ tickets as you can.

In a formal style, *many* and *much* are more common in affirmative sentences.

> The researches of **many** commentators have already thrown **much** darkness on this subject, and it is probable that if this continues we shall soon know nothing at all about it.   Mark Twain

(A) little is used with **singular** (uncountable) nouns and *(a) few* with **plurals**.
Little and *few* are rather **negative**: they mean '**not much/many**'.
A little and *a few* are more **positive**: their meaning is more like '**some**'.

> *Cactuses need **little water**.*
> *Give the roses **a little water** every day.*
> *His ideas are very difficult, and **few people** understand them.*
> *His ideas are very difficult, but **a few people** understand them.*

Little and *few* (without *a*) are rather formal; in a conversational style we more often say
only a little/few or *not much/many.*

> *Cactuses **only** need **a little** water.*   ***Not many** people understand his ideas.*

3 Write *little* or *few*.

1 There is ____ friendship in the world, and least of all between equals.   *Francis Bacon*
2 A ____ learning is a dangerous thing.   *Alexander Pope*
3 Men of ____ words are the best men.   *William Shakespeare (Henry V)*
4 Never in the field of human conflict was so much owed by so many to so ____.
   Winston Churchill
5 Never before have we had so ____ time in which to do so much.   *Franklin Roosevelt*
6 A country having a ____ inflation is like a woman being a little pregnant.
   Leon Henderson
7 We ____, we happy ____, we band of brothers;
   For he today that sheds his blood with me
   Shall be my brother.   *William Shakespeare (Henry V)*
8 Death is one of the ____ things that can be done as easily lying down.   *Woody Allen*

4 *Little* or *a little? Few* or *a few?*

1 It is ____ use trying to change her mind.
2 Could you possibly give me ____ help?
3 ____ teenagers in the village could read.
4 Slowly, ____ children began coming to school.
5 I only need ____ minutes to get ready.
6 She only wanted ____ love, ____ kindness.
7 Nadia drank ____ coffee and no alcohol.
8 Unfortunately, he had ____ friends.

Now write sentences 1, 3, 7 and 8 in a more conversational style.

**Few people can be happy unless they hate
some other person, nation or creed.**
Bertrand Russell

less and least, fewer and fewest

Less and *fewer* are **comparative** (see page 79): they are the opposite of *more*.
Least and *fewest* are **superlative** (see page 79): they are the opposite of *most*.
Less and *least* are used with **singular** (uncountable) nouns.
Fewer and *fewest* are used with **plural** nouns.

> I've got **less money** than I thought.
> Of all my friends, Jake does the **least work**.
> There were **fewer problems** than we expected.
> Ann was the person who made the **fewest mistakes** in the translation exam.

In modern English, many people use *less* with plurals (e.g. *There were **less problems** than we expected*). Some people feel this is incorrect.

1   Write *less* / *the least* / *fewer* / *the fewest*.

1   Of all British cars, this one uses ____ petrol. It also needs ____ repairs.
2   ____ girls than boys do mathematics at university. This may be because girls get ____ encouragement to study maths at school.
3   As the years went by, they had ____ things to say, and ____ interest in talking to each other.
4   Do you want more time and ____ money, or more money and ____ time?
5   Liz is very clever, but she has got ____ self-confidence of anyone I know.
6   I've had ____ days off work of anybody in the office.

Less and *least* can also be used with **adjectives** and **adverbs**.

> Ann's **less shy** than Pat.
> It was the **least successful** party we'd given.
> He drives **less carefully** than I expected.

2   Put *less* / *the least* in each blank, with one of the words in the list (or another word, if you prefer). If you are in a group, compare answers.

shy	shyly	easily	prosperous	selfish	fluently
pessimistic	politely	worried	optimistic	confident	
confidently	quickly	dangerous	religious		

1   I feel ____ about the future than I did a year ago.
2   My mother is/was ____ person you can imagine.
3   I spoke English ____ a year ago than I do today.
4   I think this country is ____ than it was a year ago.
5   People from the north of my country speak ____ than people from the south.
6   My home town is ____ place I know.

other(s) and another

When **other** is used **before a plural noun**, it does **not** have **-s**.
When **other** is used **without a noun**, it has **-s** in the plural. Compare:

> Tell the **other** people. (NOT ... ~~the others people~~.)
> Tell the **others**.
> Can you show me some **other** shoes?
> Can you show me some **others**?

1 Write *other* or *others*.

1 I could see Karima and Nedjma at their desks – but where were the ____?
2 Long after all the ____ cars had left, Dawson's BMW was still there.
3 I'll phone all the ____ if you'll phone Ted and Lucy, OK?
4 I can play the Sonata in C, but not any of the ____.
5 Do you know any ____ people who might have a reason to do this?
6 This doesn't suit me. Have you got any ____ colours?
7 Some metals are magnetic and ____ aren't.
8 The police arrested Jane, Fred and two ____.
9 I wish that girl would play more with ____ children.
10 Gerald Durrell wrote a book called 'My Family and ____ Animals'.

We can use **another** (one word) to mean **'one more'**. But with
uncountables and plurals, we do not generally use *other* to mean 'more'.
Compare:

> Have **another potato**. (NOT ... ~~an other potato~~.)
> Have some **more meat**. (NOT ... ~~other meat~~.)
> We need **more cups**.

We can use **another + few** or **another + a number** with a **plural** noun.

> Let's wait **another few minutes**. (= ... a few more minutes.)
> The job will take **another ten days**. (= ... ten more days.)

2 Write expressions with *another* or with *more*. Examples:

English → *more English*   book → *another book*   eggs → *more eggs*

clothes	friends	child	three pages	hour	mile
sleep	job possibilities	few days	hundred pounds		money
time	freedom	holidays	problem	twenty miles	

enough, too and too much

1 Look at the examples and choose the correct forms of the rules. Check your answer in the key.

*This isn't **hot enough**.* (NOT *... ~~enough hot~~.*)
*Am I going **fast enough**?*
*There is never **enough time**.*

Rules
***Enough** normally comes **(before/after)** an adjective or adverb.*
***Enough** normally comes **(before/after)** a noun.*

2 Put in words from the box together with *enough*.

big	champagne	clever	confidence	good
hard	money	time	friends	old

1 In art the best is *good enough.*   Goethe
2 I never had ____ when I was young; now I never have ____.
3 This town isn't ____ for both of us.
4 Susie hasn't got ____ to play with.
5 Bob's not ____ to travel by himself.
6 There was ____ to give everybody a glass.
7 If you work ____, you don't have to be very intelligent.
8 She was ____ to do anything she wanted, but she didn't have ____ to try.

We use ***too*** before an **adjective without a noun**, or an **adverb**.
We use ***too much/many*** before a **noun** (with or without an adjective).

*He's **too old**.* (NOT *... ~~too much old~~.*)   *She's driving **too fast**.*
*My problem is: **too much work** and **too many late nights**.*

3 Invent answers to the questions, using *too*, *too much* or *too many*.

1 Why did Jack leave his car at the pub and take a taxi home? *(beer)*
   He'd drunk too much beer.
2 Why did they drive to the cinema in two cars? *(people)*
3 Why didn't Joanna stop for lunch yesterday? *(busy)*
4 Why don't we go to the Caribbean for our holiday ? *(expensive)*
5 Why don't you let the children cycle to school? *(traffic)*
6 What went wrong in your exam? *(slowly)*
7 Why did you have the phone installed in the other room? *(noise)*
8 Can you understand what he's saying? *(quickly)*

4   Write descriptions for the pictures using *not enough* or *too much/many*.

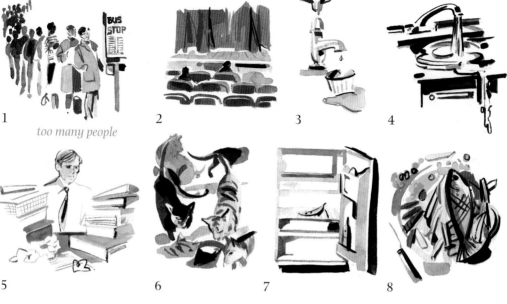

1   *too many people*

2

3

4

5

6

7

8

Note the structures *... **enough** (for ...) **to** ...* and ***too** ... (for ...) **to** ...*

*She's **old enough to vote**.   It's not **warm enough for me to swim**.*
*The box was **too heavy to lift**.   He spoke **too fast for us to follow**.*

5   Complete the sentences with *too/enough* and words from the list.

1   The food was *too spicy for the children to eat.*
2   Sally's not ___ the dog for a walk.
3   They were speaking ___ what they were saying.
4   Near some beaches the sea's not ___ in.
5   There's someone out there, but I can't see ___ if it's Emma.
6   The water was ___ anything.
7   I'll work on this tomorrow – I'm ___ it tonight.
8   I don't understand Arabic ___ to Egyptian radio.
9   He drove ___ him.

clean/people/swim
fast/police/catch
muddy/them/see
old/take
spicy/children/eat
quietly/me/hear
tired/understand
well/listen
well/decide

We can drop a noun after *enough* or *too much/many* if the meaning is clear.

*I've eaten **too much**.   'How many people live here?' '**Too many**.'*

We can use ***too much*** as an **adverb**: *He talks **too much**.*
We **don't** normally use ***too*** before **adjective + noun**.

*She doesn't like **men who are too tall**. (NOT ... ~~too tall men.~~)*

Compare: *We haven't got **enough big** nails. = We need more of them.*
         *We haven't got **big enough** nails. = We need bigger ones.*

# of with determiners

The following **determiners** have *of* before articles (*the/a/an*), possessives (*my/your* etc), demonstratives (*this/that* etc) and pronouns (*it/us/you/them*): *some, any, much, many, more, most, too much* etc, *enough, little, less, least, few, all, both, each, every one, none,* and numbers *one, two* etc.

some, any, much, more, etc	of	the, a/an my, your, *etc* this, that, *etc*	(ADJECTIVE +) NOUN

some, any, much, more, etc	of	it, us, you, them

some of the older people
most of my friends
a few of those grapes
too many of his books

none of it
every one of us
all of you
enough of them

In other cases, we use these **determiners without** *of*.

some, any, etc	(ADJECTIVE)	NOUN

some strange ideas   a little water   most people   few changes

Every and *no* are used instead of *every one* and *none*.
   every two minutes   *no time*

---

1   Put in *of* or nothing (–).

Dear Phil,

Well, some __1__ our luggage has arrived, so things could be worse. I've got the books and papers, but I've lost most __2__ my clothes. I haven't got any __3__ socks at all, and I'll have to buy some more __4__ jeans, but at least I've got enough __5__ underwear for the week. (They don't sell it here. I don't think they wear it.) I'm going to buy a few __6__ those woollen shirts that you like, and one __7__ the big coats that we looked at. They've got no __8__ shoes in my size, unfortunately, and none __9__ the jackets suit me. Anyway, I'm not alone. Every one __10__ us has lost something – in fact, three __11__ people have got no __12__ luggage at all. Well, as they say, into each __13__ life a little __14__ rain must fall.

See you on the 17th.

Andy

Note the difference between **most people** (talking about people in general) and **most of the people** (talking about particular people).

Most people *want to have children.*
Most of the people *I know live in the country.*

2   Put in *most people* or *most of the people*.

1   ____ enjoy talking about themselves.
2   ____ who wanted to see the match were disappointed.
3   I know ____ in our street.
4   ____ like music.
5   I think fishing for sport is wrong, but ____ would disagree.
6   ____ on the train had no tickets.
7   He gets on with ____.
8   ____ at the party were friends of Jan's.

3   Choose the correct versions of the cartoon captions.

'Straighten your tie, Stephen. The world is already filled with *(enough disorder / enough of disorder).'*

'Girls, girls! – *(A little less noise / A little less of noise)*, please.'

After **all** and **both**, we often **drop of** before determiners.

all (of) *my friends*   **both (of)** *his eyes*

personal pronouns: I and me etc

I, *you*, **he**, *she*, **it**, *we*, **they** are used as subjects before verbs.
Me, *you*, **him**, *her*, **it**, *us*, **them** are normally used in other cases.

SUBJECTS BEFORE VERBS:	**I like** Mary.	**We can't go** on like this.
OBJECTS AFTER VERBS:	Mary **hates me**.	**Tell us** what to do.
AFTER PREPOSITIONS:	Look **at her**.	Why is she **with him**?
	Everybody **except me** was late.	
AFTER BE:	'Who's that?' 'It**'s me**.' (NOT normally 'It is I.')	

In **short answers** we can use **me**, **him** etc (informal) or **I**, **he** etc with a verb (more formal). The same thing happens after **as** and **than**.

INFORMAL	MORE FORMAL
'I'm thirsty.' '**Me** too.' (NOT 'I too.')	'I'm thirsty.' '**I am** too.' / 'So **am I**.'
'Who's paying?' '**Her**.'	'Who's paying?' '**She is**.' (NOT 'She.')
I've got the same number **as him**.	I've got the same number **as he has**.
She gets paid more **than me**.	She gets paid more **than I do**.

1 Put an appropriate pronoun in each blank (the sentences are informal).

1 Nobody except ____ knows where the key is kept, and I'm not telling you.
2 'Who bought these flowers ?' 'It was ____. I thought you'd like them.'
3 'I haven't met Mark yet – is ____ here?' 'That's ____ over there.'
4 'I've had enough of this party.' '____ too.'
5 He's faster than ____, but I'm stronger than ____.
6 John's two years younger than Alice, but ____'s nearly as tall as ____.
7 'Who said that?' 'It was ____ – the man in glasses.'
8 You've got almost the same colour eyes as ____.
9 You may be older than ____, but I don't have to do what you say.
10 'Which is John's wife?' 'That must be ____ just getting out of the car.'

2 Change these to make them more formal or less formal. Example:

I live in the same street as him. ➜ *I live in the same street as he does.*

1 Anne's got the same car as me.
2 They've been here longer than us.
3 I'm much taller than him.
4 'He's going to Mexico.' 'Me too.'
5 'Who said that?' 'Her.'
6 We are not as old as they are.
7 He had a bigger meal than I did.
8 I am not as quick as she is.
9 'We are from York.' 'So am I.'
10 'Who wants a drink?' 'I do.'

For explanations of the words that we use to talk about grammar, see pages 298–302.

We generally use **who** as both **subject** and **object**. *Whom* is unusual, especially in questions, except in a formal style. (For *whom* in relative clauses, see page 270.)

Who *do you want to see?* (More natural than **Whom** *do you want to see?*)

We use **it** to refer to **nothing**, **everything**, **something** and **anything**. We also use **it** when **identifying** people.

Nothing *is ever the way you expect **it** to be.*
*'Who's the woman in red?' '**It**'s Chris Lewis.'* (NOT *'~~She's Chris Lewis.~~'*)

People generally use *he* and *she* for their cats, dogs, horses etc; some people use *she* for their cars, motorbikes and boats. Countries are usually *it*.
*Don't ride **him** on the main road – **he**'s a bit nervous.*
*'How's the car?' '**She**'s running beautifully.'*
*Britain imports more than **it** exports.*

3   Put in a suitable pronoun.

1   'What's your cat's name?' 'Annie. ____ understands everything we say.'
2   Thailand is quite unusual: ____ has never been ruled by another country.
3   'Do you know who the managing director is?' '____ Rose Berczuk.'
4   My bike's been giving trouble, so I'm taking ____ into the garage.'
5   Nothing happened while I was away, did ____?
6   ____ did you have lunch with?
7   'Who's that on the phone?' '____'s your father.'
8   Australia doesn't accept as many immigrants as ____ used to.
9   I don't know ____ she's going out with now.
10 Everything always happens when you don't want ____ to.

'I don't know anybody
who says "It is I".'

'Me?'

reflexive pronouns (**myself** etc)

myself, yourself, himself, herself, itself, oneself
ourselves, yourselves, themselves

We use **reflexives** when the **object** is the same person/thing as the **subject**.

> *I cut **myself** shaving this morning.* (NOT ~~I cut **me** ...~~)
> *He tried to kill **himself**.* (Different from *He tried to kill **him**.*)
> *The lights switch **themselves** on at night.*

Sometimes a reflexive pronoun refers to something that is not the subject.
> ***His** letters are all about **himself**.*   *I told **her** the truth about **herself**.*

1   Put in *myself, yourself* etc or *me, you* etc.

1   Mary bought a book and taught ____ to play the guitar.
2   John fell and hurt ____ yesterday.
3   The computer will turn ____ off if you don't use it.
4   We looked at ____ in the mirror to check our makeup.
5   Don't pay any attention to ____ – he always complains.
6   How much time do you give ____ to drive to work?
7   June can't afford to buy ____ a new car, so her dad's going to buy one for ____.
8   Who gave ____ those lovely flowers?
9   It hurt ____ when I realised Kim wasn't going to phone me.

Reflexive pronouns can also be used to **emphasise** the **subject or object** – to say 'that person/thing and nobody/nothing else'.

> *It's best if you do it **yourself**.*
> *I'll see the President **himself** if necessary.*
> *The house **itself** is nice, but the garden's small.*

2   Put in suitable reflexive pronouns.

1   No one is going to help us, so we'll have to do it ____.
2   Veronica always cuts her hair ____, and it always looks great.
3   Robert ____ is quite friendly, but the rest of his family is very cold.
4   Did you know that the Morrises built their house ____?
5   I don't trust anyone else to do my accounts; I always do them ____.
6   I got to see the gardens, but the palace ____ was closed.

For explanations of the words that we use to talk about grammar, see pages 298–302.

Note the difference between **-selves** and **each other**.

They are looking at **themselves**.   *They are looking at* **each other**.

3 Each other or -selves?

1   Hilary and June write to ____ every week.
2   Agnes and Pat have bought ____ a flat in Rome.
3   Do you and your wife tell ____ everything?
4   You will all need photos of ____ for your membership cards.
5   We've promised ____ to telephone if one of us is going to be late home.
6   We've decided to give ____ a really nice holiday this year.

4 Put in *myself* etc, *each other* or *me*, *you* etc.

1   We decided to keep most of the fruit for ____.
2   Before leaving Eric's office the robbers tied ____ up and pulled out all the
     phone wires.
3   Christine and I always take ____ to lunch on our birthdays.
4   Mum, please don't help me – I'd rather do it ____.
5   Did you ask Alice whether her brother had phoned ____ yet?
6   Don't just stand there shouting at ____ – do something!
7   I've just got up – can I phone you back when I've made ____ a cup of tea?
8   I've never met John, but we've been writing to ____ for over a year now.
9   The necklace ____ wouldn't normally be valuable, but it belonged to
     Queen Elizabeth I, so it will certainly bring a very high price.
10   When babies first start to feed ____, they usually make a big mess.
11   You can't be sure that she got the message unless you told her ____.
12   Your teenage children want to be independent – but they expect ____ to
     be ready to help ____ whenever they ask you to.

Common expressions with reflexives: *behave yourself, enjoy yourself,*
help yourself, make yourself at home, by oneself (= 'alone', 'without help').
Verbs normally used without reflexives: *wash, shave, dress, feel, hurry.*
One another can be used instead of *each other*.
Own replaces possessive reflexives: **my own** room (NOT ~~myself's room~~).

you, one and they

One and *you* can mean **'people in general'** (including the speaker and hearer).
One is more formal than *you*.

> *One/You can't learn French in a month.*
> *One dials / You dial 999 in an emergency.*
> *One's/Your own problems always seem important.*

To talk about people not including the speaker/hearer, we use *they* or a passive.

> *They speak English in this shop. / English is spoken in this shop.*
> (NOT *One speaks English in this shop.*)

They (informal) can mean 'the people around' or 'the authorities', 'the government'.

> *They don't like strangers around here.*   *They say she's pregnant again.*
> *They're always digging up the roads.*   *They don't care about old people.*

1   Write some sentences with *you* and *one*. Examples:

a card / this phone: *One needs / You need a card to use this phone.*
see her / appointment: *One/You can't see her without an appointment.*

1   get into the US / a passport   5   grow oranges / a warm climate
2   a ticket / a train   6   get a driving licence / seventeen
3   fly directly / Gdansk / Prague?   7   eat soup / a fork
4   good at maths / a physicist   8   see animals in the forest / get up early

2   Write *you*, *your*, *they* or *them*.

' 1 've put the price
of stamps up again.'

'Oh, 2 haven't,
have 3 ? 4 seem to do it more
and more often. 5 can't buy more
than a few stamps at a time, or else
 6 have to buy extra 1p stamps
to add to all 7 letters.'

'I know. And it's got
so expensive! Nowadays 8 think
twice before 9 write a letter. Of course
 10 've got special rates for businesses –
it's only ordinary people that
pay the extra.'

'I know.
It makes 11
wonder why we keep
electing 12 .'

We can also use **they**, **them** and **their(s)** to refer to a **singular indefinite person** – for example, after **somebody**, **anybody**, **nobody**, **who**, **a person**.

> **Somebody** phoned and said **they** wanted to see you.
> If **anybody** calls, tell **them** I'm out.
> **Who**'s forgotten **their** umbrella?

3 They/them/their/theirs or another pronoun?

1 Someone's left me a note, but ____ haven't signed it.
2 The person who phoned wouldn't give ____ name.
3 Nobody in the club has paid ____ annual subscription yet.
4 I can't help anybody unless ____ bring all the right documents with ____.
5 If I find out who's made this mess in the kitchen, I'll kill ____.
6 Judy says somebody's stolen ____ lecture notes.
7 Some idiot has taken my bag and left me ____!
8 If anybody can fill in this form, ____'re brighter than me.
9 Nobody will believe me unless I show ____ the picture.
10 That woman I was talking to had ____ car stolen yesterday.

Diplomacy – the patriotic art of lying for one's country.
Ambrose Bierce

They cannot scare me with their empty spaces
Between stars – on stars where no human race is.
I have it in me so much nearer home
To scare myself with my own desert places.
Robert Frost

Knowing what you can *not* do is more important than knowing what you can do.
Lucille Ball

You can get much further with a kind word and a gun than you can with a kind word alone.
Al Capone

Watermelon – it's a good fruit. You eat, you drink, you wash your face.
Enrico Caruso

Most people don't use their eyes except to keep from running into things.
Nancy Hale

You cannot feed the hungry on statistics.
David, Earl Lloyd George

If the child possesses the nationality or citizenship of another country, they may lose this when they get a British passport.
Passport application form

I was [judged] in my absence and sentenced to death in my absence, so I said they could shoot me in my absence.
Brendan Behan

Britain would be a great country if only you could roof it over.
Anonymous

No one can make you feel inferior without your consent.
Eleanor Roosevelt

I hate to spread rumours, but what else can one do with them?
Amanda Lear

one(s)

> We use **one(s)** to avoid repeating a countable noun.
>
> *'What sort of **cake** would you like?' 'A big **one** with cream.'*
> *I'd like some **shoes** like the **ones** in the window.*
> *'Could you lend me **a pen**?' 'Sorry, I haven't got **one**.'*
>
> We **don't** use **one** for an **uncountable** noun.
> *We haven't got fresh **cream**. Would you like **tinned**?*
>   (NOT ... ~~tinned **one**.~~)

1   Put in words and expressions from the box with or without *one(s)*.

> big grey leather   blue   Chinese   long sunny   new
> red woollen   sharp   solid practical   tall   unsweetened

1   'What colour cardigans would you like to see?' '*Blue ones*, please.'
2   I've lost my jacket. It's a ____.
3   'What kind of juice is that?' '____.'
4   'Which glasses do I use?' 'The ____.'
5   She doesn't sell used cars, only ____.
6   'What sort of holiday are you having this year?' 'A ____.'
7   This isn't Thai food, it's ____.
8   I don't want pretty shoes, but ____.
9   Hand me a knife, will you – a ____.
10   There's my suitcase, the____!

> **If there is no adjective:** we do not use *a* with *one*.
>
> *'What sort of cake would you like?' '**One** with cream.'* (NOT '~~A one~~ ...')
>
> We use *some/any* without *ones*. We use *mine* etc instead of *my one* etc.
> *'Could you lend me some stamps?' 'I haven't got **any**.'*
>   (NOT '... ~~any ones~~.')
> *'Which car shall we take?' '**Mine**.'* (NOT '~~My one~~.')

2   Put in *one, some, any* or *mine/yours/etc*.

1   'What sort of job would you like to do?' '____ where I travel a lot.'
2   I haven't got a train timetable, but ask Adrian – he may have ____.
3   'Is that your car or Anna's?' '____ – Anna hasn't got a car.'
4   There aren't any matches here, but there may be ____ in the kitchen.
5   I need a watch – ____ with an alarm.
6   'Where are the forks?' 'Oh, no! We didn't bring ____!'
7   Barry has put his name on this book, but Liz says it's ____.
8   If you haven't got enough plates, I'll be happy to bring ____.

pronouns and **possessives**: revision

1 **Choose the best words to complete the cartoon captions.**

'It's just natural, that's all! ____ love ____
because you're ____, like the car.'
(*we/you/they/ours/yours*)

'____ sold ____ what to ____?'
(*you/she/my/his/what/who*)

'Could ____ tell ____ if ____ glasses are ready yet?'
(*you/he/me/us/myself/my/your*)

'Have ____ seen a lady
without ____?'
(*I/you/her/me/myself*)

'Yes, of course it's important enough to
disturb ____.' (*me/him/himself*)

'Have ____ any "Do It ____" books?'
(*you/he/herself/themselves*)

countable and uncountable nouns

Countable nouns have **plurals**, and **can** be used with *a/an*.

a chair – chairs   a house – houses   an idea – ideas

Uncountable nouns have **no plurals**, and **cannot** normally be used with *a/an*. Examples: *air, water, sand, intelligence, English, weather.*

*She speaks good **English**.* (NOT *... a good English.*)
*It's terrible **weather**.* (NOT *... a terrible weather.*)

1   **Can you divide these into uncountable and countable?**

book, cup, dust, flour, flower, happiness, knowledge, love, milk, meat, mountain, music, oil, piano, rain, river, snow, song, table, wall

Some nouns can be used **both uncountably and countably.**

*Paper is made from **wood**.   I'm going out to buy **a paper**.*
*Did you remember to buy **coffee**?   I'll have **a** (cup of) **coffee**, please.*
*My mother never drinks **wine**.   Spain produces some wonderful*
                                           wines. (= kinds of wine)

2   **Uncountable, singular countable (with *a/an*) or plural? Complete the sentences.**

1   Could you pass me _____? *(glass)*
2   This table is made of _____. *(glass)*
3   I need a piece of _____. *(wood)*
4   The house was near _____. *(wood)*
5   She looked at him with _____. *(pity)*
6   It's _____ Anne isn't here. *(pity)*
7   _____ goes so quickly. *(time)*
8   She phoned six _____ yesterday. *(time)*
9   Three _____, please. *(beer)*
10   _____ makes you fat. *(beer)*
11   He hasn't got much _____. *(experience)*
12   It was _____ I won't forget. *(experience)*
13   There's _____ in the garden. *(chicken)*
14   Do you want _____ or beef? *(chicken)*

With a few uncountable nouns referring to emotional and mental activity, we use *a/an* when there is an adjective or other description.
   an excellent knowledge of German   a good education   a love of music

For explanations of the words that we use to talk about grammar, see pages 298–302.

uncountable nouns: special cases

Sometimes uncountable and countable nouns have similar meanings.

1   **Test yourself. Can you put these words in pairs (one uncountable, one countable) expressing similar ideas? Example:**

furniture – table

accommodation	advertisement	baggage	banknote
bread	cars	fact	flat	furniture	information	job
journey	loaf	money	publicity	suitcase	table
traffic	travel	work

▲ 2   **These nouns are normally uncountable. Most can be made countable by adding *piece* (e.g. *a piece of advice*). Do you know which three can be made countable by adding *a flash of*, *a stroke of* and *a clap of*?**

advice	knowledge	lightning	luck	news	research
rubbish	spaghetti	thunder			

3   **Choose the correct form of the caption for each cartoon.**

'*An advice, / A word of advice, / Some advices*, Arthur: no-one ever solved his problems by running away.'

'Doesn't it make you sick? Our *baggage has / baggages have* been sent to Jupiter.'

plurals of nouns: spelling

1   **Look at the examples and answer the questions. Check your answers in the key.**

babies	*books*	*boys*	*buses*	*buzzes*	*cars*	*chairs*
cities	*dishes*	*echoes*	*Eskimos*	*foxes*	*gases*	*heroes*
holidays	*kilos*	*ladies*	*lorries*	*matches*	*monkeys*	
photos	*pianos*	*potatoes*	*quizzes*	*radios*		
shops	*tables*	*taxes*	*times*	*tomatoes*	*watches*	
ways	*wishes*	*zoos*				

1   What is the most common way of making the plurals of nouns?
2   How do we make the plurals of words ending in **consonant + -y**?
3   How do we make the plurals of words ending in **vowel + -y**?
4   After which letters and groups of letters do we add **-es** to the singular?
5   Four common words ending in **-o** have plurals in **-es**. Can you close your eyes and remember which they are?

2   **Write the plurals of these nouns.**

address	box	brush	computer	desk	face	guy
list	loss	mess	patch	peach	play	poppy
reply	toy	tree	video	witch	worry	

3   **Write a sentence using at least two plurals from 1 above. Example:**

Foxes don't like tomatoes.

If you can work with another student, give him/her two plurals to make a sentence with.

One potatoe̸, two potatoes

IN JUNE 1992, US Vice-President Dan Quayle visited a school class in New Jersey while the children were having a spelling competition. When 12-year-old William Figueroa wrote the word *potato* correctly on the blackboard, Quayle told him he should add an *e*. William became a schoolchildren's national hero (without an *e*) and appeared on television; the Vice-President became an international laughing-stock as echoes (with an *e*) of his mistake went round the world.

plurals of nouns: special cases

▲ **1   Here are seven groups of nouns. Look in the box and find two
      more nouns to add to each group.**

> aircraft   crisis   dozen   mathematics   means   mouse
> news   police   scissors   sheep   shelf   thousand
> tooth   wolf

1   COUNTABLE NOUNS WITH SINGULAR (AND PLURAL) IN **-s**
    series   crossroads   analysis – analyses

2   OTHER NOUNS WITH SINGULAR AND PLURAL THE SAME
    trout   deer   fish   salmon

3   NOUNS THAT HAVE A PLURAL WITHOUT **-s** AFTER A NUMBER
    hundred (e.g. *two hundred*)   million

4   NOUNS WITH SINGULAR IN **–f(e)**, PLURAL IN **-ves**
    calf – calves   half   knife   leaf   life   loaf   self
    thief   wife

5   OTHER NOUNS WITH IRREGULAR PLURALS
    child – children   foot – feet   fungus – fungi   goose – geese
    man – men   medium – media   ox – oxen   penny – pence
    phenomenon – phenomena   woman – women

6   UNCOUNTABLE SINGULAR NOUNS ENDING IN **-s** (NORMALLY NO PLURAL)
    athletics   billiards   economics   gymnastics   measles
    physics   politics

7   PLURAL NOUNS WITH NO SINGULAR
    arms   belongings   cattle   clothes   congratulations
    contents   earnings   goods   outskirts   people
    remains   surroundings   thanks   troops   trousers

deer   fish

mixed **singular** and **plural**

Singular nouns for **groups** of people often have **plural verbs and pronouns** in British English, especially when we are talking about personal kinds of action. Compare:

*My **family are** very angry with me: **they** think I should go to university.*
*The average **family has** 3.5 members: **it** is much smaller than in 1900.*

*The **team are** going to lose again. **They're** useless.*
*A cricket **team is** made up of eleven players, including **its** captain.*

1 **Choose the best combination for each blank.**

class is	club has	orchestra is	school has	staff do
class are	club have	orchestra are	school have	staff does

1a   In England, a state ____ to give time to religious education.
1b   My daughter's ____ decided to hold their sports day next Saturday.
2a   The ____ given £5,000 to charity this year.
2b   The ____ fifty per cent more members than a year ago.
3a   The ____ not like the new manager.
3b   The ____ not need to be increased.
4a   Jane's ____ in Room 6.
4b   Our ____ planning a party.
5a   The ____ just tuning up – let's hurry in.
5b   An ____ composed of string, wind, and percussion instruments.

2 **Choose the correct form of the cartoon caption.**

'It's the office. Shall I tell *it/them/him* you're sick?'

The following **singular expressions** also usually have **plural verbs**:
a number of ...   the majority of ...   a couple of ...   a group of ...
a lot of + plural noun/pronoun, *the rest of* + plural noun/pronoun.

> ***A number of*** us ***are*** *worried about it.*
> ***The majority disagree****.*
> ***There are a couple*** *of children outside.*
> ***A lot of them were*** *late.*
> ***The rest of the members are*** *ill.*

Some **plural expressions** have **singular** verbs:
names of quantities, plural names of countries, compound nouns joined by
and, more than one + singular noun.

> ***Ten pounds is*** *too much to pay.*
> ***Three weeks was****n't enough holiday.*
> ***The United States is*** *smaller than Canada.*
> ***Fish and chips costs*** *£3.*
> ***More than one person disagrees****.*

We also use a singular verb after ***one of*** + **plural noun**.
> ***One of your children has*** *lost a shoe.*

3   Choose the right verb.

1   A group of teenagers in the town *(has/have)* organised a scheme to help
     old people with their shopping.
2   A number of people *(has/have)* complained about the noise.
3   Do you think three pounds *(is/are)* a big enough tip?
4   Hamburger and chips *(is/are)* not a very healthy lunch.
5   In the latest rail union vote, the majority *(has/have)* voted to go on strike;
     the rest of the members *(is/are)* expected to support the strike fairly
     solidly.
6   Two kilos *(is/are)* pretty small for a newborn baby.
7   Our teenage son thinks there *(is/are)* a number of good reasons for
     staying up late and having a good time.
8   More than one house in our street *(has/have)* been broken into recently.
9   A couple of dangerous-looking men *(is/are)* waiting for you outside.
10 One of my friends *(has/have)* just won two free plane tickets to New York.
11 Six weeks *(is/are)* a long time to wait for news of your family.
12 The majority of the children's parents *(is/are)* unemployed.
13 A lot of shops *(is/are)* opening on Sundays now.
14 The Philippines *(has/have)* signed the new human rights agreement.
15 The police think that more than one person *(was/were)* in the stolen car.
16 Tom and Rosie were late, but the rest of us *(was/were)* on time.
17 *(Is/Are)* bacon and eggs what you usually eat for breakfast?
18 We've just learnt that a couple of our club members *(has/have)* been
     chosen for the national team.

possessive 's

SINGULAR noun(s) + **'s**:	my **mother's** car, **Sarah and Henry's** house
PLURAL noun + **'**:	my **parents'** home
IRREGULAR plural + **'s**:	the **children's** names

1   **Make possessive forms from the items in List 1 to combine with items from List 2. Make fifteen combinations. Examples:**

your sister's address   my teachers' clothes

LIST 1

your sister   Jonathan   Ann and Pat   those women
my teachers   Katie   our dog   Simon and Jill
most people   doctors

LIST 2

address   car/cars   ideas   health   legs
father/fathers   nose/noses   clothes   education
fear of heights

Possessives usually **replace articles** before nouns. We can say **the** car or **Sue's** car, but not ~~**Sue's the** car~~ or ~~**the Sue's** car~~.
But a possessive word can have its own article: **the boss's** car.
Note also: *that car of Sue's; a friend of Joe's* (like *a friend of mine* – see page 28).

2   **Right or wrong? Put ✔ for correct sentences;
rewrite incorrect ones.**

1   Is this the teacher's pen?
2   Are you the Al's daughter?
3   Do you know Lesley's last name?
4   Here's the Barry's address.
5   Here's my parents' address.
6   It was the school's responsibility.
7   What's the Wilsons' number?
8   That's an old habit of Marion's.
9   It's a crazy idea of Alice.
10   Where is that brother of Carol?

Note: *We spent the evening at **Anne's**. (= ... at Anne's house.)*
       *She's at **the hairdresser's**.   I bought it at **Harrod's**.*

For explanations of the words that we use to talk about grammar, see pages 298–302.

noun + noun

We can put nouns together in three ways:
1 **noun + noun:**   *a shoe shop; a war film*
2 **preposition structure:** *the top of the hill*
3 **possessive 's structure:** *my boss's car; Ann's idea*
Usually, an idea can be expressed in only one of these ways, and it is often
difficult to know which is correct. The rules on pages 63–67 will help, but
there are exceptions – this is a very difficult point of grammar.

We often put one noun in front of another. The **first noun** is rather like an
adjective, and is usually **singular**, even if the meaning is plural.

> *a **horse** race* (a kind of race)   *a **race** horse* (a kind of horse)
> *a **shoe** shop* (NOT *a **shoes** shop*)   *a **Lancashire** man*
> *a **ten-mile** walk* (NOT *a **ten-miles** walk*)

Articles belonging to the first noun are dropped in this structure. *Officers in*
the army = army officers, NOT *the army officers*.

1 Match the expressions on the left with their meanings on the right.

1 chocolate milk   a book describing cases
2 milk chocolate   b chocolate made with milk
3 book case   c leather for making shoes
4 case book   d drawing done in ink
5 leather shoe   e garden with flowers in
6 shoe leather   f ink used for drawing
7 flower garden   g milk flavoured with chocolate
8 garden flower   h piece of furniture for books
9 ink drawing   i flower that grows in gardens
10 drawing ink   j shoe made of leather

2 What do you call these?

1 a shop that sells music   5 the clock in the station
2 a man from Birmingham   6 a rocket that goes into space
3 a frame for a picture   7 a factory that makes biscuits
4 tea made from mint   8 powder made from soap

3 Put these words into pairs to make noun + noun expressions.
   Change plural to singular if necessary.

antique	bicycle	bus	cowboy	door	film	grapes
juice	kitchen	map	newspapers	publisher	race
roads	shop	station				

noun + noun or preposition structure

We use the **noun + noun** structure for **well-known everyday combinations**.
To talk about things that do not go together so often, we usually prefer a
structure with a preposition. Compare:

a war film	*a film about a dog* (NOT ~~a dog film~~)
a history book	*a book about violins* (NOT ~~a violin book~~)
a postman	*a man from the bank* (NOT ~~a bank man~~)
road signs	*signs of anger* (NOT ~~anger signs~~)
a corner table	*the girl in the corner* (NOT ~~the corner girl~~)

**1   Eight of these ideas can naturally be expressed by 'noun + noun'.
     Which are they? Rewrite them.**

1   a cake made of chocolate
2   a child in the garden
3   a cupboard in the kitchen
4   a box for matches
5   paste for cleaning teeth
6   discussions about furniture
7   the door to the kitchen
8   a bottle designed for wine
9   a timetable of trains
10   a book about the moon
11   chairs for the garden
12   a man with a knife

**2   Look at the labels. Can you think of some more names of food
     that use the noun + noun structure?**

Newspaper headlines often save space by using the noun + noun structure
instead of the preposition structure. Strings of three or four nouns are
common.

Channel ferry safety drill leaves 18 injured

Decision day in rail dispute

Football club burglars cut home phones

noun + noun and possessive 's

We use the **noun + noun structure** to name **common kinds of thing**.
The first noun is often like an **object** (of a verb or preposition).

*a **shoe** shop = a shop that **sells shoes***
*a **war** film = a film **about war***

We use the **possessive 's structure** most often to talk about something
that **belongs to** a particular person, group, organisation, country or
animal. The first noun is often like a **subject** (usually of the verb *have*).

*my **boss's** car: my **boss has** a car*   ***Ann's** idea: **Ann had** an idea*

1   Choose the correct noun group.

1   a bus's station *or* a bus station
2   a toys' shop *or* a toy shop
3   the teacher's office *or* the teacher office
4   computer's disks *or* computer disks
5   my mother's chair *or* my mother chair
6   car's papers *or* car papers
7   Tom's plan *or* the Tom plan
8   a telephone's box *or* a telephone box
9   the dog's toy *or* the dog toy
10   a horse's race *or* a horse race

11   vegetables' soup *or* vegetable soup
12   China's history *or* the China history
13   a cowboys' film *or* a cowboy film
14   street's lamps *or* street lamps
15   the firm's office *or* the firm office
16   a bath's towel *or* a bath towel
17   that cat's tail *or* that cat tail
18   a teacher trainer *or* a teachers' trainer
19   the paper's editor *or* the paper editor
20   a glass's factory *or* a glass factory

2   Complete the cartoon caption.

MATT

'I laid 67,000 eggs last year, and if I don't
receive a _____ there'll be trouble.'

Mother Day card	Mother Day's card
Mother's Day card	Mother's Day's card

possessive 's or the of structure

We use the **possessive 's** structure especially when the first noun is the name of a **person**, **group of people**, **organisation**, **country** or **animal**. In other cases we generally prefer a structure with **of**. Compare:

my **father's** name	the name **of the book**
the **firm's** structure	the structure **of plastic**
America's influence	the influence **of alcohol**
the **dog's** leg	the leg **of the table**

We also use the possessive 's structure with common **'time when'** expressions, and in expressions of **measurement of time**.

today's paper   **tomorrow's** weather   **yesterday's** news
a month's holiday   **three hours'** delay

▲ 1   **Rewrite these using 's, ' or of the. Examples:**

the club + its monthly meeting   *the club's monthly meeting*
his parents + their car   *his parents' car*
the world + its end   *the end of the world*

Angela + her leg   the trees + their highest branches   my suitcase + its lock
your dog + its leg   the bank + its branch in Paris   your office + its floor
the table + its leg   my family + its name   the town + its atmosphere
our company + its best sales manager   the police force + its main problem
next week + its timetable   last night + its party   today + its news

▲ 2   **Make two noun groups from each set of words. Example:**

file: your secretary, legal documents:
your secretary's file, the file of legal documents

1   story: Helen, the French Revolution
2   bed: the stream, the patient
3   policy: full employment, the company
4   style: my favourite author, the 1930s
5   place: language education, women

6   ideas: modern physics, my son
7   rules: the club, football
8   view: the committee, the lake
9   head: the cat, the queue
10   arm: the chair, John

For explanations of the words that we use to talk about grammar, see pages 298–302.

▲   3   **Put together the expressions from the left-hand box, and three of the expressions from the right-hand box, to make captions for the cartoons.**

Fear?	your tests' results.
I have here	the results of your tests.
He doesn't know	the word's meaning.
Let's go. I've got	the meaning of the word.
Right, Mr Wilson.	somebody else's car
parked outside.	the car of somebody else

adjectives and adverbs

ADJECTIVES: kind, shy, cold, angry, wonderful, bad, unusual, mad
ADVERBS: kindly, shyly, coldly, angrily, wonderfully, badly, unusually, madly

We use **adjectives** to say how something **is**, **seems**, **becomes**, **looks**,
feels, **sounds**, **tastes** or **smells**.

> She **is kind**.   She **seems/appears shy**.   It's **getting cold**.
> He **felt angry**. (NOT *He felt angrily*.)   That **smells wonderful**.

We use **adverbs** with other verbs to say how something **happens** or **is done**.

> She **spoke kindly** but **shyly**. (NOT *She spoke kind*...)
> He **answered** me **coldly**.   He **closed** the door **angrily**.

1   **Complete the sentences with words from the box. More than one
    answer may be correct.**

> beautiful/beautifully   calm/calmly   cheap/cheaply
> clear/clearly   slow/slowly   soft/softly   terrible/terribly
> unhappy/unhappily

1   I suppose I should be nervous, but I've never felt so ____ in my life.
2   'I suppose we'll never see each other again,' she said ____.
3   I haven't got much money: if I travel this year, I'll have to do it ____.
4   The house is small and rather simple, but Anne has decorated it ____.
5   This soup tastes ____.
6   He spoke very ____, but she heard every word like a shout.
7   Good computers are getting quite ____ now.
8   The train was very ____; perhaps they were working on the line.
9   She sat there ____ lying about everything she had done.
10 This is a ____ house. I enjoy looking at it every time I walk past.
11 Her hair is so lovely and ____ – like a baby's hair.
12 This handwriting isn't very ____; can you read it any better than me?
13 The team played ____ last Saturday.
14 Time seemed to go so ____. When would he arrive?
15 He looks really ____: I wonder what's wrong.
16 Mary doesn't speak very ____: I often have trouble understanding her.

For explanations of the words that we use to talk about grammar, see pages 298–302.

We also use **adverbs** before **adjectives**, **past participles**, **other adverbs** and **prepositional expressions**.

> *It's **terribly cold**.* (NOT ... ~~terrible cold~~.)   *This is very **badly cooked**.*
> *You're driving **unusually fast**.*   *He was **madly in love** with her.*

2   Choose the right word.

1   Angela is *(amazing/amazingly)* good with animals.
2   As soon as I saw him I was *(sure/surely)* he had been drinking.
3   Do you think that's a *(real/really)* diamond in her ring?
4   He was wearing a *(true/truly)* astonishing tie.
5   I felt her arm *(gentle/gently)* to see if any bones were broken.
6   I read an *(amazing/amazingly)* thing in the newspaper this morning.
7   John was *(wonderful/wonderfully)* kind to me when I came to this country.
8   Keith seemed *(gentle/gently)*, but there was something cruel underneath.
9   One leg of the chair was *(slight/slightly)* damaged.
10 Sarah drives a *(real/really)* beautifully restored 1914 sports car.
11 She looked at me *(kind/kindly)*, but didn't say anything.
12 The door was *(bad/badly)* painted.
13 The food was *(wonderful/wonderfully)*, but the service was *(awful/awfully)*.
14 The room is *(clever/cleverly)* organised so three of us can work there.
15 The job was *(surprising/surprisingly)* easy.
16 He's acted *(unbelievable/unbelievably)* stupidly in the past year.

Some verbs are used with both adjectives and adverbs, with different meanings.

> *You **look angry**.* (= *You **seem** angry*.)
> *He **looked angrily** at the manager.* (= *He **turned his eyes** ...*)
> *His plan **appeared impossible**.*
> *She **suddenly appeared** in the window.*

If a thing is worth doing, it is worth doing well.
Traditional

If a thing is worth doing, it is worth doing badly.
G K Chesterton

Speak softly and carry a big stick.
President Theodore Roosevelt

Power tends to corrupt and absolute power corrupts absolutely.
Lord Acton

[You are] incredibly, inordinately, devastatingly, immortally, calamitously, hearteningly, adorably beautiful.
The poet Rupert Brooke to the actress Cathleen Nesbitt

confusing **adjectives** and **adverbs**

1 Are the words in the box adjectives, adverbs or both? Look at the sentences and decide.

daily/weekly/monthly/yearly		cowardly		deadly		early	
fast	friendly	hard	late	likely	lively	lonely	
loud	lovely	silly	ugly	well			

1 It's getting **late**.
2 *The Times* is a **daily** paper.
3 She's a **lovely, friendly, lively** person. But she seems **lonely**.
4 It doesn't seem **likely** that your children will be **ugly**.
5 The postman's **early**.
6 She speaks English very **well**.
7 We have **monthly** meetings.
8 Don't talk so **loud**.
9 If you've got a **fast** car, why don't you drive **fast**?

10 If you want me to work **hard**, you'll have to pay me more.
11 Milk is delivered **daily**.
12 The train arrived **late**.
13 I can't stand **loud** noises.
14 Don't be so **silly**.
15 She's becoming **hard** to live with.
16 I'm very **well**, thanks.
17 That was a **cowardly** thing to do.
18 Curare is a **deadly** poison.
19 I get paid **monthly**.
20 Try to come home **early**.

2 Which of the words from Exercise 1 could go in each blank?

1 a *cowardly/friendly/lovely/silly* expression
2 a ____ magazine
3 ____ music
4 She sings too ____.
5 He visits us ____.
6 a ____ thing to say
7 ____ faces
8 very ____ to rain

9 ____ flowers
10 a ____ house
11 We left ____.
12 trying ____
13 a ____ illness
14 ____ work
15 a ____ life
16 ____ phone calls

Say it loud, I'm black and proud.

Title of song by James Brown

Once the toothpaste is out of the tube, it is awfully hard to get it back in.

H R Haldeman

People tell me there are a lot of guys like me, which doesn't explain why I'm lonely.

Mort Sahl

Give us this day our daily bread.

The Lord's Prayer

This universe is not hostile, nor is it friendly. It is simply indifferent.

J H Holmes

It is better to be beautiful than to be good. But ... it is better to be good than to be ugly.

Oscar Wilde

and with **adjectives**

When adjectives come **after a verb**, we usually put ***and*** before the last. **Before a noun**, *and* is **less common**.

He was tall, dark ***and handsome***.   I'm cold, tired ***and hungry***.
a tall, dark, ***handsome*** cowboy   a tired ***(and) hungry*** child

But when adjectives (or other descriptive words) refer to **different parts** of a following noun, we use *and*.

a ***yellow and black*** dress   a ***concrete and glass*** building

1 Put in *and* if necessary.

1 The brick was rough/pink.
   The brick was rough and pink.
2 hot/breezy weather
3 untidy/red hair
4 The man was young/bearded.
5 The sea was cold/rough.
6 The church was old/ugly.
7 a quiet/tense woman
8 yellow/grey sand
9 The badges were red/blue.
10 a narrow/brown room

When you're wearing Springers ... leave your feet feeling cool and relaxed.

In the softest, lightest sandals the world is somehow brighter.

adjectives without nouns

We can use **the + adjective** (without a noun) to talk about some
social groups.

> the young   the old   the rich   the poor   the sick
> the disabled   the handicapped   the blind   the deaf
> the mentally ill   the homeless   the unemployed   the dead

These expressions are **plural**: *the blind* means 'blind people'. Compare:

> *I'm collecting money for **the blind**.*
> *Do you know **the blind person** next door?* (NOT ... ~~the blind next door?~~)
> *I met **a blind man** on the train.* (NOT ... ~~a blind~~ ...)

We can't use all adjectives in this way: we don't normally talk about *the
foreign* or *the greedy*, for example.

1   **Complete the sentences with expressions from the box.**

> the blind (twice)   the living (twice)   the poor (twice)
> the dead   the old   the rich (twice)   the young (twice)

1   In the country of ____ the one-eyed man is king.   *Anonymous*
2   Love, like youth, is wasted on ____.   *Sammy Cahn*
3   When the rich make war on each other, it's ____ who die.
      Jean-Paul Sartre
4   It's all that ____ can do for ____, to shock them and keep them up to
      date.   *George Bernard Shaw*
5   'Let me tell you about ____. They are different from you and me.'
      'Yes, they have more money.'   *F Scott Fitzgerald and Ernest Hemingway*
6   We owe respect to the dead; to ____ we owe only truth.   *Voltaire*
7   ____ have more children, but ____ have more relatives.   *Anonymous*
8   Pray for ____ and fight like hell for ____.   *Mother Jones*
9   Does it matter: – losing your sight?
      There's such splendid work for ____;
      And people will always be kind,
      As you sit on the terrace remembering
      And turning your face to the light.   *Siegfried Sassoon*

The structure is also used with the following **nationality words**: Dutch,
English, French, Irish, Scottish, Spanish, Welsh.

> **The Welsh** have a very old literary tradition.
> BUT: *I like **the Welshman** who works in the garage.*
>   (NOT ... ~~the Welsh~~...)

For explanations of the words that we use to talk about grammar, see pages 298–302.

adjectives: order before nouns

This is a complicated point of grammar. The following rules have exceptions.

Words for **colour**, **origin/place**, **material** and **purpose** go in that order.
Other adjectives come before these.

OTHER	COLOUR	ORIGIN/PLACE	MATERIAL	PURPOSE	
old	red	Spanish	leather	riding	boots
a funny	brown	German		beer	mug

Opinions often come **before descriptions**.

OPINION	DESCRIPTION	
funny	old	buildings
a terrible	little	boy
nice	new	clothes

1   **Here are descriptions from a newspaper, a journal, a biography and a novel.
Rewrite each description in the right order. Example:**

books: old, terrible   *terrible old books* (opinion + description)

1   city: Belgian, beautiful, little
2   club: jazz, local
3   dinner: excellent, cold
4   buildings: modern, industrial
5   dress: evening, red, silk
6   eyes: narrow, colourless
7   frame: flat, gold
8   furniture: old, lovely
9   ink: drawing, Swiss
10   jacket: short, leather
11   squares: brick, little
12   boots: French, ski
13   tie: blue, woollen
14   trousers: cotton, grey
15   trunks: black, nylon, swimming

WONDERFUL, tall energetic guy, 44 going on 32, would love to meet that special lady to share life with. Call phone box 53124

Good-looking, slim, kind, cheerful, mature, non-smoking Welshman, 45, interested in everything except opera and politics, seeks attractive, warm, sensitive, intelligent woman in 30s for friendship, love, who knows? Please write to Box No.781.

WOOD STREET
A pretty detached town Cottage with dining hall, living room, fitted kitchen and conservatory. Two bedrooms and bathroom. Gas heating, attractive rear garden.
£120,000

'Single green male, 214 ...'

First and **last** usually come **before numbers**:
   the ***first three*** weeks (NOT ~~the *three first* weeks~~)
   my ***last two*** holidays
Note the word order in ***something nice***; ***nothing new***.

word order: adverbs with the verb

Adverbs that go **with the verb** include words expressing **frequency** (e.g. *always*, *often*, *usually*, *never*) and **certainty** (e.g. *definitely*, *probably*). Note the exact position:

AFTER AM/ARE/IS/WAS/WERE
*You **are usually** right.*
*It **was certainly** cold.*

AFTER AUXILIARY VERBS
*She **has probably** forgotten.*
*I **can never** wake up in time.*

BEFORE OTHER VERBS
*He **always forgot** my birthday.*
*I **often get** headaches.*

NOT BETWEEN VERB AND OBJECT
*He ~~**forgot always my birthday**~~.*
*I ~~**get often headaches**~~.*

All**, **both and ***each*** can also go with the verb.
*You**'re all** wrong.*
*They **are both** studying maths.*
*We **each gave** a five-minute talk.*

1   **Make ten sentences from the box. Example:**

My father is often bad-tempered.

I am	always usually often	happy late tired
____ is	sometimes not often	friendly bad-tempered
____ are	occasionally never	depressed worried
		in love in trouble *etc*

2   **Make ten sentences beginning *I have often/never* ...**
Examples:

I have often been to America.   *I have never seen an opera.*

3   **Say how often you do some of the following things. Examples:**

I sometimes stay in bed late.   *I don't often go to the doctor.*

stay in bed late   have bad dreams   eat chocolate
get headaches   play tennis   read poetry   fall in love
go to concerts   play the piano   forget people's names
go to the cinema   cook   go to the doctor   write letters
go skiing   go swimming   get depressed   feel happy

4   **If you can work with another student:**
   - **ask him/her how often he/she does the things in Exercise 3**
   - **report his/her answer.**

Examples:

1   *'How often do you go to concerts?' 'Never.'*
2   *Maria never goes to concerts.*

5   **These sentences are all taken from real recorded conversations.
    Can you put the adverbs in the right places?**

1   You are here when something happens. *(usually)*
2   Her mum cooks a meal in the evening. *(always)*
3   We book that April holiday in January. *(usually)*
4   They think that we have got bread. *(probably)*
5   You should look where you're going. *(always)*
6   She is going to stay overnight. *(probably)*
7   Chocolate cakes are the best. *(definitely)*
8   I will be able to get it cheaper. *(probably)*
9   I have had an illness in my life. *(never)*
10 We saw sweets in those days. *(never)*
11 I remember buying some. *(definitely)*
12 Do you read upside down? *(usually)*
13 I can manage to get there. *(usually)*
14 She has done that before. *(never)*
15 Something is burning. *(definitely)*
16 She has been nervous. *(always)*
17 I feel cold in your house. *(never)*
18 They were against me. *(always)*
19 We are going to win. *(definitely)*
20 February is the worst. *(usually)*
21 It is very difficult. *(sometimes)*
22 I buy them in boxes. *(always)*
23 I have tried to find it. *(often)*
24 They are fighting. *(always)*
25 She saw this ghost. *(often)*
26 You are right. *(probably)*

'You never tell me you hate me any more.'   *Ken Pyne*

If there is more than one auxiliary verb, adverbs of **frequency** and **certainty**
usually go **after the first auxiliary**.

*The roof **has never been** repaired.*
*I **will definitely be** seeing him tonight.*

Adverbs go before or after *not*, depending on the meaning. Compare:

*She's **not often** late.*   *It's **definitely not** raining.*

focusing adverbs: even and only

Even and *only* often go **with the verb** when they focus on words later in the sentence.

He's rude to everybody. He**'s** | even | rude | to me.

(NOT ~~Even he's rude to me.~~)

He | even | plays tennis | in the rain.

I | only | liked the | first part of the concert.

They've | only | lived here | for a few weeks.

1   Put in *even* or *only*.

1   She talks to her brother.   *She only talks to her brother.*
2   I am doing this because I love you.
3   She gets up at six on Sundays.
4   He wears a suit on holiday.
5   She ate a piece of dry toast.
6   I can play very easy music.
7   He can't write his own name.
8   They make you pay for a carrier bag.
9   I was thinking of you.
10 You can ski there in summer.

Even and *only* can also go just before the words that they emphasise.

He plays tennis **even in the rain**.
He eats anything – **even raw potatoes**.
Even a child could understand it.
They've lived here **only a few weeks**.
Only you could do a thing like that.

Even does not normally go between the verb and the object.
He can **even speak Chinese**. (NOT ~~He can speak even Chinese.~~)

2   Join the beginnings and ends, and put in *even* or *only*.

BEGINNINGS	ENDS
I work every day my mother	really understands me. rats.
They do everything together	It's me! knew that he was ill.
Hello! the cat	thinks you're stupid. hated him.
She likes all animals the clock	but for a few minutes. broke the silence.
his wife his children	they brush their teeth together. on Sundays.
You can borrow it	

adverbs at the end of a sentence

At the end of a sentence we often put words and expressions which say **how**, **where** and **when**. They most often go **in that order**.

*She sang **very well at the concert last night**.*
*He works **in the garage on Tuesdays**.*
  (NOT ... *on Tuesdays in the garage.*)
*He's working **there now**.*
*The children were playing **quietly in the garden**.*
*Let's go **to bed early**.* (NOT ... *early to bed.*)

We do not normally put adverbs between a verb and its object.
*You **speak English very well**.* (NOT *You **speak very well English**.*)
*Can you **repair my watch now**?*
  (NOT *Can you **repair now my watch**?*)

1   Put the words in brackets into the sentences (not before the verb).

1   I work at night. *(best)*
2   I paid at once. *(the bill)*
3   He always moves very slowly. *(in the morning)*
4   She speaks Japanese. *(fluently)*
5   I think we'd better open the parcel. *(now)*
6   She was crying in her room. *(quietly)*
7   We talked about it briefly. *(at lunchtime)*
8   I'm going to break the eggs into the bowl. *(carefully)*
9   Ann works at the village shop. *(on Saturdays)*
10 I can't explain my feelings. *(clearly)*
11 The team played yesterday. *(brilliantly)*
12 I always worked at school. *(very hard)*
13 She practises the piano here. *(every evening)*
14 I don't think she plays tennis. *(very well)*
15 He read every word. *(slowly)*
16 Put the butter in the fridge. *(at once)*

After verbs of **movement**, the order can be different: we most often put **expressions of place first**.

*He **went upstairs quietly**.*

still, yet and already

We use **still** to talk about **situations continuing**.
We use **yet** to ask if something **expected has happened**, or to say that it **hasn't**.
Still usually goes **with the verb**; **yet** usually goes **at the end of the sentence**.

> *She's **still** asleep.   Do you **still** love me?   I **still** don't understand.*
> *Has the postman come **yet**?   Alice hasn't phoned **yet**.*

We use **already** to say that something has happened **earlier than expected**, or earlier than somebody thought. **Already** usually goes with the verb.

> *'When's your mother coming?' 'She's **already** here.'*
> *'You must go to Scotland.' 'We've **already** been.'*
> *She's only been here a week and she **already** knows all the neighbours.*

1   Put in *still*, *yet* or *already*.

1	Are you in the same job?	9	Our old car runs OK.
2	He's seventeen, but he's married.	10	Is the rice cooked?
3	Has Susan arrived?	11	She's gone to bed.
4	I've finished!	12	Is she in that little flat?
5	9 a.m., and it's dark!	13	Why are you in bed?
6	4 p.m., and it's dark!	14	I'm bored with my new job.
7	Have you had breakfast?	15	It's not time to stop.
8	Look – it's raining.	16	Have you written that letter?

'It's the waiter at the restaurant where we ate tonight.
He wants to know if everything is still all right.'

Drawing by Vietor; © 1993
The New Yorker Magazine, Inc.

**2   Write three or more sentences about yourself using *I am still* ...,
I haven't ... yet or *I have already* ...**

comparatives and superlatives

Comparative adjectives are forms like *younger*, *more expensive*.
Superlative adjectives are forms like *youngest*, *most expensive*.

1 **Look at the examples and match the beginnings and ends of the rules.**

*more/most beautiful   more/most careful   more/most distant
easier, easiest   faster, fastest   happier, happiest   later, latest
more/most intelligent   nicer, nicest   older, oldest*

Rules

To make the comparative and superlative of:	you:

one-syllable adjectives ending in -e
other one-syllable adjectives
two-syllable adjectives ending in -y
other two-syllable adjectives
longer adjectives
	put *more* and *most* in front.
	change *y* to *i* and add *-er*, *-est*.
	add *-er*, *-est*.
	put *more* and *most* in front.
	add *-r*, *-st*.

2 **Look at the examples and complete the rule correctly.**

bigger	longest	fatter	shortest	sweeter	hottest
oldest	plainer	thinnest	meaner		

Rule
Before *-er* and *-est*, we double the last letter of:

1 all adjectives.
2 adjectives that have three letters.
3 adjectives that have one vowel.
4 adjectives that end in one vowel + one consonant.
5 adjectives that end in one consonant.
6 adjectives that end in *-g* or *-t*.

3 **Check your answers to Exercises 1 and 2 in the key. Then write the comparative and superlative of:**

boring	cheap	fine	full	funny	handsome
hard	honest	interesting	lazy	light	nervous sad
safe	silly	sorry	stupid	uncomfortable	useful
violent	wet				

irregular comparison

good/well – better – best   bad – worse – worst
far – farther/further – farthest/furthest   old – older/elder – oldest/eldest
little – less – least   much/many – more – most

Farther/further and **farthest/furthest** are both used to talk about
distance.
We use **further** to mean **'additional'** in some expressions.

She lives three miles **farther/further** *away from the office than I do.*
further *education*   **further** *information*   **further** *discussion*

Elder and **eldest** are used with **brother, sister, son, daughter, grandson,
granddaughter.**

John's my **elder** *brother.* (I have one brother older than me.)
Sarah's my **eldest** *sister.* (I have more than one sister.)

1   **Answer the questions, using the words from the list at the top of
    the page.**

1   If I'm not happy with the pen I've got and money is not a problem, what
    should I do? *Buy a better pen.*
2   Three thousand people entered a poetry competition. Max's poem won.
    Why?
3   Five friends all arrived for lunch at the same time. Alice had left home an
    hour before anyone else. Why?
4   I had a cold. I went to work, but left early and went home to bed. Why?
5   I wanted to make a pear tart, but I realised all the pears were going bad. I
    used parts of some of the pears. Which three pears did I throw away?
6   Jill was born in 1970. Her sisters Liz and Sue were born in 1972 and
    1973, and her brothers Ted and Joe were born in 1971 and 1974. What
    can Liz call Jill? What can Joe call Ted? What can Sue call Jill?
7   My cousin has a medical problem. The doctors have done some tests, but
    they still can't decide what the problem is. What are they going to do?
8   Seven different plants need different amounts of water. Which one will
    grow best in a dry sunny place?
9   The Blacks have got a big house and three expensive cars. The Browns
    have got a small flat and one inexpensive car. Why?
    (*Answer in two ways*)
10   Why does it take longer for me to walk to the post office than to the park?

comparative and superlative adverbs

Comparative and superlative adverbs normally have **more** and **most**.

*Could you drive **more slowly**?* (NOT ... ~~slowlier~~?)
*French is the language he speaks **the most easily**.*

But the following adverbs have **-er**, **-est** like adjectives:
early   fast   hard   late   near   soon

Better, *best*, *worse* and *worst* can be used as adverbs.

1 **Write the comparative/superlative of a word from the box for each blank.**

1 If we don't walk ____, we'll never arrive on time.
2 She sings ____ than anyone else I've ever heard.
3 Andy's the most intelligent, but Sue works ____.
4 Eight is late – could you possibly get here any ____?
5 Of all the children, Helen writes ____.
6 I would sleep ____ if I weren't worried about Tom.
7 For the 10.20 train, ____ we can leave home is 10.
8 Mark speaks French ____ of all the boys in his class.

> beautiful
> early
> fast
> fluently
> hard
> late
> peacefully
> sensitively

2 **If you are in a class, find out some of the following things and write sentences.**

Who: sings best, sings worst, cooks better than you, cooks worse than you, can run fastest, gets up earliest, goes to bed later than you, works hardest?

3 **Complete the captions with comparative adverbs.**

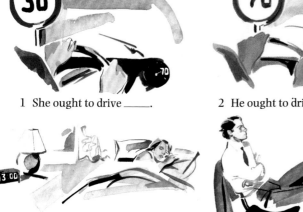

1 She ought to drive ____.   2 He ought to drive ____.

3 She should have got up ____.   4 He ought to work ____.

much etc with **comparatives**

Before comparatives, we can use *much*, *far*, *very much*, *a little*, *a bit* (informal), *a lot/lots* (informal), *any*, *no* and *even*.

He's **much/far older** than her. (NOT ~~He's very older~~ ...)
She's **very much happier** in the new job.
I feel **a little / a bit better**.
These grapes are **a lot sweeter** than the others.
The train's **no quicker** than the bus. / ... isn't **any quicker** ...
You look **even more beautiful** than usual.

1 **Write ten or more sentences comparing some of the things in the box. Try and use *much / very much / far / a little / a bit / a lot / even / no / any*. Example:**

The Taj Mahal is much older than the White House.

the Taj Mahal   the Great Pyramid   the White House a Ferrari   a Ford   a Volvo   the Amazon   the Thames the Rhône   a pen   a typewriter   a computer   a dog a cat   a parrot   a horse   living in the country living in the city   the Mediterranean   the Atlantic Europe   Africa   Asia   North America   South America you   your mother/father/friend/boss/teacher

'How about a little more coffee?'

Drawing by Gahan Wilson; © 1993
The New Yorker Magazine, Inc.

comparative or superlative?

We use a **comparative** to compare **one** person, thing, action or group with **another** person, thing etc.
We use a **superlative** to compare **one** person, thing etc with the **whole group** that he/she/it belongs to. Compare:

> Mary's **taller** than **her three sisters**.   Mary's **the tallest** of **the four girls**.
> Your accent is **worse** than **mine**.   Your accent is **the worst** in **the class**.

Some people use a **comparative** instead of a superlative when the **whole group** has **two members**.

> I like them both, but Maud's **the nicer/nicest** of **the two**.
> You can have **the bigger/biggest steak** if you like – I'm not very hungry.

1 Make two sentences for each item. Example:

a tiger   large / a leopard?   large / all the big cats?
Is a tiger larger than a leopard?
Is a tiger the largest of all the big cats?

1	this box	strong / that one?	strong / you've got?
2	Alistair	tall / anyone else / class	tall / the class
3	state of Alaska	big / other states / US	big / US
4	this wine	expensive / that one	expensive / the world
5	Al's party	good / Pat's party	good / I've ever been to

2 Compare four-wheel drive cars: here are some facts from an article about three real cars. Write at least ten sentences. Examples:

Car Z is faster than Car X. Car Y is the fastest of all / the three.

	CAR X	CAR Y	CAR Z
FAST? TOP SPEED:	106 mph	113 mph	109 mph
EXPENSIVE?	£23,382	£35,889	£36,912
ECONOMICAL?	20.1 miles/gallon	16.7 miles/gallon	15.8 miles/gallon
SAFE?	✓✓	✓✓✓	✓✓✓✓
COMFORTABLE?	✓✓✓✓✓	✓✓✓	✓✓✓✓
GOOD OFF-ROAD?	✓✓✓✓	✓✓	✓✓✓✓✓
LUGGAGE SPACE?	1,011 litres	1,100 litres	1,020 litres

comparatives: other points

We can use **double comparatives** to say that things are **changing**.

*It's getting **colder and colder**.*
*We went **more and more slowly**.* (NOT ... ~~more slowly and more slowly.~~)

1   Complete the sentences.

1   She's driving _____.   2   She's getting _____.   3   It's getting _____.

4   The maths lessons are getting _____.   5   That cat's getting _____.

6   I'm getting _____.   7   Bread's getting _____.

2   Write sentences with ...*er and ...er* or *more and more* ... Example:

My daughter's maths homework / *difficult* to understand.
My daughter's maths homework is getting more and more difficult to understand.

1   My mother's driving / *dangerous* as the years go by.
2   I heard Jeremy practising the piano yesterday – / *good*.
3   It seems as if police officers / *young*.
4   My temper / *bad*.
5   *hard* / to find time for everything you want to do.
6   Professional tennis / *boring*.
7   Restaurants / *expensive*.
8   Her holidays / *long*.

We use ***the ... the*** with comparatives to say that things change or vary together.

> ***The older*** I get, ***the happier*** I am. (NOT ~~Older I get, **more I am happy.**~~)
> ***The more dangerous*** it is, ***the more*** I like it.
> (NOT ~~The more it is dangerous~~ ...)
> ***The more*** money he has, ***the more*** useless things he buys.

3 **Complete the sentences with expressions from the box.
Use *the ... the*. Example:**

_____ Mark gets, _____ he looks like his grandfather.
The older Mark gets, the more he looks like his grandfather.

older/more	more/more	older/darker	more/angrier
warmer/more	longer/more	faster/more	more/less
more/more/less			

1   _____ he drove, _____ we laughed.
2   _____ I live here, _____ I like it.
3   _____ I get, _____ my hair gets.
4   _____ money he lost, _____ it made him.
5   _____ I learn, _____ I forget and _____ I know.
6   _____ I get to know you, _____ I understand you.
7   _____ clothes she buys, _____ clothes she wants to buy.
8   _____ it got, _____ time we spent on the beach.

4 **Circular situations: make sentences like the one in the example.**

He drives fast; he gets nervous.
The faster he drives, the more nervous he gets; and the more nervous he gets,
the faster he drives.

1   He eats ice cream; he gets fat. *(The more ice cream ...)*
2   He reads; he forgets.
3   She ignores him; he loves her.
4   She buys shoes; she wants shoes. *(Mind the word order.)*
5   We spend money; we have friends.
6   I sleep; I'm tired.
7   *(Make your own sentence.)*
8   *(Make your own sentence.)*

Why study?
The more I study, the more I know.
The more I know, the more I forget.
The more I forget, the less I know.
So why study?

superlatives: other points

After **superlatives**, we do **not** use *of* with a **singular** word for a
place or group.

> *I'm the happiest man **in the world**.* (NOT ... ***of** the world.*)
> *She's the fastest player **in the team**.*
>   (BUT ... *the fastest player **of them all**.*)

1   *Of* or *in* after a superlative?

1	all of us *of all of us*	7	the four men
2	the Army	8	the girls in her school
3	the books I own	9	the office
4	the class	10	the paintings in the gallery
5	Europe	11	Rome
6	my family	12	the school

We normally use ***the*** before **superlative + noun**, when we are comparing
one person/thing/group with others.

> *He's **the most handsome man** I know.*
> *It's **the longest day** of the year.*

We do not use *the* before **superlative without noun**, when we are
comparing somebody or something with him/her/itself in other situations.
> *He's **nicest** when he's had a few drinks.* (NOT *He's **the nicest** when ...*)
> *England is **best** in spring.*

▲ **2**   **Invent suitable beginnings for these sentences. *The* or not?**

1   ＿＿ most beautiful city in my country.
2   ＿＿ most dangerous when they're hungry.
3   ＿＿ best modern writer.
4   ＿＿ most interesting person I've ever met.
5   ＿＿ quietest in the early morning.
6   ＿＿ most efficient way to learn a language.
7   ＿＿ most comfortable when there aren't too many people around.

3   **Complete these sentences.**

1   I'm happiest when I ＿＿.
2   ＿＿ is happiest when he/she ＿＿.

than, **as** and **that**

Than is used **after comparatives**.
As is used in the structures ***as ... as*** and ***the same as***.
That is a **conjunction** used, for example, after words of saying
and thinking.
That is also a **relative pronoun**, like *which* and *who*.

> She's **taller than** me. (NOT ~~*taller as/that me.*~~)   *I'm **older than** her.*
> *It's **as cold as** ice.   The meeting's **the same** time **as** last week.*
> *I told them **that** I disagreed.   There's the house **that** I told you about.*

We can often leave out *that* (see page 243).
> *I told them I disagreed.   There's the house I told you about.*

1   *Than*, *as*, or *that*?

1   It's ____ warm ____ toast in here.
2   It's later ____ I thought.
3   I think ____ she's Czech.
4   I feel stronger ____ I did.
5   Can't you eat faster ____ that?
6   He's as funny ____ toothache.

7   It'll cost the same ____ before.
8   The car ____ I saw was too small.
9   The cat seems worse ____ yesterday.
10   There's the boy ____ broke the window.
11   It's not as cold ____ yesterday.
12   She's got the same job ____ me.

2   Complete the caption.

'There, dear! I think we've left the world a better place ____ we found it!'

as ... as

We use **as ... as** to say that people or things are **equal** in some way.

> She's **as tall as** her brother.   Is it **as good as** you expected?
> She speaks French **as well as** the rest of us.

After *not*, we can use *so ... as* instead of *as ... as*.
> He's **not so/as** successful as his father.

Other useful structures:
> I haven't got **as much** time **as** I thought.
> We need **as many** people **as possible**.
> She earns **twice as much** money **as me / as I do**.
> He went to **the same** school **as me / as I did**.
>   (NOT ... ~~to (a) same school~~ ...)

1   **Look at the information about Jake and Susie, and then write
    sentences comparing them using *as ... as*, *not so/as ... as* and
    the same ... as. Examples:**

Susie went to the same school as Jake.   Jake's not as old as her.

	JAKE	SUSIE
UNIVERSITY	Manchester	Liverpool
SCHOOL	Leeds H. S.	Leeds H. S.
HEIGHT	1.92 m	1.70 m
WEIGHT	87 kg	56 kg
JOB	accountant	accountant
BORN: WHEN? WHERE?	27.7.64 Leeds	31.3.64 Leeds
SALARY	£26,000	£52,000
WORKS FOR	IBM	Rolls Royce
HOLIDAY	5 weeks	3 weeks
ADDRESS	3 Ross Street Manchester	8 Ross Street Manchester
CHILDREN	2	2
LANGUAGES	Fluent French, some German	Fluent French, fluent German
READING	Newspapers	Newspapers, magazines, non-fiction

'There goes a car with exactly
the same number as ours.'

2 Here are the beginnings and ends of some traditional expressions with *as … as*. See how many you can put together correctly. Example:

as cold as ice

AS:			AS:		
black	cold	flat	a beetroot	gold	
good	green	hard	grass	the grave	
old	pretty	quiet	the hills	ice	iron
red	thin	warm	night	a pancake	
white			a picture	a rake	
			a sheet	toast	

Some colourful and unusual comparisons:

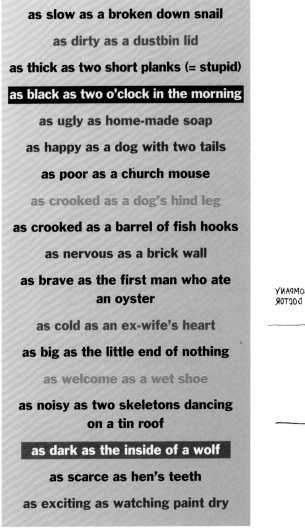

as slow as a broken down snail

as dirty as a dustbin lid

as thick as two short planks (= stupid)

as black as two o'clock in the morning

as ugly as home-made soap

as happy as a dog with two tails

as poor as a church mouse

as crooked as a dog's hind leg

as crooked as a barrel of fish hooks

as nervous as a brick wall

as brave as the first man who ate
an oyster

as cold as an ex-wife's heart

as big as the little end of nothing

as welcome as a wet shoe

as noisy as two skeletons dancing
on a tin roof

as dark as the inside of a wolf

as scarce as hen's teeth

as exciting as watching paint dry

'How d'you mean I'm as fit as a
man of thirty – I **am** thirty!'

like and as

We can use **like** and **as** to say that things are **similar**.
Like is a **preposition**, used before a **noun or pronoun**.
As is a **conjunction**, used before **subject + verb** or a prepositional expression.

> *He runs **like the wind**.*   *She looks **like me**.*
> *Nobody knows her **as I do**.*   *On Friday, **as on Monday**, we meet at eight.*

Note the common expressions *as I said, as you know, as you see, as usual*.

1   *Like* or *as*?

1   He died ____ he lived, fighting.
2   Being in love is ____ an illness.
3   It's mended, ____ you can see.
4   In Paris, ____ in Rome, traffic
    is heavy.
5   His eyes are ____ knives.

6   My brother isn't at all ____ me.
7   She left ____ she came, silently.
8   You're shy, ____ me.
9   Your smile is ____ your sister's.
10 ____ I said, you're too late.

In informal speech (but not writing), many people use *like* as a conjunction.

> *Nobody loves you **like I do**.*   ***Like I said**, she wasn't there.*

We use **as** as a **preposition** before a noun or pronoun to talk about the **jobs**, **roles** and
functions of people and things.

> *He worked **as a waiter** for a year.*   *Don't use your plate **as an ashtray**.*

Compare:
> ***As your brother**, I must warn you to be careful. (I am your brother.)*
> ***Like your brother**, I must warn you ... (We both warn you.)*

2   Choose an item from the box for each blank and write it with *like* or *as*.

1   Susan sings *like an angel.*
2   I worked ____ for five years.
3   Henry uses the dining room ____.
4   That cat snores just ____.
5   ____, next Tuesday is a holiday.
6   I've come to this meeting ____.
7   This bread tastes ____.
8   James speaks ____: carefully and precisely.
9   She's clever and passionate – ____.
10 Why don't we have ice cream ____?

| a person |
| a secretary |
| a dessert |
| a union representative |
| an angel |
| an office |
| cardboard |
| he writes |
| her mother |
| you know |

so and such

We use **so** before an **adjective** (without a noun), or an adverb.
We use **such** before **(adjective +) noun**. *A/an* comes **after such**.

> She's **so babyish**.
> I'm **so hungry** that I could eat a horse.
> ... your country, which is **so beautiful**.
>   (NOT ... your ~~so beautiful country~~.)
> I wish you wouldn't drive **so fast**.
> She's **such a baby**.
> I didn't know you had **such nice friends**.
> It was **such a comfortable bed** that I went straight to sleep.

1 Put in *such* or *so*.

1 The weather was ＿＿＿ cold that all the football matches were cancelled.
2 It was ＿＿＿ hot weather that nobody could do any work.
3 The book was ＿＿＿ boring that I stopped reading it.
4 It was ＿＿＿ a good film that I went to see it three times.
5 They've got ＿＿＿ a nice house that I always love staying there.
6 And their garden is ＿＿＿ beautiful!
7 His voice is ＿＿＿ pleasant that I could listen to him all day.
8 I don't know why she talks in ＿＿＿ a loud voice.

2 Rewrite the sentences in Exercise 1, using *such* instead of *so* or *so* instead of *such*, and making any other necessary changes.

3 Complete the sentences, using expressions with *such* or *so*.

1 It was ＿＿＿ that I couldn't see my hand in front of my face.
2 The canteen served ＿＿＿ food that nobody could eat it.
3 It was ＿＿＿ car that the police couldn't catch it.
4 The case was ＿＿＿ that nobody could lift it.
5 It was ＿＿＿ lecture that I couldn't keep my eyes open.
6 This language is ＿＿＿ that foreigners can't learn it.
7 He was ＿＿＿ person that everybody liked him.
8 I was ＿＿＿ that I went to sleep standing up.
9 I wish my ＿＿＿ wasn't/weren't so ＿＿＿.
10 I wish I hadn't got ＿＿＿.

Such and *so* emphasise. To talk about **similarity**, we prefer **like this/that**.

> Look over there. I'd love to have **a car like that**. (NOT ... ~~such a car~~.)

very and **too**

1   **Do you know the difference between *very* and *too*? Put the right
    expressions with the pictures.**

very expensive	too expensive	very fast	too fast
very hot	too hot	very slow	too slow	very small
too small	very tall	too tall

1

2

3

4

5

6

7

8

9   10

11

12

very (much) with **past participles**

We use **very much** with **past participles** when they are in **passive verbs**.

> She was **very much admired** by her students.
>   (NOT ... ~~very admired~~ ...)
> The bridge was **very much weakened** by the floods.

Very is common with **past participles** that are used as **adjectives**, especially to say how people feel – for example **worried**, **shocked**, **frightened**, **confused**, **annoyed**, **surprised**, **isolated**, **disappointed**, **thrilled**, **amused**.

> We're **very worried** about Sam. (NOT ~~We're very much worried~~ ...)
> I was **very shocked** to hear about the accident.
> She's **very frightened** of spiders.

▲ **1** **Put in very or very much.**

1   Her plans have been _____ simplified since I last told you about them.
2   I can see that you are _____ worried about something.
3   I get _____ confused when people shout at me.
4   I'll be _____ surprised if you can't answer this.
5   I'm _____ annoyed because I can't open the safe.
6   His ideas were _____ imitated by other writers.
7   Many AIDS patients feel _____ isolated.
8   My book was _____ improved by your suggestions.
9   She's been _____ photographed, written about and talked about, but nobody really knows her.
10 She's _____ respected by her colleagues.
11 The police have been _____ criticised recently.
12 They weren't _____ amused when you told that joke.
13 When I had money problems I was _____ helped by my uncle.
14 Will she be _____ disappointed if I can't come?
15 You don't sound _____ thrilled about seeing me.

Very much is used with **mistaken**.

> That's Bill's car, unless I'm **very much mistaken**.
>   (NOT ... ~~very mistaken.~~)

be: progressive forms; **do be**

We use **am being**, **are being** etc for **actions** and **behaviour**, but not feelings. Compare:

> You**'re being** stupid. (= You**'re doing** stupid things.)
> I **was being** careful. (= I **was doing** something carefully.)

> I**'m** depressed just now. (NOT I**'m being** depressed just now.)
> She **was** very cheerful yesterday. (NOT She **was being** ...)

For the use of *am being* etc in passive verbs, see page 176.

1   Put in the correct form of *be*.

1   The baby ____ very good today.
2   I ____ a bit lonely these days.
3   John ____ difficult about money again.
4   Really! The children ____ absolutely impossible this morning.
5   I don't know why I ____ so tired.
6   You ____ very careless with those glasses.
7   I didn't really mean what I said. I ____ silly.
8   She ____ excited about her birthday.

Do is used with **be** to make **emphatic imperatives** and **negative imperatives** (see page 218), but not usually in other cases.

> **Do be** careful!   **Don't be** silly!
> BUT I**'m not** often ill. (NOT I **don't** often **be** ill.)

'The dog's being impossible again.'

be: age, colour etc

Note the use of **be** to talk about **physical characteristics** and **conditions**.

AGE	*How old **is** she? He **was** my age.* (NOT *He **had** my age.*)
HEIGHT	*He must **be** six feet tall. She **is** the same height as her father.*
WEIGHT	*I wish I **was** a few kilos lighter.*
SIZE	*The room **is** ten metres by six. What size **are** your shoes?*
COLOUR	*What colour **are** his eyes?*
PHYSICAL	*I**'m** hungry. **Are** you thirsty? The baby **is** sleepy.*
CONDITIONS	*We **were** too warm/hot/cold. Don't **be** afraid.*

Note also: *to be right/wrong/lucky/ashamed.*

1   Complete the sentences.

1 I'm ____ tall.
2 I ____ the same height as ____.
3 My eyes ____.
4 My eyes ____ the same colour as ____.
5 My hair ____.
6 My shoes ____ size ____.

2   Write a sentence giving the size of the room that you are in now. If you are in a class, write sentences about some of the other students.

3   Write five or more sentences to say how you feel now. Use some of the words in the box.

cold	hot	hungry	ill	sleepy	thirsty	warm
well	wide awake					

4   Write three or more sentences beginning *I'm (not) afraid of* ...

People can have it in any colour – as long as it's black.

Henry Ford, talking about the Model T Ford car

The future is black.

James Baldwin

The so-called white races are really pinko-grey.

E M Forster

I am black, but O! my soul is white.

William Blake

Eyes too expressive to be blue, too lovely to be grey.

Matthew Arnold

The East is red.

Chinese communist slogan

do: emphatic auxiliary

Emotive emphasis: we can use *do* to make an expression **sound stronger**.

> *Do sit down.*   *You **do** look nice today!*   *I **did** enjoy our talk.*

1 **Join the beginnings and ends; make the sentences more emphatic by using *do/does/did*. Example:**

I do feel ill!

BEGINNINGS	ENDS
I agree	a lot.
I apologise	eggs and bacon.
I feel	he's really happy.
I hate	ill.
I like	cooking.
I need	tired.
Peter enjoyed	with you.
She looks	your party.
You talk	a job.
I wonder if	for disturbing you.

'Do come out, Rover, Susan won't bite.'

Contrastive emphasis: we can use *do* to show a **contrast** – between false and true, appearance and reality, or a general statement and an exception.

> *She thinks I don't love her, but I **do** love her.*
> *It looks easy, but it **does** need quite a bit of practice.*
> *There wasn't much time for shopping, but I **did** buy a couple of blouses.*

We can also use *do* to compare what is expected with what actually happens.

> *I said I was going to win, and I **did** win.*

2 Join the beginnings and ends; add the idea of contrast by using *do/does/did*. Example:

I've forgotten her name, but I do remember it began with a B.

BEGINNINGS	ENDS
I've forgotten her name,	Mind you, it has a nice big kitchen.
'You don't love me.'	They said eight o'clock, didn't they?
I may not be educated,	'I love you.'
I'll be ready in a minute,	but I remember it began with a B.
I'm not sure she'll be there,	but I have to make a phone call.
It's a small house.	She plays a bit of tennis sometimes.
My wife does the housework,	and she had a broken finger.
Although she didn't say much,	but I iron my own trousers.
She doesn't really like sport.	she gave me her phone number.
I made her go to the doctor's,	but if you see her give her my love.
There's nobody at home.	but I know something about life.

3 Make sentences like the one in the example. Use *do/does/did*.

Shakespeare didn't make films, but he did write plays.

Shakespeare	made films wrote plays sell beer
Scottish people	lend money fought against England
In England	fought against China eat potatoes
Banks	eat mice speak English speak Japanese
Cats	rains a lot snows a lot
Napoleon	

Dear ...

For the past seven years the Society has benefited from the tax rebate on your covenanted subscription but, unfortunately the covenant has now expired. We do hope you will renew it.

Dear ...

I am writing to thank you for your gift of £200.00 by banker's standing order under your covenant, received on 5th October 1992.

We do appreciate all your support – it is vital to our expanding work.

Dear ...

Thank you for your letter of 14th November. I am extremely sorry that you have been troubled and I entirely agree that writing to you was discourteous and a bad use of our funds.

We do in fact take good care to ensure that this does not happen and I am making enquiries as to why we slipped up in your case.

For *do be* in emphatic imperatives like *Do be careful!*, see page 218.

do and **make**

1　Can you work out the rule? Look at the examples and answer the questions. Then check your answers in the key.

Can you do the shopping?
Make a copy of this letter.
Dad makes wonderful omelettes.
Do something!
Could you do the ironing and the washing up?
He likes doing nothing.
I love making model aeroplanes.
I must do the accounts.

I want time to do some reading.
Once my father and I made a boat.
Shall I make a cake?
She's always making crazy plans.
He did something really funny.
Time to do some work.
We did a lot of walking and swimming.
What shall we do now?

1　Do we use *do* or *make* to talk about **work**?
2　Which do we use to talk about **building** and **creating** things?
3　Which do we use when we **don't say exactly** what the activity is?
4　Which do we use before **determiner + *ing* form**, to talk about longer or repeated activities (mostly jobs and hobbies)?

2　Learn these fixed expressions:

do: good, harm, business, one's best, (someone) a favour, one's hair, one's duty, 100 mph/kph
make: an attempt, an effort, an offer, an excuse, a suggestion, a decision, an exception, enquiries, a phone call, a mistake, a fuss, a noise, arrangements, a journey, progress, money, a profit, a fortune, love, a bed, a fire, war, peace

3　Complete the cartoon caption.

'Pembroke, have you been trying to _____ decisions again?'

4 Try to complete the sentences without looking at the opposite page.

1 He's *doing* the shopping.

2 She's ____ the ironing.

3 She's ____ her accounts.

4 He's ____.

5 He's forgotten to ____.

6 He's ____.

7 He's going to ____.

8 They're ____.

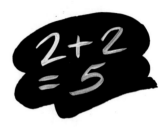

9 She's forgotten to ____.

10 This car will ____.

11 Somebody's ____.

12 'I'm just going ____.'

have: actions

We often use **_have_** to talk about **actions**, especially in an informal style.

typical expressions:
have breakfast, lunch, coffee etc
have a wash, bath etc
have a rest, sleep, lie-down, dream etc
have a good time, bad day, nice evening, day off, holiday etc
have a good flight/trip/journey etc
have a talk, word, conversation, disagreement, quarrel, fight etc
have a swim, walk, dance, ride, game etc
have a try, a go, a look
have difficulty/trouble in ...ing
have a baby
have an accident, an operation, a nervous breakdown

In this structure, _have_ is an ordinary verb with progressive forms, and with
_do_ in questions and negatives.
    '_Where's Jane?_' '_She**'s having** a bath._'   _What time **do you have** lunch?_

1   **What can you do with these things / in these places? Use _have_**
    with the words in the box.

dinner   a drink   a game of cards   a game of tennis
a rest   a shave   a shower   a swim   tea

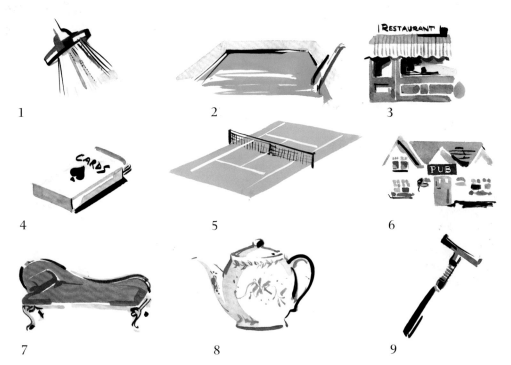

1   2   3

4   5   6

7   8   9

2   What are they going to do? Use *have* with the words in the box.

| an accident   a baby   a fight   a nervous breakdown |
| an operation |

1   2   3

4   5

'Yes, this seems quite a clear bit, have a nice day.'

'You have a go in ours, and we'll have a go in yours, okay?'

'This is your captain speaking … I apologise for the
bumpy ride. We are now flying at about ten feet …
Mr Tatlow's had a go … who's next?'

have (got): possession etc

Have can be used to talk about **possession**, **relationships**,
characteristics and similar ideas.
The short forms *I have*, *have I?*, *I have not* etc are **unusual** in
an informal style.
Instead, we generally use forms with *have got* or *do ... have*.

INSTEAD OF	WE USE
I/you/*etc* have	I've got, you've got *etc*
have I/you? *etc*	have I got? *etc* OR do I have? *etc*
I/you *etc* haven't	I haven't got *etc* OR I don't have *etc*
had I/you? *etc*	did I have? *etc*
I/you/*etc* hadn't	I didn't have *etc*

1   Can you complete the examples?

1   I've _____ a new boyfriend. (*More natural than* I have a new boyfriend.)
2   _____ your sister got a car? OR Does your sister _____ a car?
    (*More natural than* Has your sister a car?)
3   I haven't _____ your keys. OR I _____ have your keys.
    (*More natural than* I haven't your keys.)
4   The school does not _____ adequate sports facilities.
    (*More natural than* The school has not adequate sports facilities.)
5   _____ you _____ good teachers when you were at school?
    (*More natural than* Had you good teachers ... ?)
6   She _____ _____ children. (*More natural than* She hadn't children.)

**2   If you're *homeless*, you *haven't got a home*. Write sentences using
    If you're ..., you haven't got a/any ... to explain these words:**

1	bald	4	unemployed	7	starving
2	penniless	5	toothless	8	an orphan
3	childless	6	lonely	9	unmarried

I have got is not present perfect in this use. It means exactly the same as *I have*.
Got- forms are most common in the present.
The past forms *I/you/etc had* are common without *got*.
    I had a bad cold last week.

Do and *got* are not used together. NOT ~~Do you have got any children?~~
Progressive forms of *have* are not possible with these meanings.
    NOT ~~Are you having any children?~~

3   Complete the conversations, using *have got*, *has got* etc.

1   '____ an aspirin? ____ a terrible headache.' 'I'll just look. I think ____ some in my bag. Oh, no, sorry, ____ any.'
2   'How many brothers and sisters ____?' 'Just one brother.'
3   'We ____ a new car.' 'Really?' 'Yes. ____ four-wheel drive, power steering and anti-lock braking.' 'Fascinating.'
4   'I'm afraid ____ some bad news for you.' 'Oh, no. What is it this time?'
5   'Why ____ dark glasses on?' '____ something wrong with my eyes.'
6   '____ dirt on my nose?' 'No, but ____ something funny in your hair.'
7   'Sally ____ a new boyfriend.' 'What's he like?' 'Very good-looking. He's quite tall, and ____ big dark brown eyes and a lovely smile. But she says ____ a terrible temper.'

4   Here are some 'contact' advertisements from a magazine. Write sentences about some of the things that the people have got. Example:

The man in the first advertisement has got an athletic build.

handsome, intelligent male, 6ft, 31, athletic build, Porsche, seeks attractive girlfriend, under 30, for fun and friendship. Box 329.

natural woman, 37, intelligent, fun loving, tall, brown hair, blue eyes, good sense of humour, enjoys cinema, theatre and travel, seeks sincere, well educated man, 35–55, for honest, caring relationship. Ring 093 22815.

attractive, professional black lady, slim, 5ft 6in, nice smile, own apartment, likes long hair, brains in a man. Ring 038 9734.

successful businessman, 35, attractive, tanned, nice home, yacht, requires exciting, slim female. Photograph. Ring 045 37943.

5   Complete some of these sentences.

1   I've got plenty of ____.
2   I haven't got a ____.
3   I haven't got much ____.
4   I haven't got many ____.
5   I haven't got any ____.
6   I've got too much ____.
7   I've got too many ____.
8   I've got enough ____.
9   I haven't got enough ____.

6   If you can work with another student, ask him/her ten questions using *have you got?* Then write a report on what you have found out.

have: habitual and repeated actions

Got-forms are **not** generally **used** to talk about **habits and repeated actions**.

*We **have** meetings on Mondays.* (NOT ~~**We've** got meetings on Mondays.~~)
***Do** you often **have** colds?* (NOT ~~**Have** you often **got** colds?~~)

1   Here is a child's school timetable. Write ten or more sentences beginning *She has ... / She doesn't have ...*   Examples:

She has maths at nine o'clock on Mondays.
She has economics once a week.
She doesn't have French on Wednesdays.

	M	T	W	Th	F
9.00–10.00	maths	French	English	maths	physics
10.15–11.15	history	maths	chemistry	French	chemistry
11.30–12.30	biology	physics	Russian	geography	English
2.00–3.00	English	geography	sociology	Russian	maths
3.15–4.15	games	economics	games	English	games

2   Write some sentences about what happens in your week. Examples:

I have staff meetings on Wednesday mornings.
I have English lessons three times a week.
I usually have a lie-in on Sunday mornings.

American influence on British usage

In British English, present-tense *do*-forms have traditionally been used mostly to talk about habitual and repeated actions; *got*-forms have been used in other cases. (Compare: *I don't usually have colds*; *I haven't got a cold.*)

In standard American English, *got*-forms are unusual in questions and negatives, and *do*-forms are common for all meanings. (*I don't have a cold.*)

But modern British English usage is becoming more similar to American usage.

have + object + verb form

Have something done: **arrange** for something to be done.

> I must **have my watch repaired**.   We need to **have the curtains cleaned**.

1 **Make sentences using *have* + object + the past participles in the box.**

changed	cleaned	cut	put in	redecorated	repaired	reproofed
re-strung	serviced	sharpened	valued			

1 When did you last (your hair)?
   When did you last have your hair cut?
2 We (our knives) once a year.
3 We're going to (the roof) next summer.
4 I must (my jacket). And I'd better (my raincoat).
5 'Do we need to (the car)?' 'Well, we ought to (the oil).'
6 When she (her jewellery), she found it wasn't actually worth much.
7 You need to (your tennis racket).
8 Shall we (the kitchen), or shall we do it ourselves?
9 It would be nice to (some more electric sockets).

This structure can also be used to refer to kinds of **experience**:
Have something happen: **experience** something that **happens/happened**/etc.
Have something happening: **experience** something that **is/was happening**.
Have something done: **experience** something that **is/was done**.

> We **had a strange man come** to the door yesterday.
> We suddenly realised we **had water coming** through the ceiling.
> He **had his car stolen** while he was shopping.

'If you don't mind, I'm going to stop this conversation right now and turn on the television.
If I've got to have my intelligence insulted, then I'd rather it were done by an expert.'

modal auxiliary verbs: basic rules

The 'modal auxiliary verbs' are **can**, **could**, **may**, **might**, **shall**, **should**, **will**, **would**, **must** and **ought**.
They are used **before other verbs**, and in **tags** and **short answers**.

'You **can speak** Japanese, **can't you?**' 'Yes, I can.'
'You **shouldn't** be here, **should** you?' 'No, I **shouldn't**.'

DO IT YOURSELF

1 Compare the modal verbs and the ordinary verbs in the examples, and answer the questions. Check your answers in the key.

Could you help me?	Do you expect to see her?	Do you want to stop?
He must be happy.	He seems to be happy.	I can't sing.
I hope to see him.	It may rain.	Shall we stop?
She will not go home.	She doesn't know much.	She wants to go home.
They didn't ask to be here.	They shouldn't be here.	We ought to tell her.

1 Which sort of infinitive is used after modal verbs? Which is the exception?
2 What is special about the third person present (he/she/it ...) of modals?
3 What is special about the question and negative forms of modals?

2 Use infinitives from the box to complete the sentences.

be	to be	do	to do	finish	to finish	get
to get	go	to go	make	to make	pass	to pass
play	to play					

1 Can you _play_ the piano?
2 She seems _to be_ better today.
3 I want _to do_ some shopping.
4 We may _go_ to France soon.
5 When will you _finish_ school?
6 She hopes _to get_ a new car.
7 Must you _make_ so much noise?
8 Could you _get_ the salt?

3 Make these sentences into questions, and change the pronouns as shown. Example:

I can swim. (you) ➔ Can you swim?

1 She can stay here. (I)
2 I must go. (you)
3 They will understand. (he)
4 I shall drive. (we)
5 He could do it. (she)
6 I would like to. (you)

For explanations of the words that we use to talk about grammar, see pages 298–302.

Modal auxiliary verbs have **no infinitives or participles**. Instead, we use other expressions like **be able to**, **be allowed to**, **have to**.

4   Can you complete the examples with expressions from the box?

> be able to   to be able to   been able to   been allowed to
> have to   to have to   had to

1   He'd like _to be able to_ travel abroad more. (NOT He'd like to can ...)
2   I've never _been able to_ understand maths. (NOT I've never could ...)
3   The child has always _been allowed to_ go out alone. (NOT She's always could ...)
4   I'm sorry ____ tell you this ... (NOT I'm sorry to must ...)
5   We've ____ get new shoes for both the kids. (NOT We've must ...)
6   One day, everybody will ____ travel where they want.
7   I'm afraid you will ____ work next weekend.
8   I would hate ____ live in a big city.
9   I would have enjoyed the holiday more if I had ____ speak Spanish.

5   Complete some of these sentences.

1   I've never been able to _sing well._
2   I'd like to be able to _be a good listener._
3   One day, people will be able to _know me as a good singer_
4   I wouldn't like to have to _take a training._
5   I've always had to _go walking._
6   I've never had to _go by car._
7   When I am President of the World, people will have to _follow me._

6   What do you think are the missing words in the cartoon caption?

'But the good news is that you'll never ____ smoke, drink or drive a car again.'

must, **can**, **may**, **might**: how certain?

We can use **must** to say that something is **logically necessary**, or that we **suppose** it is **certain**. The **negative** is **cannot** or **can't**, not ~~must not~~.

> If A is bigger than B, and B is bigger than C, then A **must** be bigger than C.
> Mary **must** have a problem – she keeps crying.
> There's the doorbell. It **must** be Roger.
> No, it **can't** be Roger. It's too early. (NOT ... ~~it mustn't be Roger~~ ...)

Can is used in **questions**.
> There's the phone. Who **can** it be?

1   Rewrite these sentences using *must* or *can't*.

1   I'm sure she's at home.   *She must be at home.*
2   I'm certain you're crazy.
3   I know that isn't Janet – she's in America.
4   I'm sure she thinks I'm stupid.
5   I bet I look silly in this coat.
6   They're always buying new cars – I'm certain they make a lot of money.
7   I'm sure he's not a teacher – he's too well dressed.
8   You're an architect? I'm sure that's an interesting job.
9   I'm sure you're not serious. I know you're joking.
10   I'm sure he's got another woman: he keeps coming home late.

'She must be blind. She's smiling.'

JUMP, BOY!

GOD, YOUR LIFE MUST BE DULL.

C.Barsotti

May suggests that something is **possible**. *Might* suggests a **weaker possibility**.

> *She **may** be at home.* (perhaps a 50% chance)
> *Ann **might** be there too.* (a smaller chance)
> *According to the radio, it **may** rain today. It **might** even snow.*

2 Look at the pictures and write sentences with ***must/may/might/ can't***. Example:

1 *She must be ill.* OR *She can't be well.*

1   2   3   4

5   6   7   8

9   10

Note the difference between ***may/might not*** and ***can't***.

> *The game **may/might not** finish before ten.* (Perhaps it won't.)
> *The game **can't** finish before ten.* (It's not possible.)

must, **should** etc: obligation

Must is used for **orders** and for **strong suggestions**, advice and opinions.
Should is used for **less strong suggestions**, advice and opinions.

> *You **must** stop smoking or you'll die.*
> *You really **should** stop smoking, you know. It's bad for you.*
>
> *People **must** realise that the world is in serious trouble.*
> *People **should** drive more carefully.*

Ought is similar to *should*, but is followed by *to*.
> *People **ought to** drive more carefully.*

Orders and instructions can be made more polite by using *should*.
> *Applications **should** be sent before 30 June.*

1   Which do you think is better – *must* or *should*?

1   You know, I think you _____ take a holiday.
2   Tell Mark he _____ tidy his room at once.
3   Visitors are reminded that they _____ keep their bags with them.
4   I'm sorry, but you _____ go. We don't want you here.
5   I really _____ go on a diet. I'll start today!
6   I suppose I _____ write to Aunt Rachel one of these days.
7   You absolutely _____ check the tyres before you take the car out today.
8   All officers _____ report to the Commanding Officer by midday.
9   You _____ have your hair cut at least once a week.
10 I think men _____ wear jackets and ties in restaurants.

'For your first effort you should write about something you understand.
Don't try to write about yourself.'

2   Complete some of these sentences with your own ideas.

1   I think people should _be independent_
2   I don't think people should _do too_
3   I think children should ____.
4   I don't think children should ____.
5   I really must ____.
6   People really must realise that ____.
7   My father/mother should ____.
8   My husband/wife really must ____.

We often use ***should*** in **questions** when we are **wondering what to do**.

Should *I change my job or stay where I am?*

3   Write questions for people who don't know:

1   how much cheese to buy.
    How much cheese should I buy?
2   whether to move to London.
3   what she should call her baby.
4   where to put his bicycle.
5   when to pay her tax bill.
6   whether to invite his mother.
7   how to cook a crab.
8   whether to go to the police.
9   whether to take a taxi.
10 whether to take a holiday.
11 how long to wait.
12 what to do at the weekend.

4   Write some similar questions for yourself. Example:

Should I go on studying English?

'Should we walk upright? Should we continue to live in trees?
Should we try to make things? Decisions, decisions!'

must and **have (got) to**: obligation

Must usually expresses the **feelings** and **wishes** of the **speaker/hearer**.
Have (got) to often expresses **obligations** that come from **somewhere else**.
Compare:

> I **must** stop smoking. (**I** want to.)
> I**'ve got to** stop smoking – **doctor's** orders.
>
> **Must** you wear those dirty jeans? (Is that what **you** want?)
> Do you **have to** wear a tie at work? (Is there a **rule**?)

1   Put in *must* or *have/has (got) to*.

1   I'm tired. I _ _must_ _ go to bed early.
2   John _ _has to_ _ go to school on Saturdays.
3   We _must_ get another dog soon.
4   'This is a great book.' 'I _____ read it.'
5   A soldier _ _has to_ _ obey orders.
6   We _____ go to London for a meeting.
7   I think we _____ pay in advance.
8   You really _must_ visit us soon.
9   I _____ try to spend more time at home.
10   You _____ go through Carlisle on the way to Glasgow.

▲ **2   Read this with a dictionary; see how *must* reflects the hearer's wishes.**

(In a dream, Mrs Ogmore-Pritchard is talking to her two dead husbands,
Mr Ogmore and Mr Pritchard.)

MRS O-P: Tell me your tasks in order.
MR O: I must put my pyjamas in the drawer marked pyjamas.
MR P: I must take my cold bath which is good for me.
MR O: I must wear my flannel band to ward off sciatica.
MR P: I must dress behind the curtain and put on my apron.
MR O: I must blow my nose in a piece of tissue-paper which I afterwards burn.
MR P: I must take my salts which are nature's friend.
MR O: I must boil the drinking water because of germs.
MR P: I must make my herb tea which is free from tannin.
MR O: I must dust the blinds and then I must raise them.
MRS O-P: And before you let the sun in, mind it wipes its shoes.

> *Dylan Thomas: Under Milk Wood* (adapted)

Unlike *have to*, **must** has **no infinitive**, **participles** or **past tense**.

> When you leave school you**'ll have to** find a job. (NOT ~~You'll must~~ ...)
> I don't like **having to** cook every evening.
> We**'ve had to** change our plans for the summer.
> Joe **had to** go home yesterday. (NOT ~~Joe must/musted~~ ...)

must not, **do not have to** etc

> We use **must not** in **prohibitions** (negative orders).
> We use **do not have to**, **do not need to** or **need not** to say that something is
> **unnecessary**.

> Students **must not** leave bicycles in front of the library.
> Passengers **must not** speak to the driver.
> Friday's a holiday – I **don't have to** work. (NOT ~~I mustn't work.~~)
> You **needn't** pay now – tomorrow's OK. (NOT ~~You mustn't pay now~~ ...)

1 **Complete the sentences, using must not / mustn't or do not / don't have to.**

1 Campers _____ play music after 10 p.m.
2 Students _____ ask permission to stay out after midnight.
3 Bicycles _____ be parked in the front courtyard.
4 Residents _____ hang washing out of the windows.
5 British subjects _____ get visas to travel in Western Europe.
6 Passengers _____ lean out of the windows.
7 You _____ pay for your tickets now.
8 It's rained a lot, so we _____ water the garden.
9 You _____ disturb your sister while she's working.
10 You _____ knock before you come into my room.

2 **Make sentences, using must not or do not need to.**

BEGINNINGS	ENDS
In rugby football	touch the ball with your hands.
In tennis	lift your stick above your shoulder.
In chess	hit your opponent below the belt.
In boxing	pass the ball forwards.
In athletics	look at other people's cards.
In hockey	touch a piece if you aren't going to move it.
In baseball	start before the gun.
In football	hit the ball before it bounces.
In bridge	hit the ball after its second bounce.
	throw the bat.

can (ability): special problems

Future: We can use *can* if we are **deciding now** what to do in the future. **In other cases**, we have to use *will be able to*.

> *I* ***can*** *see you tomorrow morning for half an hour.*
> *One day we* ***will be able*** *to live without wars.*
> (NOT ~~One day we~~ ***can*** ~~live~~ *...*)

Conditional: We can use *could* to mean **'would be able to'**.

> *You* ***could*** *get a better job if you spoke a foreign language.*

1   Put in *can* or *can't* if possible; if not, use *could* or *will be able to*.

1   I ____ pick it up tonight, if that's convenient.
2   I think I ____ speak English quite well in a few months.
3   'We need some more oil.' 'OK, I ____ let you have some this week.'
4   Dr Parker ____ see you at twelve on Tuesday.
5   She ____ walk again in a few weeks.
6   If we took the wheels off, we ____ get it through the back door.
7   Do you think one day people ____ travel to the stars?
8   This week's no good, but I ____ bring the car in next week.
9   If I practised a bit, I ____ be pretty good at tennis.
10 In a few years, computers ____ think better than we do.
11 She ____ give you a lesson this evening.
12 I'm free at the weekend, so the kids ____ come round.
13 I'll post your letter, but I don't think the postman ____ read the address.
14 I ____ do your job with no trouble at all.
15 We're busy this week, but we ____ repair it by next Thursday.

Past: We do **not** use *could* to say that we managed to do something **on one occasion**. Instead, we use, for example, **managed to** or **succeeded in ...ing**.

> *I* ***managed to*** *get up early today.* (NOT ~~I could get up early today.~~)
> *After six hours, we* ***succeeded in*** *getting to the top of the mountain.*
> (NOT ~~After six hours, we~~ ***could*** ~~get~~ *...*)
> BUT: *She* ***could*** *read when she was four.* (Not one occasion.)
> *He* ***couldn't*** *find the ticket office.* (He didn't manage it.)

2   Complete the sentences with *could*, *couldn't* or *managed to*.

1   I ____ speak French really well when I lived in Paris.
2   He ____ repair the car, but it took him a long time.
3   At last I ____ make her understand what I wanted.
4   We wanted to go to the opera, but we ____ get tickets.
5   I ____ swim across the river, but it was harder than I expected.
6   All three children ____ ride as well as they ____ walk.
7   Fortunately, I ____ get her address from her office.
8   I don't know how the cat ____ get through the window, but it did.
9   He ____ already walk when he was ten months old.
10 After the accident, she somehow ____ walk home.

> We often use *can* and *could* with *see*, *hear*, *feel*, *smell* and *taste*, with the
> same meaning as a **progressive** form.
>
> I *can see* Susan coming. (NOT ~~I'm seeing~~ ...)
> What's in the soup? I *can taste* something funny.
> Through the window, I *could hear* a man singing.

3   Complete the sentences.

1   I ____ something burning. What do you think it is?
2   He opened his eyes, but to his horror he ____ nothing.
3   Through my study window I ____ mountains.
4   I ____ Susan practising the piano next door; it sounds nice.
5   This isn't my coffee – I ____ sugar in it.
6   He thought he ____ something crawling up his leg, but when he looked
    he ____ anything.
7   Spring is coming: you ____ snowdrops in all the gardens.
8   I ____ the cats fighting in the kitchen: can you go and put them out?

**4   Look around you, and write five sentences beginning *I can see* ...
    Listen to the noises around you, and write five sentences
    beginning *I can hear* ...**

'I can see why they made February
the shortest month of the year.'

can, could, may: permission etc

We use **can** to **ask for** and **give permission**, and **cannot/can't** to **refuse** it.

'**Can** I ask you a question?' 'Yes, of course you **can**.'
I'm sorry, you **can't** come in here.

We also use *could* to ask for permission; it is more polite.
Could I have a look at your newspaper?

May is used in the same way. It is more formal and less common.
May I help you, sir?

We use *can* and *could* (but not usually *may*) to talk about what is normally allowed.
Can you park in this street on Sundays? (NOT **~~May you park~~** ...?)

1   Rewrite these sentences using *can*, *could* or *may*.

1   I'd like to talk to you for a minute, Bill. *(friendly)*
     Can I talk to you for a minute, Bill?
2   I would like to use your phone. *(more polite)*
3   I would like to stop work early today. *(formal)*
4   Take my bike if you want to.
5   Are children allowed to go into pubs?
6   I don't want you to come into my room.
7   I would like to speak to Jane, if she's there. *(polite)*
8   I would like to have a beer. *(friendly)*
9   Are students allowed to use this library?
10 I would like to pay you tomorrow. *(polite)*

'Dad, can I borrow the gun tonight?'

Drawing by Mankoff; © 1993
The New Yorker Magazine, Inc.

We use **can** in **offers**, **requests** and **instructions**.

> **Can** I carry your bag?
> I **can** baby-sit for you this evening if you like.
> **Can** you put the children to bed?
> When you've finished the beds you **can** clean up the kitchen.

Could sounds **less definite**; it is common in suggestions and requests.
> I **could** do some shopping for you, if that would help.
> 'I'm bored.' 'You **could** go for a bike ride.'
> **Could** you help me for a few minutes?

Common structures in **polite requests**:
> **Could you possibly** help me?
> **I wonder if you could** help me?

2   **Rewrite these sentences, beginning with *I can ...*, *Can I ...?***
   You can ...*, *Can you ...?* *Could you ...?* or *I wonder if you could ...?

1   Would you like me to take your coat?
2   Start cooking supper now, please.
3   I'd be glad if you would translate this for me. *(friendly)*
4   I'd be glad if you would translate this for me. *(polite)*
5   Why not watch a video if you don't know what to do?
6   Why don't you spend the day with us if you're free on Saturday?
7   I don't mind feeding the horses, if you'd like me to.
8   I'd be glad if you would lend me £5. *(polite)*
9   Tell me when it's time to go. *(friendly)*
10   I'd be grateful if you would tell me when it's time to go. *(polite)*

3   **Put the words of the caption in the right order.**

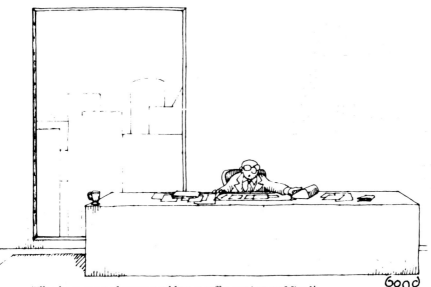

'Ellis, here my and come could pass coffee me in you Miss ?'

will: willingness etc

Will can express **willingness** and **intentions**.
We often use *will* to **announce a decision at the moment when we make it**.

I really **will** give up smoking tomorrow!
We**'ll** buy the tickets if you**'ll** make supper after the show.
There's the doorbell. **I'll** go. (NOT ~~I go.~~)

I'll have ... is often used when people order in cafés, restaurants etc.
I'll have a black coffee, please.

Will you ...? can introduce **instructions**, **orders** and **requests**. *Would you ...?* is softer,
and can be used to make requests more polite.
Will you get me a paper while you're out?
Will you be quiet, please?
Would you watch the children for a few minutes?

Won't can be used to talk about **refusals**.
He **won't** talk to anybody.
The car **won't** start.

1 **Put the beginnings and ends together. Example:**

I'll drive if you'll map-read.

BEGINNINGS	ENDS
I'll drive	I will.
I'll wash up	I'll answer it.
I'm tired. I think	I'll go to bed now.
If you see Ann,	if you'll dry.
She won't tell us	if you'll map-read.
The cat	in the oven at 5.30?
The phone's ringing.	shouting?
This video	to this address, please?
Who's going to get the tickets?	what's wrong.
Will you deliver the furniture	when you're ready to leave?
Will you let me know	won't eat.
Will you stop	won't play.
Would you put the meat	would you tell her I got her letter?

We can use **will** to make **threats** and **promises**. The simple present is not possible in this case.

> **I'll** hit you if you do that again. (NOT ~~I hit you if~~ ...)
> You**'ll** get your money tomorrow. (NOT ~~You get~~ ...)
> I promise **I'll** stop smoking. (NOT ~~I promise I stop smoking.~~)

2   **A boy left home for the first time to go to university. Look at the pictures, and write the promises he made to his parents. Begin: *I promise I'll ...* or *I promise I won't ...***

1   2   3

4   5   6

7   8   9

10   11   12

For *will* as a future auxiliary, see page 130.

will and **would**: typical behaviour

We can use **will** to talk about **habits** and **typical behaviour**.

She'll sit talking to herself for hours.
*If something breaks down and you kick it, it **will** often start working again.*

If we stress *will* it can sound critical.
*She **will** fall in love with the wrong people.*

Would is used to talk about the past.
*On Saturdays, when I was a child, we **would** all get up early and go fishing.*
*He was a nice boy, but he **would** talk about himself all the time.*

1   Complete the sentences with *will/would* + verbs from the box.

be	drive	fall	keep	listen	make	play	ring
take	talk	tell					

 1 'Dad, I've broken my watch.' 'Well, you ____ playing with it.'
 2 On Sundays when we were kids, Mother ____ us pancakes for breakfast.
 3 He's no trouble – he ____ by himself for hours.
 4 She's nice, but she ____ about people behind their backs.
 5 People ____ to you if you listen to them.
 6 We lived by a lake, and sometimes Dad ____ us fishing.
 7 I'm not surprised you had an accident – you ____ too fast.
 8 If you drop toast, it ____ butter side down every time.
 9 If you're having a bath, the phone ____. And if you answer it, it ____ a
    wrong number.
10 He ____ you one thing one minute and the opposite the next – he's crazy.

2   Here are some laws of nature. Join the beginnings and the ends.

BEGINNINGS	ENDS
After you have bought something,	it will.
If anything can go wrong,	somebody will.
If there are two good TV shows,	they will both be on at the same time.
If you explain so clearly that nobody can misunderstand,	will always move faster.
If you throw something away,	will fall asleep first.
No matter how much you do,	you will find it somewhere else cheaper.
The one who snores	you'll need it the next day.
The other queue	you'll never do enough.

shall in questions

> ***Shall I/we ...?*** can be used to **ask for instructions** and **decisions**, and to **make offers** and **suggestions**.
>
> *What on earth **shall we** do?*   *What time **shall we** come and see you?*
> ***Shall I** carry your bag?*   ***Shall we** go out for a meal?*

1   Can you complete the sentences? (They are from a discussion about holiday plans.) Use *shall we?*

1   where?   *Where shall we go?*
2   seaside/mountains?
     Shall we go to the seaside
     or the mountains?
3   this country/abroad?
4   when?
5   how long for?

6   fly/train/drive?
7   hotel/camp?
8   stay in one place / travel around?
9   take Granny?
10   go with the Jacksons?
11   what do with dogs?

2   Write three questions asking for advice for yourself. If you can work with other students, ask them your questions and get their advice.

What shall I say
when our neighbours
want us to come to tea?
They don't know you're not with me.
What shall I say?

What shall I say
when the phone rings
and someone asks for you?
They don't know I ask for you too.
What shall I say?

How can I hide the tears inside?
How can I face the crowd?
I can make lips of mine be still,
but my heart sighs too loud.

I could explain that
you're gone for only a week to shop.
But after the week is up
What shall I say?

Peter Tinturin

For *shall* as a future auxiliary, see page 130.

should have, could have etc

We can use **should have**, **could have** etc + past participle to talk about
'unreal' past situations that are the opposite of what really happened.

> *You **should have been** here an hour ago. (But you weren't.)*
> *Alice **should** never **have bought** that car. (But she did.)*
> *I was so angry I **could have killed** her. (But I didn't.)*
> *She **could have married** anybody she wanted to. (But she didn't.)*
> *Jumping out of the window like that – he **could/might have broken** his leg.*
> *If I'd known you were coming, I **would have stayed** in.*

We can use this structure to criticise people for not doing things.
> *You **could have helped** me! (Why didn't you?)*
> *You **might have let** me know you weren't coming – I stayed in all evening.*

**1   Complete the sentences with *should have ...*, *could have ...*, *might
    have ...* or *would have ... * More than one answer may be possible.**

1   He _____ me last week. *(pay)*
    He should have paid me last week.
2   You _____ somebody, driving like that. *(kill)* could have killed .
3   I _____ you, but I didn't have your number. *(phone)*
4   If my parents hadn't been so poor, I _____ to university. *(go)*
5   It's his fault she left him; he _____ nicer to her. *(be)*
6   I _____ more garlic in the soup. *(put)*
7   If you needed money, you _____ me. *(ask)*
8   'We got lost in the mountains.' 'You fools – you _____ a map.' *(take)*
9   It's a good thing they got her to hospital in time. She _____. *(die)*
10 When he said that to me I _____ him. *(hit)*
11 You _____ me you were bringing your friends to supper! *(tell)*
12 You _____ my jeans after you borrowed them. *(wash)*

This structure can also be used to talk about **things that are not certain
to have happened**, or that we **suppose** (but don't know definitely) have
happened. *May have ...* is common in these senses.

> *I **may have left** my keys here this morning – have you seen them?*
> *He **should have arrived** home by now. Let's phone him.*
> *So you went to Australia. That **must have been** nice.*
> *Where is she? She **can't have gone** out – the door's locked.*

2 **Complete the sentences with *may have ...*, *should have ...*, *must have ...* or *can't have ...* More than one answer may be possible.**

1 'Where's Phil?' 'I don't know. He _____ home.' *(go)*
2 'How are the builders getting on?' 'They _____ by now. I'll go and see.' *(finish)*
3 'Ann isn't here.' 'Surely she _____ – I reminded her yesterday.' *(forget)*
4 The garden's all wet. It _____ in the night. *(rain)*
5 'We went to Dublin for the weekend.' 'That _____ a nice change.' *(be)*
6 'Who phoned?' 'She didn't give her name. It _____ Lucy.' *(be)*
7 He _____ all his money. I gave him £10 only yesterday! *(spend)*
8 I _____ a new job. I'll know for certain tomorrow. *(find)*
9 The car's got a big dent in the side. Bernie _____ an accident. *(have)*
10 They're not at home. They _____ away for the weekend. *(go)*

> Note the differences between *may not have ...* and *can't have ...*, and between *had to ...* and *must have ...*
>
> *They **may not have arrived** yet.* (= Perhaps they haven't arrived,)
> *They **can't have arrived** yet.* (= They certainly haven't arrived.)
>
> *Joe **had to** go home.* (= It was necessary for him to go home.)
> *Joe **must have gone** home.* (= It seems certain that he has gone home.)

3 **Put in *may not have ...*, *can't have ...*, *had to ...* or *must have ...***

1 Shakespeare _____ been to Australia because it hadn't been discovered.
2 King Arthur _____ existed – nobody's sure.
3 Castles in the Middle Ages _____ been cold places.
4 People in those days _____ get their water from wells and streams.
5 Poor people five hundred years ago _____ had easy lives.
6 But they _____ been unhappier than us.

'All the exits have been sealed off. He must have got out through the entrance.'

For *will have ...* (future perfect tense), see page 139.
For *would have ...*, see page 262.

revision of **modal verbs**

1   Correct the mistakes.

1   I don't can sing.
2   I would like to can travel more.
3   He should to work harder.
4   Could you telling me the time?
5   I must work last Saturday and Sunday.

2   Choose the best form. (Sometimes both may be possible.)

1   We ____ win, but I don't think there's much chance. *(may, might)*
2   I ____ ask you to help me later. *(may, might)*
3   That ____ be her daughter – they're nearly the same age. *(can't, mustn't)*
4   We ____ decide to go camping again at Easter. *(can, may)*
5   There ____ be enough room for everybody on the bus – we'll have to wait and see. *(may not, can't)*
6   You ____ get in without a ticket – not a chance. *(may not, can't)*
7   You absolutely ____ go and see Liz. *(should, must)*
8   I think you ____ try to relax more. *(should, must)*
9   You ____ pass a special exam to be a teacher. *(must, have to)*
10   In this country, boys ____ do military service. *(must not, don't have to)*
11   I ____ see you at eight tomorrow. *(can, will be able to)*
12   One day, everybody ____ say what they like. *(can, will be able to)*
13   It took a long time, but I ____ repair the car. *(could, managed to)*
14   When I was younger I ____ sing quite well. *(could, was able to)*
15   At what age ____ you get a driving licence? *(can, may)*
16   I promise I ____ smoking. *(stop, will stop)*
17   I don't know why she's not here. She ____ have got my message. *(may not, can't)*
18   He's not answering the phone. He ____ have got home yet. *(may not, can't)*
19   When I was eighteen we ____ two years in the army. *(had to do, must have done)*
20   She ____ very quietly – I didn't hear her go. *(had to leave, must have left)*

3   Write sentences about three things that you should have done last week but didn't, and three things that you shouldn't have done but did.

For explanations of the words that we use to talk about grammar, see pages 298–302.

4 Complete the cartoon captions with expressions from the box.

he might be	it may not be	can this be	it can be
you could	I'll		

'_____ the same man who pulled Excalibur out of a stone?'

'Yeah, they're all right, _____ take them.'

'Oh my God! His report says _____ Prime Minister one day!'

'Provided you eat sensibly, stay off the beer, cigarettes and whisky, don't take any strenuous exercise and keep away from women, _____ live for another twenty minutes.'

'Frankly, Wallace, I think you'd better stop telling it. If no one laughs, _____ a joke.'

'It's a Valentine's card. I wonder who _____ from!'

need

Need can sometimes be used like a **modal verb**, (questions and negatives without *do*), especially to say what is (not) **necessary at the time of speaking**.

> **Do I need to** *pay now?* OR **Need I** *pay now?*
> *He* **doesn't need to** *go.* OR *He* **needn't** *go.*

1   Complete these sentences with *needn't*, using a verb from the box.

come	get	laugh	phone	ring	take	think	try
worry	write						

1   You ____ – my haircut's not as funny as all that.
2   You ____ up yet, because there's no school today.
3   He ____ everything down. Just the name and phone number will do.
4   She ____ and see me if she doesn't want to; I don't mind.
5   You ____ about me. I'm fine.
6   You ____ I care about you, because I don't.
7   Tell him he ____ the bell; he can just walk straight in.
8   I'd like to see her today, but it ____ very long.
9   Just come when you like, any time. You ____ first.
10 You ____ to explain. I'm not interested.

Compare **didn't need to ...** and **needn't have ...**

> *We* **didn't need to hurry**; *we had lots of time.*
>   (It was unnecessary to hurry.)
> *We* **needn't have hurried** *– we got there much too early.*
>   (It was unnecessary to hurry, but we did.)

2   Complete the sentences with *didn't need to ...* or *needn't have ...*

1   I ____ the flowers; I could see that Anne had already done it. (*water*)
2   You ____ supper for me; I've already had something to eat. (*cook*)
3   I ____ all that work, because nobody appreciated it. (*do*)
4   We ____ the encyclopaedia; the kids never look at it. (*buy*)
5   We had enough petrol, so I ____. (*fill up*)
6   I ____ so much about Granny. When I got there she was fine. (*worry*)
7   Luckily we had plenty of food, so I ____ shopping. (*go*)
8   I ____ long; she arrived just after me. (*wait*)
9   I ____ Latin at school; it hasn't been any use to me since. (*study*)

had better

Had better (not) is followed by an **infinitive without *to***.
We use *had better* to give **strong advice** to people (including ourselves).
Had better is not past or comparative – the meaning is '**It would be good to ...**'

> You'**d better** turn that music down before your Dad gets angry.
> It's seven o'clock. I'**d better** put the meat in the oven.
> You'**d better** not say that again.

Had better refers to the immediate future. It is more urgent than *should* or *ought*.
> '*I* **ought** to go and see Fred one of these days.' 'Well, you'**d better** do it soon.
> He's leaving for South Africa next month.'

1   Complete the sentences with verbs from the box, using '*d better*.

do	not forget	get	give	have	invite	not let
open	start	not tell				

1   The plane's at six o'clock. You ____ packing, hadn't you?
2   I suppose I ____ up and put some clothes on.
3   You ____ the door and see who it is.
4   Tell Sheila she ____ my birthday this time!
5   We ____ Pat her camera back, hadn't we? She might need it.
6   We ____ John round soon; we owe him a meal.
7   I ____ some washing, or we won't have anything to wear.
8   You ____ Jane what's happening; she'll get too upset if you do.
9   You don't look well. You ____ some whisky and honey.
10 You ____ your father see that magazine – he'll kill you.

2   What advice might you give to a friend who:

1   feels very ill?
2   is very tired?
3   feels cold?
4   feels tense?
5   has been working too hard?
6   seems very unhappy?
7   is going to work in China and Japan?
8   can't sleep?
9   has got an exam next week?
10 smokes too much?
11 thinks she saw burglars breaking
    into the house next door?

Had better is quite direct; it is **not** used in **polite requests**. Compare:

> *Could you* help me if you've got time? (NOT ~~You'd better help me~~ ...)
> *You'd better* help me or there'll be trouble.

used to ... (/'juːst tə/)

We use **used + infinitive** to talk about past habits and long-lasting situations which are now finished or different.

> I **used to smoke** like a chimney.   She **used to live** in Liverpool.

Used to ... is only past. For present habits, we use the simple present tense.
> My sister **smokes** occasionally. (NOT ~~My sister **uses to smoke** ...~~)

In an informal style, questions and negatives are generally made with *do*.
> **Did** you **use** to collect stamps?   I **didn't use** to like her.
> I **used not** to like her. (More formal.)

1   Complete the text with words from the box, using *used to* ...

buy	go	have	keep	look after	look at	live
play	stand	take				

Recently we took our 15-year-old son Joe to the place in Paris where we __1__ when he was a baby. We showed him the house, with the balcony where he __2__ and make speeches to imaginary crowds. Then we went inside, and believe it or not, there was Mme Duchène, who __3__ Joe when we were working. She didn't look a day older. We couldn't get into the flat, but we saw the garden where Joe __4__. Then we visited the park where we __5__ him for walks, the zoo where he __6__ the lions and tigers, and the lake where we __7__ boating. Not much had changed in the area: most of the shops were still there, including the wonderful old grocer's where we __8__ delicacies like cherries in brandy. But the friendly butcher who __9__ the best pieces of meat for us was gone, and so was the restaurant with the bad-tempered old waitress where we __10__ Sunday lunch. I found it strange to go back: it made me feel happy and sad at the same time. But Joe was delighted with the trip.

2   Make sentences with *used to* and *didn't use to* about how people lived hundreds of years ago.

1   travel / horse
2   cook / wood fires
3   live so long
4   fight / spears
5   hunt / bows and arrows
6   believe / ghosts and devils
7   be able / vote
8   think / earth was flat
9   bigger families
10   children / work

3   Write some sentences about things that you used to or didn't use to do/think/ believe when you were younger. If you can work with other students, find out what they used to do/think/ believe.

supposed to (/sə'pəʊst tə/)

Be supposed + infinitive can be used to talk about what is **generally believed**.

He**'s supposed to be** rich.   This stuff **is supposed to kill** flies.

Another meaning is: what people are expected to do, or what is intended.
You**'re supposed to start** work at 8.30 in the mornings.
She **was supposed to be** here an hour ago. Where is she?
You**'re not supposed to park** on double yellow lines.
That's a strange picture. What**'s** it **supposed to be?**

1   Put the beginnings and ends together.

BEGINNINGS	ENDS
Aspirins are supposed	at the cash desk on the way out.
Catholics are supposed	but I can't find them.
You were supposed	in food shops.
It's supposed to have instructions with it,	supposed to come today?
Wasn't my computer magazine	the shower with shoes on.
What am I supposed to do	to cure headaches.
You're not supposed to go into	to go to church on Sundays.
You're not supposed to smoke	to come and see me yesterday.
You're supposed to be good at geography	with all this chicken salad?
I think you're supposed to pay	– where the hell are we?

2   What do you think these are supposed to be?

1

2

3

4

It's supposed to be a house.

5

6

7

8

future: will (and shall)

| I will (*or* shall) work
you **will work**
he/she/it **will work**
we **will** (*or* shall) **work**
they **will work** | *Questions:* **will/shall** I **work?** *etc*
Negative: I **will/shall not work** *etc*

Contractions: I'll, you'll *etc*; won't /wəʊnt/, shan't /ʃɑːnt/ |

I/we will and *I/we shall* are used with no difference of meaning in most situations in modern British English. (But see page 121.) *Will* is more common than *shall*.

We use **will/shall** to **give or ask for information about the future**, in cases where there is no reason to use a present verb-form (see pages 132–136).

> We **will** need the money on the 15th.
> **Will** all the family be at the wedding?
> It **will** be spring soon.
> She**'ll** be here in a few minutes.

We often use **will/shall** to **predict** the future – to say what we **think**, **guess** or **calculate** will happen.

> Tomorrow **will** be warm, with some cloud in the afternoon.
> Who do you think **will** win?
> You**'ll** never finish that book.

1   Here are some sentences taken from recorded conversations. Can you put the beginnings and ends together?

BEGINNINGS	ENDS
Buy the cat food here.	about you.
Don't give her your keys.	and then your kids will laugh at you.
Get John to have a look at the TV.	He'll fix it.
'He'll grow up one day.'	he'll be dead in five years.
He'll need somebody	he'll drink it.
'How's June?'	he'll get hit on the nose with a ball.
I must get back to work,	'I hope you're right.'
If he doesn't stop drinking,	It'll be cheaper.
If we give her a shout,	on May 12th.
If you put lemon in it,	otherwise I'll get the sack.
Knowing his luck, if he plays golf	'She'll be OK.'
No good sending her a bill, is it?	She'll just refuse to pay.
One day you'll be old,	She'll only lose them.
She'll be fourteen	she'll come and help.
She'll forget	to help him.

2   Complete the sentences with your own predictions.

1   It *will / will not rain* next week. *(rain)*
2   England *will / will not win* the next football World Cup. *(win)*
3   The weather ____ much warmer in the next few years. *(get)*
4   There ____ a world government before the year 2050. *(be)*
5   There ____ a world war before the year 2050. *(be)*
6   Private cars ____ before the year 2100. *(disappear)*
7   English ____ the world language in the year 2100. *(be)*
8   Everybody / Not everybody ____ a computer in the year 2100. *(have)*
9   Everybody / Not everybody ____ enough to eat in the year 2100. *(have)*
10 Clothes ____ very different in the year 2100. *(be)*
11 In the year 2100, people ____ the same things as they do now. *(eat)*
12 *(Write your own prediction.)*

3   Look at the map and complete the weather forecast. Use some of the words in the box.

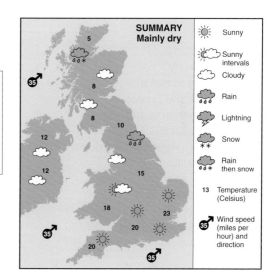

be	cold	dry	earthquakes
east	hurricanes	ice	
lightning	north	rain	
snow	south	thunder	
warm	west	wet	will
will be	winds		

Tomorrow will ____ mainly ____, but there ____ some ____ in the north. There ____ be strong ____ from the south-west later in the day. It will be quite ____ in the south, but Scotland ____ cold, and in the ____ of Scotland the rain ____ turn to ____ during the afternoon.

For *will* after *if*, see pages 137, 256. For *will* in requests, promises etc, see page 118.

future: going to

We often use **present verb-forms** to talk about the **future**. For example, we say that something **is going** to happen. This is common when we talk about **plans**, **decisions** and **firm intentions**, especially in an informal style.

We're going to get a new car soon.
When are you going to get your hair cut?
I'm going to keep asking her out until she says 'Yes'.

1   **Here are some of the plans of various members of a family. Can you put the sentences together, using *going to*? Example:**

Jane is going to study music in Vienna.

BEGINNINGS	ENDS
Jane / study	a professional pianist.
She / try to become	a year learning German.
But first, she / spend	as a pilot.
Max / do maths and science	decorate the house.
Then he / train	for his final exams.
Jennifer's eight, and she doesn't know	music in Vienna.
One day she says	she / be a dancer.
And the next she says she /	the summer learning to fly.
This summer, Jane /	start her own business.
Max / spend	stay with her aunt in America.
Their parents / spend	two weeks walking in Scotland.
Then they /	what she / do.

'Right, children, there are going to be a few changes this term.'

'This is going to put the magic back into our marriage.'

Going to is common when we predict the future by using **present evidence** – when we can see that a future event is on the way, or starting to happen.

*Look – it's **going to rain**.*   *Look out – we're **going to crash**!*

2   What is going to happen?

1

2

3

4

5

6

7

8

9

10

future: present progressive

> The **present progressive** is common when we talk about future **personal arrangements** and **fixed plans**; we often give the **time, date, and/or place.**
>
> *'What **are** you **doing** this evening?' '**I'm washing** my hair.'*
> *My car**'s having** a service next week.   We**'re going** to Spain in June.*
> *Did you know I**'m getting** a new job?   What **are** we **having** for dinner?*

1   Look at the diary and correct the sentences.

1   She's playing tennis on Sunday afternoon.
2   She's having lunch with James at 12.30 on Tuesday.
3   She's flying to Rotterdam on Thursday.
4   She's meeting Mrs Parsons in the London office.
5   She's driving to the meeting with Mrs Parsons.
6   She's going to a funeral on Wednesday afternoon.
7   She's meeting the accountants at 12.00 on Monday.
8   She's going to the theatre on Saturday evening.
9   She's spending Friday at the races.
10   Matthew is coming to see her on Sunday morning.

2   Write some sentences about your plans for the coming week. If you can work with other students, find out about their plans.

'Ili, it's me. Listen. It's David's birthday, so a few million of us are going out for a meal. Are you interested?'

AUGUST   WEEK 34

22 Sunday
Tennis with Barbara 10am
Matthew afternoon

23 Monday
10.15 Mrs Parsons
Oxford office (9.00 train)
Accountants 4.00 pm

24 Tuesday

25 Wednesday
George's funeral 9.00
Lunch James 12.30

26 Thursday
To Amsterdam KLM 147, 8.00
Back 18.50 KLM 156

27 Friday

Theatre Royal with Polly
28 Saturday
RACES

future: comparison of structures

We can often use more than one structure to talk about the same future event.
Present forms emphasise present ideas like **intention**, **certainty** and **plans**.
We prefer **will/shall** when we are **not** emphasising **present ideas**. Compare:

> *Next year **is going to be** different – I promise.* (present intention)
> *Next year **will** probably be different.*

> *What **are** you **doing** next year? You haven't told me your plans.*
> *What **will** you **do** next year – do you know?*

We prefer **present forms** when we are talking about **future events** that have some
present reality. Compare:
> *I'm seeing Pete on Tuesday.* (There is an arrangement now.)
> *I wonder if he**'ll recognise** me.* (No present idea.)

In **predictions**, we prefer **present forms** when there is **outside evidence** for what will
happen – when we can see something coming.
We prefer **will** when we are talking more about what is **inside our heads**: our beliefs,
guesses, knowledge etc.

> *Look out – we**'re going to** crash!* (I can see it coming.)
> *Don't lend him your car – he**'ll crash** it.* (I know him.)

▲ **1   Which form do you feel is best?**

1   Here's the builder's estimate. It *(will cost / is going to cost)* £7,000 to
    repair the roof.
2   I think it *(will cost / is going to cost)* about £3,000 to rebuild the garage.
3   Alice *(will have / is going to have)* a baby.
4   With a bit of luck, the baby *(will have / is going to have)* Alice's eyes.
5   *(I will play / I'm playing)* tennis with Stan on Sunday.
6   *(He'll win. / He's winning.)* He always does.
7   Don't tell her. *(She'll tell / She's going to tell)* everybody else.
8   What's happening? The train *(won't stop / isn't going to stop)*!
9   One day everybody *(will have / is going to have)* proper housing.
10 *(She'll get married / She's getting married)* on Friday at the local church.
11 *(It will rain / It's going to rain)* – look at those clouds.
12 If it gets any colder, *(it will snow / it's going to snow)*.

'Separate futures, please.'

future: simple present

We sometimes use the **simple present** to talk about the future. This
happens mostly when we talk about **timetables**, routines and schedules.

> Next term **starts** on 6 April.
> My train **leaves** at 3.17.
> What time **does** the bus **arrive** in York?
> **Do** you **have** classes next Saturday?

The simple present can also be used to give and ask for instructions.

> When you get to the office you **go** up to the first floor, you **knock** on the first
>   door on the right and you **ask** for Mrs Alstone. OK?
> What **do** we **do** now?
> Where **do** I pay?

In other cases we **don't** use the **simple present** in main clauses to talk about
the **future**. (For subordinate clauses after conjunctions, see page 244.)

> Lucy's **coming** for a drink this evening. (NOT ~~Lucy comes~~ ...)
> I'**ll phone** you – I promise. (NOT ~~I phone you~~ ...)
> There's the doorbell. I'**ll go**. (NOT ... ~~I go.~~)

1   Choose the best tense.

1   When *(does / will)* school start?
2   The plane *(arrives / will arrive)* at 10.00.
3   I *(write / will write)* soon.
4   We *(go / are going)* to Spain some time soon.
5   You *(go / will go)* next door for the tickets.
6   I *(stop / will stop)* smoking after Christmas.
7   How *(do / will)* I switch this on?
8   The exams *(are / will be)* in June.
9   I *(have / will have)* a lecture at 9.00 tomorrow.
10   The train *(won't / doesn't)* stop at Oxford.
11   I *(come / will come)* round after 7.00.
12   Where *(do / will)* I go for my interview?
13   I *(play / am playing)* football tomorrow.
14   What time *(does / will)* the concert end?
15   I *(post / will post)* your letters.

'– And please hurry. My credit card expires
at midnight.'

future: tenses after **if** and **when**

After **if** and **when**, we normally use **present tenses** to talk about the **future**.

> **If I'm** there tomorrow, I'll phone you.
> **When it's** ready I'll give it to you.

1 Put in *if* or *when* with the present tense of a verb from the box.

be   come   not find   grow up   pass   rain   say
not want

1 What are you going to be ＿＿ you ＿＿?
2 We won't play ＿＿ it ＿＿.
3 I'll try again ＿＿ I ＿＿ older.
4 I'll be surprised ＿＿ she ＿＿ the exam.
5 ＿＿ you ＿＿ your keys, you can use mine.
6 I'll hit you ＿＿ you ＿＿ that again.
7 Pete will take the job ＿＿ Ann ＿＿ it.
8 We'll all be happy ＿＿ the weekend ＿＿.

When I grow up I'm going to be unemployed...

If and **when** can be followed by **will** in **indirect** and **direct questions**.

> **I don't know if I'll** be there.
> **They haven't said when it'll** be ready.
> **When will** I see you again?

We can also use **will** after **if** in **polite requests**.

> **If** you **will** just come this way ...

And we use **if ... will** to say 'if this will happen **as a result**'.

> All right. I'll give up smoking **if it will make you happy**.
> We can come tomorrow evening **if it won't upset your plans**.

▲ **2 Put in the correct verb form (present tense or will ...).**

1 If you ＿＿ there first, keep a seat for me. *(get)*
2 I'll see you again when I ＿＿ next in London. *(be)*
3 I don't know when I ＿＿ a job. *(find)*
4 Give her some more chocolate if it ＿＿ her quiet. *(keep)*
5 I'll open the window when it ＿＿ raining. *(stop)*
6 You can borrow my coat if you ＿＿ it back. *(bring)*
7 If you ＿＿ a seat, I'll see if the doctor's free. *(take)*
8 All right. I'll apologise if it ＿＿ you feel better. *(make)*
9 Can you tell me when Mr Ellis ＿＿ here next? *(be)*
10 Come back again soon if you ＿＿ a chance. *(get)*

future progressive

✔	I **will be working** *etc*
?	**will** you **be working?** *etc*
✗	she **will not be working** *etc*

We can use the **future progressive** to say that something will be **going on at a certain time in the future**.

> *This time tomorrow I'**ll be skiing**.*
> *Good luck with the exam. We'**ll be thinking** of you.*

The future progressive is also used for planned or expected future events.

> *Professor Asher **will be giving** another lecture at the same time next week.*
> *I'**ll be seeing** you one of these days, I expect.*

In polite enquiries the future progressive suggests 'What have you already decided?', giving the idea that we are not trying to influence people. Compare:

> ***Will** you **be staying** in this evening?* (just asking about plans)
> ***Are** you **going to stay** in this evening?* (perhaps pressing for a decision)
> ***Will** you **stay** in this evening?* (request or order)

1 Make future progressive questions to ask somebody politely:

1 what time they are planning to get up.
2 what they plan to wear.
3 how they intend to travel to work.
4 how soon they intend to leave.
5 whether they expect to take the car.
6 whether they plan to have lunch out.
7 what time they intend to come back.
8 where they are planning to sleep.
9 how they intend to pay.
10 when they plan to go back home.

2 Complete the cartoon caption, using a future progressive.

'My name is Mr Collins. I *(teach)* you English literature, and I'm armed.'

future perfect

	SIMPLE	PROGRESSIVE
✔	I **will have worked** *etc*	I **will have been working** *etc*
?	**will** you **have worked?** *etc*	**will** you **have been working?** *etc*
✗	she **will not have worked** *etc*	he **will not have been working** *etc*

We can use the **future perfect** to say that something will have been **completed by a certain time in the future**.

> *The builder says he'**ll have finished** the roof by Saturday.*
> *The car **will soon have done** 100,000 miles.*

We can use the **future perfect progressive** to say **how long** something will have continued by a certain time.

> *Next Christmas I'**ll have been teaching** for twenty years.*

1 **Use the future perfect to put the beginnings and ends together.**

BEGINNINGS	ENDS
I *(not finish)* the report by Monday, In a couple of years the children *(leave)* home On our next wedding anniversary When I get home tonight When I retire	and we'll be able to get a smaller house. and it's needed for Monday morning. I *(drive)* for fourteen hours non-stop. I *(work)* for forty years. we *(be)* married for twenty-five years.

2 **A romantic novelist writes 300-page books. She writes ten pages a day, and takes no holidays. Use the future perfect to answer the questions.**

1   How many pages will she have written after ten days? After a month? After a year? After ten years?
2   If she starts today, how soon will she have finished her first book? How many books will she have written a year from now?
3   How long will she have been writing when she has written 120 books?
4   She earns £100,000 per book. How much money will she have made altogether after her 120th book?

3 **How long will you have been learning English / working / going to school / living in your present house by next summer? (Write sentences with the future perfect progressive.) If you can work with other students, ask them the same questions.**

future: I am to ...

We can talk about the future by saying that something **is to happen**.
We often use this structure to talk about **official plans** and fixed **personal arrangements**.

*The President **is to visit** Scotland in September.*
*We **are to get** a wage rise.*
*I felt nervous because I **was** soon **to leave** home for the first time.*

1   Write sentences about President Morton's schedule. Example:

The President is to arrive at Star City at 08.00.

Schedule for Presidential Visit to Northland
Monday 27.6

08.00	Arrive Star City Airport. Inspect guard of honour.
09.00	Working breakfast with President Jensen.
11.00–13.00	Tour of Star City; meet mayor and civic leaders.
13.00–14.00	Lunch with Foreign Minister Svendsen and guests.
14.00–16.00	Visit inner city schools; open new eye hospital.
16.00–20.00	Meet business leaders; rest.
20.00–23.00	Attend State Dinner as guest of President and Mrs Jensen.

You are (not) to can be used (for example by parents) to **give orders**.

*You**'re to do** your homework before you watch TV.*
*She can go out, but she**'s not to be** back late.*

2   Put together sentences that a parent might say to a child, using expressions from the two boxes and *You're (not) to* ...   Example:

You're to clean up your room.

clean up	do	give chocolate	go to bed	learn how to use
leave dirty	leave empty	make	make your own	
open door	write			

at nine o'clock	bed	Christmas thank-you letters	
crisp-packets lying around		hour-long phone calls	
piano practice	room	socks on floor	to cat
to strangers	washing machine		

future in the past

> When we are talking about the past, we often want to say that something
> was still **in the future at that time**. To express this idea, we can use the
> **past progressive (was ...ing), was going to ..., would ... or was to**.

1 Put the beginnings and ends together.

BEGINNINGS	ENDS
Carola and I hardly noticed each other that first evening.	and she still hadn't started packing.
He was to regret that conversation	arrived one Friday morning.
I was going to ring you yesterday,	but I forgot.
She was leaving in two hours,	for many years to come.
So this was the school where I would spend the next five years.	I didn't like it.
The letter that was to change my life	Two weeks later we would be married.

▲ **2 These sentences are from C S Forester's novel _The General_, set in
   the First World War. Complete the sentences with expressions
   from the box.**

would stand   would make   would return   was going to be
was going to say   was marrying   were to find   were to lose

1   The parlourmaid was in the room and her presence caused Lady Emily
    not to say immediately what she _____.
2   As the Duchess had said, the fact that Emily _____ a General was a very
    adequate excuse for so much ceremony at the wedding.
3   There was going to be no muddling in _his_ Corps. Everything _____ exact,
    systematic, perfect.
4   (This was) the front line of the British trench system – in it many men
    _____ their lives for the barren honour of retaining that worthless ground.
5   There were six men bending over that map, and five of them _____ their
    graves at the point where the General's finger was stabbing at the map.
6   A vivid flash of imagination, like lightning at night, revealed the future to
    Curzon. He _____ to England a defeated general, one of the men who had
    let England down. Emily _____ by him, but he did not want her to have to
    do so. Emily whom he loved _____ it all the worse. He would rather die.

the two **present tenses**

	SIMPLE PRESENT	PRESENT PROGRESSIVE
✔	I/you/we/they **work** he/she/it **works**	I **am**, you **are** *etc* **working**
?	**do** I/you/we/they work? **does** he/she/it work?	**am** I, **are** you *etc* **working?**
✗	I/you/we/they **do** not work he/she/it **does** not work	I **am** not, you **are** not *etc* **working**

You **live** in North London, don't you?
No thanks. I **don't smoke**.
Chetford Castle **stands** on a hill outside the town.
Alice **works** for an insurance company.
What **do** frogs **eat**?
I **play** tennis every Wednesday.
The sun **rises** in the east.

My sister**'s living** with me just now.
Look – Ann**'s smoking** a cigar.
Why **is** that girl **standing** on the table?

Phil**'s working** in Japan at the moment.
Hurry up! We**'re waiting** for you.
'What **are** you **doing**?' 'I**'m writing** letters.'
Why **are** you **crying**? What's wrong?

DO IT YOURSELF

1   Study the above examples, and then look at the words and expressions in the
    box. Which of them go best with the simple present, and which go with the
    present progressive? Check your answer in the key.

| permanent   temporary   habit   just around now   always |
| usually   just at this moment   these days but not for very long |

DO IT YOURSELF

2   Write a rule in your own language to explain the difference
    between the two English present tenses. If you can work with
    other students who speak your language, compare your rule
    with theirs.

'I am standing under your foot.'

We **don't** use a **present tense** to say **how long** something has been going on.
I've known her for years. (NOT ~~I know her for years.~~) See page 156.

3 **Here are some exchanges from an interview between an American journalist and a French film star. Can you complete them with the correct tenses?**

1 'How do you start work on a film?' 'I *(read)* the script and *(make)* notes.'
2 'I *(make)* notes of our interview. I hope you don't mind.' 'No, that's OK.'
3 'What languages *(you speak)?*' 'English, French and Spanish.'
4 'I'm glad we *(do)* this interview in English. My French isn't very good.'
5 'Who *(play)* that guitar?' 'My son, when he has time.'
6 'Who *(play)* the piano upstairs?' 'My sister. She's got a concert tomorrow.'
7 'What *(she play)?*' 'I think it's a piece by Mozart.'
8 '*(She play)* anything else?' 'The violin. She's very musical.'
9 'Your daughter's very keen on sport, isn't she?' 'She *(play)* tennis.'
10 'Where is she now?' 'She *(play)* tennis, as usual.'
11 'What's that delicious smell?' 'My husband *(cook).*'
12 'Is that usual?' 'Yes, normally I *(shop)* and my husband *(cook).*'
13 'What a lovely clock!' 'It *(not work)*, I'm afraid – it's been broken for years.'
14 'Could I use your phone?' 'I'm afraid it *(not work)* at the moment.'

4 **Choose the correct forms of the cartoon captions.**

'Of course, he still has his hobby.
He *(collects / is collecting)* dust.'

'So *(how's everything going / how does everything go)?*'

Drawing by Gahan Wilson; © 1993
The New Yorker Magazine, Inc.

Repeated actions not only around the moment of speaking: **simple present**.
Repeated actions around the moment of speaking: **present progressive**.

*I **go** to the mountains about twice a year.*   *Water **boils** at 100° Celsius.*
*Why **is** he **hitting** the dog?*   *Jake**'s seeing** a lot of Felicity these days.*

present tense stories etc

We often tell stories with present tenses in an informal style.
We use the **simple present** for **events** – things that happen one after another.
We use the **present progressive** for **background** – things that are already happening when the story starts, or that continue through part of the story.

*There's this Scotsman, you see, and he's **walking** through the jungle when he **meets** a gorilla. And the gorilla's **eating** a snake sandwich. So the Scotsman **goes** up to the gorilla and **says** ...*

1   **Put the story in order and put in the correct forms of the verbs.**

ask	close	go	hold	keep	notice	open	say
sit	start	take	throw	work			

The man ____ another orange out of his bag and ____ opening the
   window.
'But there are no elephants in these mountains,' ____ the woman.
Suddenly the man ____ the window, ____ out the orange and ____ the
   window again.
'Because we ____ through the mountains. Oranges ____ the elephants
   away.'
A woman ____ in a railway carriage when she ____ that the man
   opposite her ____ an orange in his hand and looking out of the
   window.
'You see?' says the man. 'It ____.'
'Excuse me,' the woman ____, 'but why did you do that?'

2   **You probably know a better story than this. Write it, or tell other
    people.**

We use the **simple present** to describe events that happen **one after
another** in **commentaries** and **demonstrations**.
We also use the simple present to ask for and give **instructions**.

*Calvin **passes** to Peters, Peters to O'Malley, Lucas **intercepts**, Lucas to
   Higgins, Higgins **shoots** – and it's a goal!*
*First I **put** a lump of butter into the frying pan and **light** the gas; then while
   the butter's melting I **break** three eggs into a bowl ...*
*'How **do** I **get** to the station?' 'You **go** straight on for half a mile, then you
   come to a garage, you **turn** left and then you **take** the first right.'*

For explanations of the words that we use to talk about grammar, see pages 298–302.

3   Look at the map and follow the directions. Where do you get to?

When you come out of the station you turn right. Then you take the
first left and keep straight on till you come to a T-Junction. You turn
right and keep straight on till you get to a crossroads, and then turn
right again.

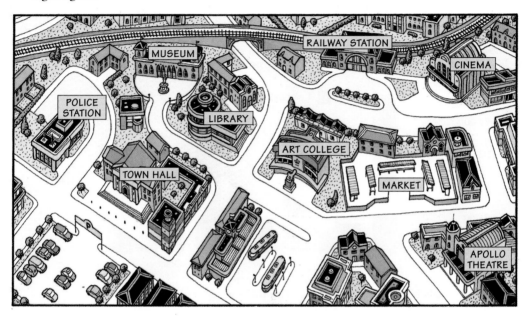

**4   Write similar directions to tell somebody how to get from the
station to the Apollo Theatre.**

**5   If you can work with other students, give them directions to
another place on the map. See if they can work out where it is.**

6   Look at the pictures and write the instructions for boiling an egg.

7   Write the instructions for cooking something else.

present progressive for changes

We use the **present progressive** for **changing** and **developing** situations.

*The climate **is getting** warmer.* (NOT *~~The climate **gets** warmer.~~*)
*That child**'s growing** bigger every day.*
*The universe **is expanding**, and has been since its beginning.*

1   Look at the graph and say what is happening.

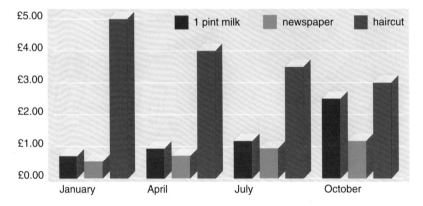

2   Say what is happening to some of the following.

the world's population	you (age)	your English	prices
days (length) pollution	roads	trains cars	air travel
the world's forests wildlife		the political situation	children
cities medical care	teenagers	unemployment	sprinters
men women older people		people's holidays	

3   Complete the cartoon captions

'Seems all right. How *(your English / get on)* ?'

'That funny noise *(get)* louder.'

simple present: spelling

DO IT YOURSELF

1 **Look at the examples of third person singular (*he/she/it* ...) forms and answer the questions. Check your answers in the key.**

catches	*cooks*	*does*	*eats*	*enjoys*	*fixes*	*flies*
goes	*lives*	*makes*	*misses*	*passes*	*plays*	*pushes*
reads	*replies*	*says*	*shops*	*smokes*	*speaks*	*stands*
teaches	*thinks*	*tries*	*waits*	*washes*	*works*	

1   What is the most common way of making the third person singular?
2   What happens with words ending in **vowel + -*y*?**
3   What happens with words ending in **consonant + -*y*?**
4   After which consonants and groups of consonants do we add **-*es*?**
5   Which two other common words add **-*es*?**

2 **Write the third person singular of these verbs.**

box	brush	buy	complete	cry	defend	deny
destroy	excite	expect	fry	guess	look	pray
reach	receive	rush	spend	want	watch	

3 **Complete the quotations with the verbs in the box.**

come	do *(twice)*	get	happen	hate *(twice)*	love	
make	sing	start	teach	wait	wash	

1   He who can, ____. He who cannot, ____.   *G B Shaw*
2   It's not that I'm afraid to die. I just don't want to be there when it ____.
    Woody Allen
3   He's fanatically tidy. After he takes a bath, he ____ the soap.
    Hugh Leonard
4   Opera is when a guy ____ knifed in the back and, instead of bleeding, he
    ____.   *Ed Gardner*
5   Never marry a man who ____ his mother; he'll end up hating you.
    Jill Bennett
6   The brain is a wonderful organ. It ____ working the moment you get up
    in the morning, and it ____ not stop until you get to the office.
    Robert Frost
7   A man who ____ whisky and ____ kids can't be all bad.   *W C Fields*
8   The man who ____ no mistakes does not usually make anything.
    E J Phelps
9   Everything ____ to him who ____.   *Traditional*

non-progressive verbs

Some verbs are **not** normally used in **progressive forms**.

*I **know** what you **mean**.* (NOT *I'm knowing what you're meaning.*)
*You **seem** worried.* (NOT *You're seeming ...*)

1 **These verbs aren't normally used in progressive forms. Use some
or all of them to complete the sentences. More than one answer
may be possible.**

believe	belong	contain	forget	hate	like	love
matter	need	own	prefer	realise	remember	
suppose	understand	want				

1 This book ____ to me.
2 I ____ you're right.
3 ____ you ____ this music?
4 His father ____ a chain of hotels.
5 She says she ____ to see Fred.
6 I ____ a drink of water.
7 I ____ you don't ____ me.

8   I ____ how old she is.
9   She ____ me and I ____ her.
10 Money doesn't ____ to me.
11 'Beer?' 'I ____ water.'
12 I ____ his face, but not his name.
13 That bottle ____ petrol.

Some verbs have **progressive forms with one meaning** but not with
another. The following do not usually have progressive forms:
have (= 'possess'); ***appear*** (= 'seem'); ***look*** (= 'seem');
see (= 'understand'); ***think*** (= 'have the opinion that');
feel (= 'have the opinion that').

2 **Choose the correct form (simple present or present progressive).**

1   I *(have)* a great time.
2   She *(have)* plenty of money just now.
3   He *(appear)* at the Fortune Theatre next week.
4   She *(appear)* to have a problem.
5   Why *(you look)* at me like that?
6   It *(look)* as if it's going to rain.
7   I *(see)* what you're trying to say.
8   I *(see)* the manager this afternoon.
9   I *(think)* you're right.
10 What *(you think)* about?
11 I *(feel)* very tired today.
12 I *(feel)* she's making a mistake.

'I think we've got a leadership problem.'

he's always borrowing money etc

If something **is always happening**, it happens **often**, but is **unplanned**.

*I'm **always losing** my keys.*
*Granny's **always giving** us little presents.*
*He's **always borrowing** money.*

Compare:
*When Alice comes, I **always meet** her at the station.* (planned meetings)
*I'm **always meeting** Alan Forbes in the supermarket.* (unplanned)

1   **Here are some sentences taken from real conversations. Can you
    put the beginnings and ends together?**

BEGINNINGS	ENDS
Dad is always teasing me	a party in one of the houses.
He's always arguing	about my clothes.
He's always giving people	and chest problems.
Her best friend is always	her family.
dropping in	making up stories about people.
I hate those cartoons	new products.
Jamie is always having colds	or fighting.
My wife's always buying	she wishes she was prettier.
She's always criticising	small presents.
She's always saying	to criticise the way she lives her life.
Someone is always giving	where Tom is always chasing Jerry.
That old bitch is always	

DO IT YOURSELF

2   **This structure usually expresses an emotion. Which emotion is
    most common in the examples in Exercise 1 – interest, criticism,
    surprise or admiration? Check your answer in the key.**

3   **Use this structure to write sentences describing people you know
    who often do some of the following things (or others):**

worry about nothing lose their temper lose things		
complain about their health forget things cry fall in love		
change their job buy new clothes quarrel talk nonsense		

revision of **present tenses**

1   Put in the correct tense (simple present or present progressive).

1   Vegetarians are people who *(don't eat / are not eating)* meat.
2   Look out! My husband *(comes / is coming)*.
3   Some people still think the sun *(goes / is going)* round the earth.
4   I *(play / 'm playing)* tennis every weekend.
5   Who *(sits / 's sitting)* in my chair?
6   What *(happens / is happening)* in golf if you lose the ball?
7   An alcoholic is a person who *(drinks / is drinking)* too much and
    can't stop.
8   Look! *(She wears / She's wearing)* the same shoes as me.
9   'What *(are you looking / do you look)* at?' 'A strange bird.'
10   I *(stay / 'm staying)* with John for a few weeks until my flat's ready.
11   We *(usually stay / 're usually staying)* with Peggy when we go to Chicago.
12   Can you explain why water always *(runs / is running)* downhill?
13   What *(do you do / are you doing)* with my coat?
14   Nobody *(gets / is getting)* up early for fun.
15   Not many passenger planes *(fly / are flying)* faster than sound.

2   Match the questions and answers.

1	What do you do?	a	Actually, that's the radio.
2	What are you doing?	b	French – she's from Belgium.
3	Where do you work?	c	I want to get this car started.
4	Where are you working?	d	I'm an architect.
5	Does your son play the violin?	e	I'm in Cardiff this week.
6	Is your son playing the violin?	f	In a big insurance company.
7	What language does she speak?	g	It sounds like Russian.
8	What language is she speaking?	h	Me – can I have some more?
9	Who drinks champagne?	i	Me, when I can afford it.
10	Who's drinking champagne?	j	No, the piano.

3   Put in the correct tense (simple present or present progressive).

1   I *(think)* he's away.
2   You *(know)* what I *(mean)*.
3   She *(always complain)*.
4   We *(always start)* at nine.
5   While the butter *(melt)*, you *(take)* three eggs and *(break)* them
    into a bowl.
6   I *(think)* about your father.
7   Scientists *(believe)* the weather *(change)*.
8   I *(not see)* what the problem is.
9   Why *(you look)* at me like that?
10   Now I *(understand)* what she wants.

For explanations of the words that we use to talk about grammar, see pages 298–302.

simple present perfect: introduction

✔	I **have seen**, you **have seen** *etc*
?	**have** I **seen**? **have** you **seen**? *etc*
✗	I **have not seen**, you **have not seen** *etc*

X - →X
past   **present**

The simple present perfect **connects the past and the present**.
We use it especially for **finished actions that are important now**.
They have **results now**, or they are **news**.

RESULTS NOW	NEWS
*I can't walk – I've **hurt** my leg.*	***Have** you **heard**? He's **arrived**!*
*Look – he **hasn't drunk** his tea.*	*You**'ve passed** your exam!*

Compare: *Brutus **killed** Caesar.* (NOT *... ~~has killed~~ ...* – no present meaning.)

We can often change a present perfect sentence into a present sentence with
more or less the same meaning.

*I**'ve hurt** my leg. = I **have** a bad leg.*   *Sue**'s come** back. = Sue **is** home.*
*He**'s lost** his keys. = He **can't** find them.*   *He**'s gone**. = He **isn't** here.*

**1   Change these present perfect sentences into present sentences
with similar meanings.**

1   The Foreign Minister has died.
2   Lucy's had a baby.
3   You've torn your coat.
4   I've broken my leg.
5   He's lost his address book.
6   Have you made tea?
7   I've done the washing up.
8   She's gone to work for the BBC.
9   We haven't found out where he is.
10   The noise has stopped.
11   I've forgotten your name.
12   She's learnt French.

**2   Complete the cartoon caption. Can
you make a present-tense sentence
about the situation in the cartoon?**

'First the good news. His temperature (*go*) down.'

present perfect and **past**: news

	SIMPLE PRESENT PERFECT	SIMPLE PAST
✔	I **have seen** *etc*	I **saw** *etc*
?	**have** I **seen**? *etc*	**did** I **see**? *etc*
✗	I **have not seen** *etc*	I **did not see** *etc*

We often **announce** a piece of news with the **present perfect**.
We can use ***just*** to say that something has happened **very recently**.

*A light passenger plane **has crashed** in Surrey.*
*Andy's **just found** a flat!*

1 **Join the beginnings and ends to make pieces of news. Which
sentence goes with which picture?**

BEGINNINGS	ENDS
A parachutist has just	a baby girl.
Lucy has had	gone into hospital again.
My poor old father has	into our garden gate.
Polly and Simon have	just got married.
Some people have bought	landed on the roof.
Somebody has just crashed	lost £30 million this year.
The firm has	the cup again.
United have won	the house next door.

1   2   3   4

5   6   7   8

When we give **more details**, we usually change to the **simple past**.

'I've had a terrible day at the office, dear. My secretary went home sick, we lost three major contracts and a funny little dwarf turned me into a banana.'

2   **Choose the right tenses and put the sentences in pairs to make news items. Example:**

A light passenger plane has crashed in Surrey. According to eyewitnesses, the aircraft hit a tree while coming in to land.

A light passenger plane *(crash)* in Surrey.
Five thousand fans *(be)* at the airport.
According to eyewitnesses, the aircraft *(hit)* a tree while coming in to land.
Ana Gomez, of Peru, *(set)* a new record for the marathon.
He *(say)* I was just the person he needed.
Novelist Maria Santiago *(marry)* actor Tony Delaney.
Peter *(just offer)* me a new job!
Police *(find)* missing schoolgirl Karen Allen.
She *(cover)* the 42 km in just over 2 hours and 16 minutes.
She *(be)* at a friend's house in Birmingham.
The World Cup team *(arrive)* home.
They *(fall)* just before reaching the summit of Mont Blanc (4,807 m).
They *(meet)* while working on the screenplay for the film *Sun in the Morning*.
They *(steal)* dustmen's uniforms and walked out through the main gate.
Three climbers *(die)* in the Alps.
Two prisoners *(escape)* from Caernarvon high security prison.

Note that we use the **simple past** to talk about the **origin** of something present.

> *Who **wrote** that?* (NOT *Who **has written** that?*)
> *Bill **gave** me this necklace.*   ***Did** you **put** this here?*
> *Whose idea **was** it to come here on holiday?*

present perfect and **past**: time words

To talk about **finished actions**, we can use the **present perfect or the
simple past**. It often depends on the **kind of time expression** that is used.
We do **not** normally **use** the **present perfect** with expressions which refer
to a **finished time**, like *yesterday, last week, three years ago, then, when.*
We normally **use the present perfect** with expressions which refer to
'**any time up to now**', like *ever, never, before, recently, often, already, yet.*
Compare:

> *I **saw** Kate **yesterday**.* (NOT ~~I **have seen** Kate yesterday.~~)
> ***Have** you **seen** Rob **recently**?*
> *You **were** here **last week**, weren't you?*
> *You**'ve been** here **before**, haven't you?*
> *She **studied** Chinese **when she was at university.***
> *He**'s never studied** any foreign languages.*

1   Finished or unfinished time? Put the expressions in two lists.

a long time ago	before I was born	in 1991	in my life
just after I got up	last year	lately	this year	today
when I was nine			

2   Choose the correct tense.

1   I *(haven't seen / didn't see)* much of Al lately.
2   'Who is she?' 'I *('ve never seen / never saw)* her before.'
3   I *('ve done / did)* a lot of stupid things in my life.
4   She *(has left / left)* school last year.
5   When *(have you got / did you get)* married?
6   I'm sorry. I *(haven't finished / didn't finish)* yet.
7   I *('ve often wondered / often wondered)* what he does for a living.
8   He *(has caught / caught)* the plane at eight this morning.
9   I *('ve read / read)* a lot of her books when I was at school.
10   *(Have you seen / Did you see)* any good films recently?

Just now (meaning 'a moment ago') is used with the **simple past**.
Compare:

> *She **has just phoned**.   She **phoned just now**.*

For explanations of the words that we use to talk about grammar, see pages 298–302.

We can **think of a finished time** even without using a time expression.
We can **think of 'any time up to now'** even if we don't say so.

Did you *see* 'Hamlet'? (It was on TV **last night**.)
Have you *seen* 'Hamlet'? (= Have you **ever** seen 'Hamlet'?)

3   Put in the most suitable tense (simple past or present perfect).

1   You *(be)* a beautiful baby.
2   I *(not read)* her latest book.
3   *(you visit)* India?
4   My great-grandmother *(live)* in Glasgow.
5   Columbus *(not discover)* America: the Indians already *(know)* where it
    was.
6   Amazing news! Scientists *(discover)* a new planet!
7   Who *(give)* Shakespeare his first job?
8   How many times *(you be)* in love?
9   I *(never enjoy)* a holiday as much as this one.
10 '*(you hear)* the thunder?' 'No, nothing wakes me up.'

**4   Complete the three questions in your own words. If you can, ask
     somebody else and report the answers.**

Have you ever ...?
How often have you ...?
When did you last ...?

5   Complete the cartoon captions correctly.

'Oh yes! I *met* / *'ve met* your sort before.'

'When *did you last feed* / *have you last fed*
that goldfish?'

present perfect: situations 'up to now'

past ▨s▨i▨t▨u▨a▨t▨i▨o▨n▨ ▶ **present**

> We use the **present perfect** to talk about situations **continuing up to now**, especially when we say **how long** they have lasted.
>
> Alex **has worked** with children **all her life**.
> He went to Rome on holiday ten years ago, and he**'s lived** there
>   **ever since**.
> She**'s always wanted** to go to Australia, but she**'s never had** time.
>
> We **do not** use a **present** tense to say how long something has lasted.
>
> I**'ve known** Joe **for years**. (NOT ~~I know Joe for years.~~)
> How long **have you been here** for? (= 'Since when ...?')
> Compare: How long **are** you here for? (= 'Until when ...?')

1   Read the sentences and answer the questions.

1   'How long has Ann lived in Spain?' *Does Ann still live in Spain?*
2   'How long did Bill live in Italy?' *Does Bill still live in Italy?*
3   'Joe worked with me for two years.' *Does Joe still work with the speaker?*
4   'Sue has worked with me for two years.' *Does Sue still work with the speaker?*
5   'I've had a headache all day.' *Has the speaker got a headache?*
6   'I had a headache all day.' *Has the speaker got a headache?*

2   Put the bracketed expressions into the sentences and choose the correct tenses.

1   I *(like)* sport. *(always)*   I have always liked sport.
2   I'm sorry for her. She *(have)* bad luck. *(all her life)*
3   I *(want)* to be a doctor. *(until I was fifteen)*
4   He *(be)* unemployed. *(ever since he left school)*
5   *(you live)* in this town? *(How long)*
6   I *(not work)* very hard. *(when I was at university)*
7   He was ill before Christmas, but he *(be)* fine. *(since then)*
8   I *(have)* trouble sleeping. *(all this week)*
9   I *(have)* trouble sleeping. *(all last week)*
10   I *(learn)* a lot. *(in this job)*
11   I *(not learn)* much. *(in that job)*
12   My boyfriend and I *(know)* each other. *(for ages)*
13   He *(live)* in Durban. *(for a year before he got married)*
14   I *(spend)* three days in hospital. *(last month)*

We often use the **present perfect** for actions **repeated up to now.**
Compare:

> *Benjamin's been to Africa several times this year.* ('up to now')
> *I went to Africa three times last year.* (not 'up to now')
>
> *I've climbed a lot of mountains, but I've never been up Mont Blanc.*
> *In 1861 he climbed most of the highest mountains in France.*

3   Complete the sentences with the present perfect or simple past.

1   I *(play)* a lot of tennis this year.
2   She *(have)* six different jobs since she left school.
3   He *(run)* away from school three times when he was fourteen.
4   How many cups of coffee *(you drink)* today?
5   In those days, Andrew *(come)* to stay with us most weekends.
6   Shakespeare *(write)* poems as well as plays.
7   Since my brother lost his job, he *(write)* two books.
8   I'm not cooking today – I *(cook)* all the meals yesterday. In fact, I *(cook)*
    most of the meals this week.
9   Would you believe I *(make)* twenty-three phone calls today?
10 Our team are rubbish. They *(just lose)* eight games one after the other.

4   Complete these sentences in any way you like.

1   I've always ____.
2   I've often ____.
3   I often ____ when I was a child.
4   All my life I have ____.
5   I've known ____.
6   I've had my ____ since ____.
7   I've lived ____.
8   I've never lived ____.
9   I've ____ times this year.
10 I ____ times last year.

**5   Choose the correct version
of the cartoon caption.**

'I've spent / I spent twenty-five years
making a name for myself and now
you want me to CHANGE it?!'

With most verbs, we can also use the **present perfect progressive** to talk
about situations continuing up to now. For details, see pages 158–159.

> *Have you been waiting long?*

present perfect progressive

✔	I **have been working** *etc*
?	**have** you **been working?** *etc*
✗	he **has not been working** *etc*

We often use the **present perfect progressive** to talk about actions **continuing up to now**, especially when we say **how long** they have lasted. We **do not** use a **present** tense to say how long something has lasted.

> It **has been snowing** since Tuesday.
>   (NOT ~~It *is snowing* since Tuesday~~.)
> How long **have** you **been learning** English?
>   (NOT ... ~~*are you* *learning* ...?~~)

For the difference between the progressive and simple tenses, see page 160.

1 **Complete the sentences with verbs from the box. Use the present perfect progressive. Which sentences go with the two cartoons?**

cry	learn	live	play *(twice)*	rain	wait *(twice)*
walk	work				

1 It ____ all day.
2 I ____ English since I was six.
3 She ____ tennis professionally for ten years.
4 We ____n't ____ in this house for very long.
5 That man ____ up and down the street for ages.
6 I ____ very hard this week.
7 She ____ non-stop since she got his letter.
8 He ____ that music for hours. I wish he'd stop.
9 ____ you ____ long, sir?
10 They call me waiter, but you ____ for half an hour.

A

B

We can also use the **present perfect progressive** to talk about long or
repeated actions that have finished recently, and which have **present
results**.

'You look hot.' 'Yes, I've been running.'

2 Put together the beginnings and ends of the conversations.

BEGINNINGS	ENDS
'Aren't you hungry?'	'Helen's been looking at them.'
'Is it true that Philip's been arrested?'	'I've been gardening all afternoon.'
'Janet seems very cheerful.'	'I've been swimming.'
'She's very dirty.'	'I've been talking to Henry, and he just goes
'Why are my books all over the floor?'	on and on.'
'Why's your hair wet?'	'No, I've been eating all day.'
'You all look very miserable.'	'She's been cleaning the cellar.'
'You look tired.'	'She's been skiing with Roger for the last
'You're very late.'	week.'
'Your hair's all white.'	'Yes, he's been stealing things from shops.'
	'Yes, I've been painting the ceiling.'
	'Yes, we've been telling each other our life
	stories.'

3 Write sentences about the pictures, to say what has been happening.

1

2

3

4

5

6

present perfect progressive or simple?

To talk about recent long actions and situations:
the **present perfect progressive** looks at the **continuing situation itself**; the **present perfect simple** says that something is **completed, achieved.**

*I've **been reading** your book: I'm enjoying it.*
*I've **read** your **book.** (= I've finished it.)*

We use the **simple present perfect** to say **how often** something has happened (because of the idea of completion). Compare:
*I've **played** tennis three times this week.*
*I've **been playing** a lot of tennis recently.*

We prefer the **simple present perfect** to talk about permanent or very long-lasting situations. Compare:
*He's **been living** in Doncaster for the last few months.*
*I've **lived** here all my life.*

1   Put in the present perfect progressive or simple.

1   That man *(stand)* outside for hours.
2   The castle *(stand)* on that hill for 900 years.
3   Ann *(garden)* all afternoon. She *(plant)* a lot of rose bushes.
4   James *(go)* out every night this week.
5   He *(see)* a lot of Alexandra recently.
6   How long *(you wait)*?
7   I *(wait)* long enough. I'm going.
8   Her family *(farm)* this land since the tenth century.
9   She *(only farm)* for two years, but she's doing very well.
10   I *(learn)* German for six years.
11   I *(learn)* most of the irregular verbs.
12   My mother *(do)* all her Christmas shopping.
13   I *(do)* Christmas shopping all day.
14   I *(clean)* the car. Doesn't it look nice?
15   'You look tired.' 'I *(wash)* clothes all day.'

Remember that some verbs are not used in progressive forms even if the meaning is one for which a progressive form is more suitable (see page 148).

*He's only **known** her for two days.* (NOT ~~He's only been knowing her~~ ...)
*How long **have** you **had** that cold?* (NOT ... ~~have you been having~~ ...?)

since and for

1 Do you know the difference between *since* and *for*? Look at the examples and try to make a rule. Then check this in the key.

*He's been here **since ten o'clock**.*   *He's been here **for two hours**.*
*We've had this car **since December**.*   *We've had this car **for six months**.*
*I've known her **since university**.*   *I've known her **for a very long time**.*

2 Complete the expressions.

since yesterday = for 24 hours
for 200 years = since the 18th century
since 1980 = _____   for 20 years = since _____
since Tuesday = _____   for five days = _____
since six o'clock = _____   for the last two hours = _____
since my birthday = _____ the last _____ days/weeks/months

3 Complete the sentences with *since* or *for*.

1 I've had this job _____ a month.
2 He's known her _____ April.
3 She's been ill _____ years.
4 I haven't seen him _____ ages.

5 I've lived here _____ 1992.
6 He's been away _____ a long time.
7 I haven't slept _____ two nights.

4 Write sentences about these situations with *since* and *for*.

1 Jake runs a small business. He started doing this five years ago.
2 Andy lives in Dublin. He moved there last year.
3 Helen plays the piano. She started two years ago.
4 Rob has a Mercedes. He bought it five years ago.
5 Jan is living with Pete. This started in 1994.
6 Sammy is learning Turkish. He started four years ago.

5 Complete the sentences in your own words.

1 I've had this _____ for _____.
2 I've known _____ since _____.

3 I haven't _____ for _____.
4 I haven't _____ since _____.

6 If you can work with other students, ask them questions beginning 'How long have ...' They should answer 'Since ...' or 'For ...'

tenses with **since** and **for**

Sentences with *since* usually have a **perfect** tense. But **past tenses** are possible in the **time expression after *since*.** Compare:

> *I've known her since 1980.*
> *I've known her since we were students.*

1 Choose the right tenses.

1 It *(is / was / has been)* snowing since I *(have got up / got up).*
2 Things *(have been / were)* difficult since Carol *(has lost / lost)* her job.
3 Since Jake *(has taken up / took up)* the trumpet, nobody *(has / has had / had)* any peace.
4 He *(has been / was)* quite different since he *(has got / got)* married.
5 Since she *(has gone / went)* to live in France we *(haven't heard / didn't hear)* anything from her.
6 He *(has been / was)* strange ever since he *(has had / had)* the accident.

A **present tense** is sometimes used in the main clause to talk about **changes**.
Note also the structure ***It is ... since ...***

> *She looks quite different since her illness.*
> *It's a long time since lunch.*

2 Put the beginnings and ends together. (Different answers are possible.)

BEGINNINGS	ENDS
He looks much younger	since he had a job.
It's nearly three years	since he shaved off his beard.
It's only a week	since I met her, but it seems like years.
It's too long	since she stopped going out with Pete.
She's a lot happier	since we got our own flat.
Things are better	since we last had a proper talk.

Sentences with *for* have a **perfect** tense when the meaning is **'time up to now'**, but other tenses are used with other meanings.

> *I've known her for ages.*
> *I was in that school for three years.*
> *She's staying for another week.*
> *He'll be in hospital for a month.*

present perfect and **past**: revision

1   Tenses and time expressions. Which rule is true? Check your answer in the key.

1   **Present perfect (simple or progressive)** with longer periods of time; **simple past** with shorter periods.
2   **Present perfect** with expressions of finished time; **simple past** with expressions of unfinished time.
3   **Present perfect** with expressions of unfinished time; **simple past** with expressions of finished time.
4   **Present perfect** with repeated actions; **simple past** with actions that are not repeated.

2   Put in the correct forms.

Dear Eileen

Hope things are OK with you. The doctor (1 *come*) yesterday. He (2 *not like*) my cough. I (3 *lie*) in bed looking at the ceiling since Tuesday, and I can tell you, I'm fed up with it. I (4 *never be*) ill like this before – don't know what's happening to me. And the weather's terrible. It (5 *rain*) all day, and I can't even have a cup of tea to cheer myself up, because the milkman (6 *not come*) this morning. Don't know why – I'm sure I (7 *pay*) his bill.

Alice (8 *get*) married last week, so now all Mary's kids (9 *leave*) home. She won't know what to do with herself, will she?

Lucy Watson (10 *move*) to Doncaster. Since Fred (11 *die*) she (12 *be*) all alone. It (13 *be*) a heart attack, apparently. I'm sorry she (14 *go*) – we (15 *be*) neighbours (16 *since/for*) over thirty years, and she (17 *always be*) friendly and ready to help out.

Amy (18 *leave*). My cleaning lady, you remember? I'm glad. She (19 *not be*) much use, and I (20 *not trust*) her since she (21 *break*) all those plates and (22 *say*) it (23 *be*) the cat.

There (24 *not be*) much change in the village. Some new people (25 *take*) over the shop. They seem quite nice. Hope they're more efficient than old Joe.

No more news. Write when you've got the time.

Love

Emma

past progressive

✔	I **was working** *etc*
?	**were** you **working?** *etc*
✗	she **was not working** *etc*

What **were you doing**   As I **was walking** down the road
---------x----------   ---------------x---------------
       at 1.00?   I **saw** Bill.

> We use the **past progressive** to say that something was going on **around a particular past time**.
>
> *'What **were you doing** at 1.00 last night?' 'I **was watching** TV.'*
> (NOT *'What **did you do**...?' 'I **watched** TV.'*)

> We can use the **past progressive and simple past** together.
> **Past progressive**: longer **background** action or situation.
> **Simple past**: shorter action that **interrupted it** or happened in the middle.
>
> *As I **was walking** down the road I **saw** Bill.*
> *The phone **rang** while I **was having** dinner.*

1   Put in the correct tenses.

1   At six o'clock this morning I *(have)* a wonderful dream, but then the alarm *(go)* off.
2   This time yesterday I *(lie)* on the beach.
3   When I walked in they *(all talk)* about babies.
4   I saw Sid when I *(come)* to work this morning. He *(shop)*.
5   She *(meet)* her husband while she *(travel)* in Egypt.
6   While I *(talk)* to Mrs Singleton somebody *(walk)* into my office and *(steal)* the computer.
7   When Jake *(come)* in everybody *(stop)* talking.
8   I *(look)* out of the window and *(see)* that we *(fly)* over the mountains.
9   I *(wake)* up to find that water *(pour)* through the bedroom ceiling.
10 He *(break)* his leg while he *(play)* football.
11 I *(go)* to see how she *(be)* and found she *(cry)*.
12 She *(tell)* me she *(have)* a bad time with her husband.

2   **Look at the pictures, and write sentences to say what was happening and what happened.**

▲   **3**   **Complete the text with the verbs in the box (there is one verb too many). You will need five past progressives and three simple pasts.**

ask	come	dance	grin	hold	not dance	order
play	throw					

On the dance floor half a dozen couples __1__ themselves around. Most of them __2__ cheek to cheek, if dancing is the word. The men wore white tuxedos and the girls wore bright eyes, ruby lips, and tennis or golf muscles. One couple __3__ cheek to cheek. Mitchell's mouth was open, he __4__, his face was red and shiny, and his eyes had that glazed look. Betty __5__ her head as far as she could get away from him without breaking her neck. It was very obvious that she had had about all of Mr Larry Mitchell that she could take.

A Mexican waiter in a short green jacket and white pants with a green stripe down the side __6__ up and I __7__ a double Gibson and __8__ if I could have a club sandwich.   *Raymond Chandler: Playback* (adapted)

Progressive forms are used mostly for **temporary** actions and situations. For longer, more **permanent** situations we prefer the **simple past**. **Compare:**

> *When I walked in I found that water **was running** down the walls.*
> *Explorers believed that the river **ran** into the Atlantic.*

We do **not** normally use the **past progressive** to talk about **past habits**, or to say **how often** something happened.
> *I **played** a lot of tennis when I was younger. (NOT I **was playing** ...)*
> *She **rang** the bell three times. (NOT She **was ringing** ...)*

Remember that some verbs are not used in progressive forms (see page 148).
> *I tried the cake to see how it **tasted.** (NOT ... how it **was tasting.**)*

past perfect

✔	I **had worked** *etc*
?	**had** you **worked?** *etc*
✗	he **had not worked** *etc*

DO IT YOURSELF

1   **Look at the examples. Which of rules 1–5 gives the best explanation for the use of the past perfect? Check your answer in the key.**

*When I got to the car park I realised that I **had lost** my keys.*
*She told me she **had worked** in France and Germany.*
*He arrived late; he **hadn't realised** the roads would be so icy.*
*She was upset because Andrew **hadn't telephoned**.*

Do we use the **past perfect**:
1   mostly in **indirect speech**?
2   to show that a past action was **completed**?
3   when we are already talking about the past, and want to talk about an **earlier past** for a moment?
4   to talk about things that happened a **very long time ago**?
5   to say **why** something happened?

2   **Put in the simple past or past perfect.**

1   I *(be)* sorry that I *(not be)* nicer to him.
2   Nobody *(come)* to the meeting because Angela *(forget)* to tell people about it.
3   I *(see)* her before somewhere – I *(know)*.
4   Because he *(not check)* the oil for so long, the car *(break)* down.
5   She couldn't find the book that I *(lend)* her.
6   All the people we *(invite)* turned up, and some that we *(not invite)*.
7   They *(never find)* where he *(hide)* the money.
8   It was a firm that I *(never hear)* of.
9   When she *(come)* in, we all knew where she *(be)*.
10   The lesson *(already start)* when I *(arrive)*.

TENSES: PERFECT AND PAST **167**

3 Choose the correct tense (simple past or past perfect).

When I (1 *go*) to Paris last spring for a job interview, I (2 *not be*) there for five years. I (3 *arrive*) the evening before the interview, and (4 *spend*) a happy hour walking round thinking about the good times I (5 *have*) there as a student.

As I was strolling by the Seine, I suddenly (6 *see*) a familiar face – it was Nedjma, the woman I (7 *share*) a flat with when I was a student, and whose address I (8 *lose*) after leaving Paris. I could tell she (9 *not see*) me, so I (10 *call*) her name and she (11 *look*) up. As she (12 *turn*) towards me, I (13 *realise*) that she (14 *have*) an ugly scar on the side of her face. She (15 *see*) the shock in my eyes, and her hand (16 *go*) up to touch the scar; she (17 *explain*) that she (18 *get*) it when she was a journalist reporting on a war in Africa.

She (19 *not be*) uncomfortable telling me this; we (20 *feel*) as if the years (21 *not pass*), as if we (22 *say*) goodbye the week before. She (23 *arrive*) in Paris that morning, and she (24 *have*) a hospital appointment the next day. The doctors (25 *think*) that they could remove the scar, but she would have to stay in Paris for several months. Both of us (26 *have*) the idea at the same time: if I (27 *get*) the job, we could share a flat again. And we could start by having a coffee while we (28 *begin*) to tell one another everything that (29 *happen*) to us in the past five years.

> We often use the **past perfect** after **when** and **after** to show that something was **completely finished**.
>
> When he **had painted** the kitchen and bathroom, he decided to have a rest.
> After I **had finished** the report, I realised that it was too late to post it.

4 Join the beginnings and ends to make sensible sentences.

BEGINNINGS	ENDS
After he had tried on six pairs of shoes	he decided he liked the first ones best.
After Mary had done all the shopping	he started going through the cupboards downstairs.
When I had washed and dried the last plate	she took a short walk round the park.
When Mark had looked through all the drawers in his room	he went to the café in the square for a cup of coffee.
When he had finished eating lunch	Paul came in and offered to help.

5 Use *when* or *after* to make one sentence for each situation.

1 I wrote to my boyfriend. Then I watched television for an hour or so.
2 Everybody had a chance to say what they thought. Then we took a vote.
3 I posted the letter. Then I felt much better about everything.
4 She stopped trying to lose weight. She looked much healthier.
5 He bought presents for everyone in his family. Then he bought something for himself as well.

past perfect progressive

✔	I **had been working** *etc*
?	**had** you **been working?** *etc*
✗	she **had not been working** *etc*

DO IT YOURSELF

1 **Look at the examples and think about when we use the past perfect progressive instead of the (simple) past perfect.**

> *All the roads were blocked: it **had been snowing** all night long.*
> *After I **had been walking** for an hour, I decided to have a rest.*
> *She fell ill because she **had been working** too hard.*
> *Mary could see that the child **had been crying** for some time.*

DO IT YOURSELF

2 **Look at these diagrams. Which one represents the (simple) past perfect, and which represents the past perfect progressive? Check your answers in the key.**

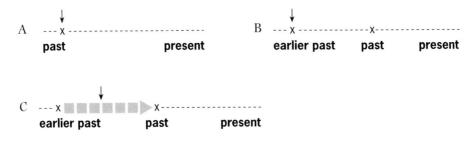

3 **Complete the text with past perfect progressives: choose verbs from the box.**

drive	lie	repair	work

John Latton, 39, an engineer at Felton Plastics in Upton, had a lucky escape after an accident on the A34 in the early hours of the morning. Mr Latton fell asleep while driving and crashed into a pile of sand left by workers who __1__ the road.

When he left Felton Plastics at 3.00 this morning, Mr Latton __2__ for 72 hours without any sleep.

A passing motorist discovered the accident after the engineer __3__ in his car with a broken leg for half an hour. Ambulance workers said that if Mr Latton __4__ any faster his injuries might have been much worse.

4 Read the story.

On Tuesday afternoon, everyone in my family was very busy – except me. During the afternoon Helen repaired her car; John practised his karate; Kate did some gardening; Stephanie played tennis; Roger swam for half an hour; Pam went horse-riding; Philip painted the ceiling in his room light blue. I spent the afternoon sitting reading.

Now answer the questions.

1 Who had black grease on her hands at teatime? Why?
   Helen, because she had been repairing her car.
2 Who had dirt on her hands and knees? Why?
3 Who was wearing a short white skirt? Why?
4 Who was wearing a white jacket and trousers and a black belt? Why?
5 Who was wearing high boots and a hard hat? Why?
6 Whose hair had light blue streaks in it? Why?
7 Whose hair was all wet? Why?

5 In a murder investigation, some suspects were asked by police what they had been doing at eight o'clock the previous evening. They all told lies. Write sentences to explain what they told the police they had been doing, and what they had actually been doing. Example:

Mrs Oliver said she had been reading, but actually she had been watching the neighbours through binoculars.

NAME	TOLD POLICE HAD BEEN DOING	TRUTH
Mrs Oliver	reading	watching neighbours through binoculars
Mr Lucas	watching TV	stealing cars
Mrs Allen	talking on the phone	making a bomb
Mr Nash	washing clothes	forging £5 notes
Alice	playing cards	selling drugs
Pete	studying chemistry	fighting
Aunt Jane	writing letters	planning a bank robbery
Miss Fry	washing her hair	out dancing with her sister's boyfriend
Rob	painting his flat	playing roulette

perfect tenses with this is the first etc

We use a **simple present perfect** tense in sentences with *this/it/that is the first/second/third/only/best/worst* etc.

> This is the first time that I've **heard** her sing.
> (NOT ~~This is the first time that I **hear** her sing.~~)
> This is the fifth time you've **asked** me the same question.
> (NOT ~~This is the fifth time you **ask** ...~~)
> That's the third cake you've **eaten** this morning.
> It's one of the most interesting books I've ever **read**.

1 Complete the sentences correctly.

1   This is the first time I *(see this film)*.
2   That's the eighth time you *(sing that song)* today.
3   This is the only time this week I *(feel happy)*.
4   This is the third serious mistake you *(make)* in this job.
5   This is the only time I *(ever see)* her cry.
6   That's the tenth cup of coffee you *(drink)* since breakfast.
7   It's the first time all the family *(be together)* since Sue's wedding.
8   This is the best meal I *(eat)* this year.
9   'Excuse me.' 'That's the first thing you *(say)* to me all day.'
10 These are the first clothes I *(buy)* myself since Christmas.

When we talk about the **past**, we use a **past perfect tense** in these structures.

> It was the third time he **had been** in love that year.
> (NOT ~~It was the third time he **was** in love ...~~)

2 Read the text and make sentences beginning *It was the first time.* Example:

It was the first time he had been away from home.

John didn't enjoy his first week in the army. He had never been away from home before; he had never worn uniform; he had never had to make his own bed; he had never cleaned his own boots; he had never fired a gun, and he hated the noise; he had never walked more than a mile.

Can you make some more examples?

For explanations of the words that we use to talk about grammar, see pages 298–302.

past and **progressive** in **requests** etc

Past tenses can make requests, questions and suggestions **more polite**. (They sound less direct than present tenses.)

> I **wondered** if you **were** free this evening.
> How much **did** you **want** to spend, sir?

The past modal forms **would**, **could** and **might** are often used in this way.
> I **thought** it **would** be nice to have a picnic.
> **Could** I ask you to translate this for me?
> You **might** see if the consulate can help you.

Past progressives can make **requests** less direct, and so **more polite**.
> I **was wondering** if I might use your phone.

In other kinds of sentence, **present progressives** can sound **casual and friendly**.
> We**'re hoping** you'll come and stay with us soon.
> I**'m looking** forward to hearing from you.

▲ **1 Make these sentences less direct.**

1   How many days do you intend to stay? (➤ *past*)
2   I hope you can lend me £10.
    (➤ *past progressive and past modal*)
3   I wonder if you have two single rooms.
    (➤ *past progressive and past*)
4   Are you looking for anything special?
    (➤ *past progressive*)
5   Can you give me a hand? (➤ *past modal*)
6   I look forward to seeing you again.
    (➤ *present progressive*)
7   I think I'll borrow your bike for the afternoon,
    if that's OK. (➤ *past progressive and past modal*)
8   We can ask Peter to help us. (➤ *past modal*)
9   I wonder if I can ask you a small favour.
    (➤ *past progressive and past modal*)
10 I think it will be a good idea to invite Simon.
    (➤ *past and past modal*)

'Hi! I thought you'd be sick
of chocolates and flowers.'

Another way of making requests **less direct** is to use a **future** verb form.

> I'm afraid you**'ll need** to fill in this form.
> I**'ll have** to ask you to wait a minute.

revision of **past** and **perfect tenses**

1 Choose the right tenses (present perfect, past or past perfect; simple or progressive).

1 Reports are coming in that a train *(crash)* near Birmingham. According to eyewitnesses, it *(hit)* a concrete block which somebody *(put)* on the line.

2 Halfway to the office Paul *(turn)* round and *(go)* back home, because he *(forget)* to turn the gas off.

3 I *(do)* housework all day today. I *(clean)* every room in the house.

4 I *(lie)* in bed thinking about getting up when the doorbell *(ring)*.

5 It wasn't surprising that she *(start)* getting toothache. She *(not go)* to the dentist for two years.

6 I *(play)* a lot of bridge recently.

7 When I *(get)* home everybody *(watch)* TV.

8 We *(not see)* your mother for ages.

9 How long *(you learn)* English?

10 London *(change)* a lot since we first *(come)* to live here.

11 'How many times *(you see)* this film?' 'This is the first time I *(see)* it.'

12 'Who's that?' 'I *(never see)* him before in my life.'

13 I hear Joe *(get)* married last summer.

14 I *(often wonder)* where she *(get)* her money.

15 *(You read)* Pam Marshall's latest book?

16 They *(just discover)* a new fuel – it's half the price of petrol, and much cleaner.

17 *(You hear)* the storm last night?

18 My sister *(be)* married three times.

19 While she *(talk)* on the phone the children *(start)* fighting and *(break)* a window.

20 He used to talk to us for hours about all the interesting things he *(do)* in his life.

21 You know, she *(stand)* looking at that picture for the last twenty minutes.

22 The old cross *(stand)* on top of the hill as long as anybody can remember.

23 I *(spend)* a lot of time travelling since I *(get)* this new job.

24 When I *(be)* at school we all *(study)* Latin.

25 After he *(finish)* breakfast he *(sit)* down to write some letters.

26 When I *(meet)* him he *(work)* as a waiter for a year or so.

27 I *(never learn)* to ski.

28 *(you finish)* with the bathroom yet?

29 We *(live)* in Scotland until I *(be)* eighteen.

30 She *(have)* a hard life, but she's always smiling.

For explanations of the words that we use to talk about grammar, see pages 298–302.

2 Choose the right tenses (present perfect, past or past perfect; simple or progressive).

Going to the Pictures

That afternoon we all (1 *get*) ready to go to the pictures. We (2 *get*) a 63 bus to take us to the Elephant and Castle, because the pictures are just next door. There (3 *be*) a great big queue waiting to go in and we (4 *be*) at the very back. Soon we (5 *get*) in. The picture (6 *already start*) and it was very dark in there. We had to go down some stairs to get to our seats but instead of walking down them we (7 *fall*) down them. Soon we were in our seats. We (8 *sit*) there watching the film when something (9 *hit*) me on the head. It was an ice-cream tub. I (10 *turn*) round to see who it was and a little boy who (11 *sit*) two rows behind me said, 'I am very sorry. It wasn't meant to hit you. It was meant to hit the boy in front.'

Anonymous child

The Little Girl and the Wolf

One afternoon a big wolf (12 *wait*) in a dark forest for a little girl to come along carrying a basket of food to her grandmother. Finally a little girl did come along and she (13 *carry*) a basket of food. 'Are you carrying that basket to your grandmother?' asked the wolf. The little girl said yes, she was. So the wolf (14 *ask*) her where her grandmother lived and the little girl (15 *tell*) him and he (16 *disappear*) into the wood.

When the little girl (17 *open*) the door of her grandmother's house she (18 *see*) that there was somebody in bed with a nightcap and nightgown on. She (19 *approach*) no nearer than twenty-five feet from the bed when she (20 *see*) that it was not her grandmother but the wolf, for even in a nightcap a wolf does not look in the least like anybody's grandmother. So the little girl (21 *take*) an automatic pistol out of her basket and (22 *shoot*) the wolf dead.

Moral: It is not so easy to fool little girls nowadays as it used to be.

James Thurber: Fables for Our Time (adapted)

Rioting students battle against police

May 7 (1968).   In the last two days, Paris (23 *see*) the worst street-fighting since the Liberation in 1944. Up to 30,000 students, locked out of their own campus yesterday by the Sorbonne rector, Jean Roche, (24 *fight*) the tear gas of the riot police with barricades, bricks, paving stones and Molotov cocktails.

The trouble (25 *be*) fermenting for some time. On March 20, six students (26 *be*) arrested after an anti-American demonstration; the next day, a mass sit-in at the Nanterre campus (27 *begin*). Last Friday, the police – whose alleged brutality is said to have sparked off the violence – forcibly evicted the students, who were led by Daniel Cohn-Bendit.

All day yesterday, the Latin Quarter (28 *be*) the arena for running street fights centred on the Boulevard St Germain.

Chronicle of the 20th Century   ▶

3 Complete the cartoon captions with the expressions from the box, and put in the right tenses.

> another bit of metal, Maureen.
> Could you tell us, please, where we *(go)*?
> I *(start)* leaving my husband an hour ago.
> *(do)* this job, is it?
> this fear of heights, Mr Winthrop?
> what, exactly, *(you do)*?
> you *(die)*.
> All his batteries *(run)* down.

A   Look, Mary, I must go;

B   How long *(you have)*

C   You *(book)* us a holiday abroad during the summer

D   I *(find)*

E   Good Lord, Fenton, I had no idea

F   First time you

G   Perhaps I could help you choose, sir –

H   He has nothing to do.

passive structures

PASSIVE TENSE	STRUCTURE	EXAMPLE
simple present	*am/are/is* + past participle	English **is spoken** here.
present progressive	*am/are/is being* + pp	Excuse the mess: the house **is being painted**.
simple past	*was/were* + pp	I **wasn't invited**, but I went.
past progressive	*was/were being* + pp	I felt I **was being watched**.
present perfect	*have/has been* + pp	**Has** Mary **been told**?
past perfect	*had been* + pp	I knew I **had been forgotten**.
will future	*will be* + pp	You**'ll be told** soon.
future perfect	*will have been* + pp	Everything **will have been done** by Tuesday.
going to future	*am/are/is going to be* + pp	Who**'s going to be invited**?

Examples of passive infinitives: *(to) be told; (to) have been taken.*
Examples of passive *-ing* forms: *being told; having been taken.*
Future progressive passives (*will be being* + pp) and perfect progressive
    passives (e.g. *has been being* + pp) are unusual.
Two-word verbs can have passive forms (e.g. *The meeting **has been put off***).

1   Find the passive verbs in this text. What tenses are they?

IN DENMARK, 24 people were left hanging upside down when a roller coaster car made an unscheduled stop.

The passengers were stranded 60 ft in the air for 20 minutes before firemen arrived with ladders.

An official for the fairground, at Aalborg in Western Denmark, said the riders had been firmly locked in and had not been in danger.

'They were given their money back,' the official said.

The **subject** of a **passive verb** corresponds to the **object** of an **active verb**.

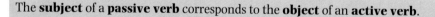

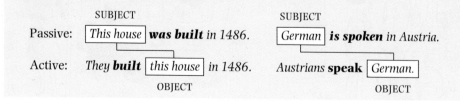

	SUBJECT			SUBJECT	
Passive:	*This house*	**was built** in 1486.		*German*	**is spoken** in Austria.
Active:	*They* **built**	*this house* in 1486.		*Austrians* **speak**	*German.*
		OBJECT			OBJECT

2   Write passive sentences.

1 Chinese *(speak)* in Singapore.
2 The Taj Mahal *(build)* around 1640.
3 The new hospital *(open)* next year.
4 She *(interview)* now.
5 I realised I *(follow)*.
6 *(you invite)* to Andy's party?
7 He found that all his money *(steal)*.
8 These computers *(make)* in Korea.
9 Passengers *(ask)* not to speak to the driver.
10 Sorry about the noise – the road *(mend)*.
11 The village church *(burn down)* last year.
12 A Roman pavement *(just find)* under Oxford Street.

With a passive, we can use **by + noun** if we need to say who does the action.

This house was built in 1486 **by Sir John Latton***.*

---

3   Make the sentences passive. Use *by* … only if it is necessary to say who does/did the action.

1 Shakespeare wrote 'Hamlet'.
2 They have arrested her for shoplifting.
3 They are repairing your car now.
4 People in Chile speak Spanish.
5 Has anybody asked Peter?
6 My mother made this ring.
7 Electricity drives this car.
8 Somebody will tell you where to go.
9 A drunken motorist knocked her down.
10 Liverpool beat Manchester 3–0 yesterday.
11 The Chinese invented paper.
12 You need hops to make beer.
13 They don't sell stamps in bookshops.
14 The directors are still considering your application.

4   Choose the correct version of the cartoon caption.

'Bad news, Cromwell – *you're replaced /
you're being replaced / you were replaced* by a machine.'

reasons for using **passives**

1   **Rule study. Read the text and then do the rest of the exercise.**

A DRIVER has been sent to jail for 90 days for driving with excess alcohol.

Graham Smith, 29, of North Street, Barton, was stopped by police officers near his home last November and was found to have drunk almost twice the legal limit for drivers, Didcot magistrates heard on Thursday.

Twelve months earlier Smith had been disqualified from driving for three years for drink-driving.

He was disqualified for twelve months in 1986 for a similar offence.

Mr Peter Jones, defending, said Smith had used the car to visit a sick friend.

He said Smith was depressed after the visit, and went to a pub and drank five or six pints before driving home.

He was caught by police during a routine speed check in Wantage Road, Barton.

The following expressions in the text have passive verbs. Would it be easy to rewrite the text with active verbs (e.g. ... *sent a disqualified driver to jail; police officers stopped Graham Smith*)?

A disqualified driver **has been sent** to jail
Graham Smith ... **was stopped** by police officers
... **was found** to have drunk almost twice the legal limit
Smith **had been disqualified** from driving
He **was banned** for twelve months
He **was caught** by police

Which two rules are best? Check your answers in the key.

1   We use passives when we are interested in **what happens**, not **who it happens to**.
2   Passives are common when we are thinking about what **is done** to the person or thing that we are interested in, not about what he/she/it **does**.
3   Passives can help us to go on talking about the **same thing**, in cases where an active verb would need an **unwanted new subject**.
4   Passives are best in a **formal** style. Actives are more **informal**.

2 Choose the best way of continuing after each sentence.

1 He lives in a small house.   a. Somebody built it about forty years ago.
   b. It was built about forty years ago.
2 English is worth learning.   a. People speak it in a lot of countries.
   b. It is spoken in a lot of countries.
3 He got a sports car, but he didn't like it.   a. So he sold it again.
   b. So it was sold again.
4 My nephew is an artist.   a. He has just painted another picture.
   b. Another picture has just been painted by him.
5 The new Virginia Meyer film is marvellous.   a. They are showing it at
   our local cinema.   b. It is being shown at our local cinema.

▲ **3 Choose the best sentence from each pair to build up a continuous text.**

1 a. HOW BOOKS ARE MADE
   b. HOW PEOPLE MAKE BOOKS
2 a. First of all, the printers print big sheets of paper.
   b. First of all, big sheets of paper are printed.
3 a. Each sheet contains the text of a number of pages (e.g. 32).
   b. The text of a number of pages (e.g. 32) is contained in each sheet.
4 a. People fold and cut the sheets to produce sections of the book.
   b. The sheets are folded and cut to produce sections of the book.
5 a. These sections are called signatures.
   b. We call these sections signatures.
6 a. The printers put all the signatures together in the correct order.
   b. All the signatures are put together in the correct order.
7 a. Then they are bound together and their edges are trimmed.
   b. Then they bind the signatures together and trim the edges.
8 a. Finally, the cover – which has been printed separately – is attached.
   b. Finally, they attach the cover – which they have printed separately.
9 a. Now the publishers can publish the book.
   b. Now the book can be published.

DO IT YOURSELF

**4 Change these sentences as in the example. Then think about why
   this makes them better, and check your answers in the key.**

1 That she had not written to her parents for over two years surprised me.
   I was surprised that she had not written to her parents ...
2 That nobody was prepared to take him to hospital shocked us.
3 That Mary wanted to tell everybody what to do annoyed me.
4 That George rang me up at three o'clock in the morning to tell me he was
   in love again didn't please me.
5 The fact that he looked completely different from the last time I had met
   him confused me. (*I was confused by ...*)

passives: verbs with two objects

Verbs with two objects (see page 183) have **two** possible **passive** structures.

ACTIVE	PASSIVE
They gave **the winner a prize**.	**The winner was given** a prize.
They gave **a prize to the winner**.	**A prize was given** to the winner.

We choose the structure which fits best with what comes before and after (see page 178). The structure with the **person** as subject is probably more common.

1   Change the structure.

1   Nothing was sent to me.   *I was sent nothing.*
2   Papers were brought to us to sign.
3   A clock was given to Henry when he retired.
4   Stories were read to the children.
5   £5,000 is owed to me.
6   A new job has been offered to me.
7   French is taught to us by Mrs Lee.
8   A car has been lent to me for the week.
9   A full explanation was promised to us.
10   A lot of lies were told to me by the secretary.

2   Complete the text with expressions from the box.

had been given②   had been told①   had never been taught ⑥
was given *(twice)*③④   was offered⑤   was promised ⑦   was sent
was shown   wasn't being paid⑨

I'll never forget my first day at that office. I __1__ to arrive at 8.30, but when I got there the whole place seemed to be empty. I didn't know what to do, because I __2__ no information about the building or where I was going to work, so I just waited around until some of the secretaries began to turn up. Finally I __3__ a dirty little office on the fifth floor, where I __4__ a desk in a corner. Nothing happened for an hour; then I __5__ some letters to type on a computer by one of the senior secretaries. This wasn't very successful, because I __6__ how to use a computer. (In the letter I __7__ when I __8__ the job, I __9__ computer training, but they'd obviously forgotten about this.) By lunchtime things hadn't got any better, and I decided that I __10__ enough to put up with this nonsense, so I walked out and didn't go back.

3   Complete these sentences any way you like.

1   I was given _____ last Christmas / for my last birthday / _____.
2   I have often been given _____.
3   I have never been given _____.

passives: progressive, perfect etc

Further practice on some passive verb forms.

1   **Present progressive passive. Imagine you are in a busy hotel at
    midday. Make sentences to say what is being done, using words
    from the two boxes and the present progressive passive. Example:**

Beds are being made.

beds	bills	coffee	drinks	food	luggage		money
new guests		reservations		rooms	tables		

bring down		change	clean	lay	make	order	pay
prepare	serve	take	welcome				

2   **Present perfect passive. Imagine that, rich and famous, you
    return to your old home town after fifty years. A lot of things are
    different. Make sentences, using words from the boxes and the
    present perfect passive. Example:**

The Café Royal has been turned into a casino.

Café Royal	houseboats	new car park	new schools
opera house	old fire station	ring road	station streets
town centre	statue of you	Super Cinema	your house

build	modernise	put up in park	rebuild	widen
turn into casino / floating restaurants / museum / supermarket /				
theatre / pedestrian precinct				

3   **Infinitives and *-ing* forms. Make some sentences beginning
    I (don't) like ... ing or *I (don't) want to ...*, using verbs from the box.
    Examples:**

I like being talked to.   I don't want to be forgotten.

admire	criticise	forget	give presents	ignore
invite out	laugh at	like	listen to	look at love
need	shout at	take seriously	talk about	talk to
undervalue				

passives: complex structures

A   active object complement → passive subject complement

ACTIVE	PASSIVE
The Queen considered **him a genius**.	**He** was considered **a genius**.
They elected **Mrs Robins President**.	**Mrs Robins** was elected **President**.
The others call **him stupid**.	**He** is called **stupid** by the others.
You've made **me very happy**.	**I** have been made **very happy**.

B   structure with introductory it: *It is thought/believed* etc *that* ...
> **It is thought that** the Minister will resign.
> At the time, **it was believed that** illnesses were caused by evil spirits.
> **It is expected that** the company will become profitable in the New Year.

C   subject + passive verb + infinitive
... *is thought/believed/said/asked/seen/made* etc *to* ...
> She **is thought to have** left home.   He **is believed to be** in Wales.
> They **are said to be** millionaires.   I **was asked to help**.

Note that we use *to*-infinitives in the passive after *see, hear* and *make*.
> He was seen **to enter** the bank.   I was made **to tell** them everything.

D   structure with *there is*: *There is thought/said* etc *to be* ...
> **There are thought to be** fewer than twenty people still living in the village.
> **There were said to be** ghosts in the house, but I never heard anything.

▲ **1   Make these sentences passive, using one of the above structures.**

1   People think the government will fall.
2   We appointed Mr Evans secretary.
3   The villagers called her a witch.
4   People believed that fresh air was bad for sick people.
5   Some people say that there are wolves in the mountains.
6   Police think the man holding the hostages is heavily armed.
7   They say he is in an agitated state.
8   Everybody considered her strange.
9   We expect that the rate of inflation will rise.
10   They say he is somewhere in Germany.
11   Somebody saw Harris leave the plane in Ontario.
12   People think that she died in a plane crash.
13   People believed that the earth was the centre of the universe.
14   They think that there is oil under Windsor Castle.
15   They made me give them details of my bank accounts.

verbs with **two objects**

Many verbs can have **two objects** – one direct and one indirect.
Usually the **indirect object refers** to a **person**, and this often **comes first**.

>   He gave **his wife a camera**.   I wish **you a Merry Christmas**.

If we put the **indirect object last**, we use a preposition (usually **to** or **for**).
>   I passed my licence **to the policeman**.
>   Mother bought the ice cream **for you**, not for me.

1   **Change the structure. Examples:**

I gave my sister some flowers.
I gave some flowers to my sister.
Let me make some tea for you.
Let me make you some tea.

1   Could you send me the bill?
2   I've bought a present for you.
3   Leave me some potatoes.
4   I lent Bill £5 yesterday.
5   Show Granny your picture.
6   Read the letter to me, will you?
7   She teaches adults French.
8   I took the report to Mrs Samuels.
9   Would you get me a beer?
10   We owe £20,000 to the bank.

'Get me the Zoo, please, Miss Winterton.'

2   **Write five sentences with two objects beginning** *I would like to*
give/send **..., using verbs from the box.**

Common verbs with two objects:								
bring	buy	cost	get	give	leave	lend	make	offer
owe	pass	pay	play	promise	read	refuse	send	show
sing	take	teach	tell	wish	write			

Explain, **say**, **suggest** and **describe** do **not** have the **indirect object first**.

>   Can you **explain the plan to us**? (NOT ~~Can you explain us the plan?~~)
>   I've come to **say goodbye to you**. (NOT ...~~to say you goodbye.~~)
>   I **suggested a new method** to her. (NOT ~~I suggested her a new method.~~)
>   **Describe your wife** to me. (NOT ~~Describe me your wife.~~)

verbs with prepositions and particles

PREPOSITIONS:
after   *at*   *during*   *for*   *from*   *into*   *of*   *out of*   *to*
with   *without*

(ADVERB) PARTICLES:
ahead   *aside*   *away*   *back*   *forward*   *home*   *out*

BOTH PREPOSITIONS AND PARTICLES:
about   *across*   *along*   *(a)round*   *before*   *behind*   *by*
down   *in*   *inside*   *near*   *off*   *on*   *outside*   *over*
past   *through*   *under*   *up*

English has many **two-word verbs**, made up of a **verb** and a **small word**
like **at**, **in**, **on**, **up**. Two-word verbs are very common in an informal style.

▲ 1   **Match the two-word verbs and the more formal one-word verbs.**
       Example:

look for – seek

blow up	break up	get up	give up	go away
go into	look for	put off	send back	talk about
think over	turn up			

abandon	arrive	consider	discuss	disintegrate
enter	explode	leave	postpone	return	rise	seek

The small word in a two-word verb may be a **preposition** or an **adverb
particle**. (A good dictionary will tell you which.) There are some
differences.

VERB **+** PREPOSITION	VERB **+** ADVERB PARTICLE
Look at *this.*	**Look out!**
Don't **sit on** *that chair.*	**Sit down**.
She **climbed up** *the ladder.*	*She* **cut** *the wood* **up** / **cut up** *the wood.*
I **fell in** *the river.*	*I* **filled** *the form* **in**. / *I* **filled in** *the form.*
He **got off** *the bus.*	**Switch** *the light* **off**. / **Switch off** *the light.*

For explanations of the words that we use to talk about grammar, see pages 298–302.

DO IT YOURSELF

2   Which three rules are correct? Check your answers in the key.

1   Verbs with prepositions are normally followed by objects.
2   Some verbs with prepositions don't have objects.
3   Verbs with adverb particles are normally followed by objects.
4   Some verbs with adverb particles don't have objects.
5   Prepositions can come just after their objects.
6   Adverb particles can come just after their objects.

An **adverb particle** must go **after a pronoun object**.

>   *She cut **it up**.* (NOT ~~*She cut **up it**.*~~)   *Switch **it off**.* (NOT ~~*Switch **off it**.*~~)

Compare the word order with a preposition and a pronoun object.

>   *She climbed **up it**.* (NOT ~~*She climbed **it up**.*~~)   *He got **off it**.*

▲   **3   Change the object to a pronoun; change the word order if necessary. Examples:**

>   Sit on the wall. ➔ *Sit on it.*
>   Switch on the light. ➔ *Switch it on.*

1   We talked about the accident. *(preposition)*
2   I put off the meeting. *(adverb particle)*
3   Could you look after the children? *(prep.)*
4   We broke off our relationship. *(adv. part.)*
5   Can you clean up the kitchen? *(adv. part.)*
6   She put the dress on. *(adv. part.)*
7   I'm looking for my bag. *(prep.)*
8   I wrote down the address. *(adv. part.)*
9   I sent the steak back. *(adv. part.)*
10 I stood on the table. *(prep.)*

▲   **4   Look at the adverb particles in the following sentences, and choose the best meaning from the box for each one.**

away	further	higher	into pieces	louder	quieter
on paper	to various people		working	not working	

1   He drove off.
2   Write it down.
3   The heater's off.
4   Turn the radio down.
5   Can you cut up the onions?
6   I've sent out the invitations.
7   Go on.
8   Prices are going up.
9   Is the printer on?
10 Who turned the music up?

Note the position of **prepositions** and **particles** in **passive sentences**:
after the main verb. (See also page 292.)

>   *Their wedding has been **put off**.*   *All the lights were **switched on**.*
>   *She likes to be **looked at**.*   *He's already been **spoken to**.*

Some verbs have both prepositions and particles: e.g. *get on with, look out for*.

structures with **get**

> *Get* has **different meanings** in **different structures**.
>
> | | |
> |---|---|
> | *Where can I **get some stamps?*** | *She **got a letter** from her mother.* |
> | *It's **getting late**.* | *The problem is **getting worse**.* |
> | *What time do you usually **get up?*** | *It takes me an hour to **get to** work.* |

DO IT YOURSELF

1 **Look at the examples above, and decide which structure goes with which meaning. Check your answer in the key.**

STRUCTURES	MEANINGS
get + direct object *get* + adjective *get* + adverb particle / preposition	move, change position receive, obtain, fetch, buy ... become

2 **Can you match the expressions with *get* and their more formal equivalents? Example:**

get older – age

get across	get better	get bigger	get off	get older
get on	get out of	get over	get smaller	get to get up

age   alight from, leave (public transport) board (public transport)   cross   decrease, shrink improve   increase, grow   leave   reach   recover from rise (from bed)

3 **Complete the sentences using expressions with *get*.**

1 My English is ＿＿ing ＿＿.
2 Ann ＿＿ her car and drove away.
3 ＿＿ the bus opposite the cinema, and ＿＿ at the second stop.
4 What are you doing in my room? ＿＿!
5 If you go out in the rain without a coat, you'll ＿＿.
6 If you don't put on a sweater, you'll ＿＿.
7 I don't want to ＿＿; I'm going to die young.
8 If I don't have breakfast, I ＿＿ really ＿＿ about eleven o'clock.
9 I'm ＿＿ing ＿＿. I think I'll go to bed.
10 It ＿＿ very early in winter.

For explanations of the words that we use to talk about grammar, see pages 298–302.

> ***Get*** is often used with a **past participle**.
>
> Common expressions:
> > *get dressed   get changed   get lost   get married*
> > *get divorced   get broken   get drowned*
>
> This structure can be similar to a passive verb.
> > *Joe **got arrested** for drunken driving last week. (= ... was arrested ...)*
> > *They had a dog, but it **got run over**.*
> > *We never **get invited** anywhere.*

4   **Put together the beginnings and ends, using a structure with**
   ***get* + past participle. Example:**

'Ann and Bill are getting divorced.' 'But they've only been married a year.'

BEGINNINGS	ENDS
'Ann and Bill are *(divorce)*.'	'But they've only been married a year.'
'Shall we go swimming?'	'Eight o'clock.'
'What time do the animals *(feed)*?'	'OK. I'll just go and *(change)*.'
Every time he goes walking in the country	and go to bed.
His glasses *(break)*	but we *(cut off)*.
I was talking to her on the phone	he *(lose)*.
I'm going to *(undress)*	in the fight.
If you leave your bag there,	it'll *(steal)*.
That child takes an hour	next April.
They're going to *(marry)*	to *(dress)* in the morning.

> We can often add a direct object to structures with *get*. Compare:
>
> | | |
> |---|---|
> | ***Get out*** *of here!* | ***Get him out*** *of here!* |
> | *I can't **get warm**.* | *I can't **get my feet warm**.* |
> | *You'd better **get dressed**.* | *You'd better **get that child dressed**.* |

'I still say she's too young to get married.'

infinitives

There are **simple**, **progressive**, **perfect** and **passive** infinitives, with and without *to* (see page 190).

SIMPLE:	*I want **to see** the manager.*	*It may **rain**.*
PROGRESSIVE:	*It's nice **to be sitting** here.*	*You must **be joking**.*
PERFECT:	*I'm glad **to have seen** her.*	*She could **have told** us.*
PASSIVE:	*She likes **to be liked**.*	*It will **be posted** today.*

There are also perfect progressive and perfect passive infinitives.

PERFECT PROGRESSIVE:	*I'd like **to have been sitting** there when she walked in.*
PERFECT PASSIVE:	*You could **have been killed**.*

Negative infinitives are made with ***not (to)***.
*Try **not to be** late.* (NOT ~~Try **to don't be** late.~~)
*I'm sorry **not to have phoned**.*
*You should **not worry**.*

1 Put in the right kind of infinitive.

1　I ought *(work)* right now.
2　Your watch will *(repair)* by Tuesday.
3　I'd like *(go)* home early today.
4　I'd like *(see)* her face when she opened the letter.
5　She must *(have)* a shower – I can hear the water running.
6　It's important *(listen)* to people.
7　She hopes *(choose)* for the national team.
8　Try *(not be)* back late.
9　You should *(tell)* me you were ill.
10　He doesn't like *(interrupt)* while he's working.

2 Say what you think the woman in the pictures is doing. Begin *She could/may/must be ...ing* or *She seems to be ...ing*. Example:

1 *She may be cycling.*

perfect infinitives (to have gone etc)

Perfect infinitives have the same kind of meaning as **perfect or past tenses**.

> *I'm glad **to have left** school. (= ... that **I have left** school.)*
> *She was sorry **not to have seen** Bill. (= ... that **she had not seen** Bill.)*
> *We hope **to have finished** the job soon. (= ... that **we will have finished** ...)*
> *I seem **to have annoyed** Anne yesterday. (= It seems that **I annoyed** ...)*

1   Rewrite these sentences using perfect infinitives.

1   I'm glad I've met you.
2   I was sorry I had disturbed him.
3   I expect I'll have passed all my exams by June.
4   It seems that you made a mistake. *(You seem ...)*
5   I'm happy that I've had a chance to talk to you.
6   I was disappointed that I had missed the party.
7   It seems that she's got lost.
8   She was pleased that she had found the house.

With ***was/were***, ***would like*** and ***meant***, perfect infinitives often refer to **unreal situations** that are the opposite of what really happened.

> *He **was to have gone** to art college but he fell ill.* (He didn't go.)
> *I'**d like to have been sitting** there when she walked in.* (I wasn't there.)
> *I **meant to have telephoned** but I forgot.*

2   Rewrite the sentences as shown.

1   She didn't marry a friend of her parents. *(was to)*
    She was to have married a friend of her parents.
2   I didn't see his face when he realised what had happened. *(would like to)*
3   He didn't finish all his work by three o'clock. *(mean)*
4   We didn't spend a week skiing. *(were to)*
5   It wasn't the happiest week of my life. *(was to)*
6   She didn't say goodbye to everybody before she left. *(mean)*
7   I didn't live in the seventeenth century. *(would like)*
8   He didn't play in the Cup Final. *(was to)*

For perfect infinitives after modals (e.g. *should have gone*), see page 122.

infinitive with and without **to**

We use the **infinitive without *to*** after the **modal verbs** *can, could, may, might, must, shall, should, will* and *would*, and after *had better* and *needn't*.

>   ***Could*** you ***help*** *me?* (NOT ~~*Could you* ***to help*** *me?*~~)
>   *You* ***should try*** *to forget about it.*
>   *'**Can** I **give** you a lift?' 'No, thanks, I'**d** rather **walk**.'*
>   *She'**d better go** home now.*
>   *You* ***needn't worry***.

Note also the structure with *Why (not) ...?*
>   ***Why worry***?
>   ***Why not give*** *him socks for Christmas?*

In most other cases, we use the infinitive with *to*.

>   *I* ***want to have*** *a rest.* (NOT ~~*I* ***want have*** *a rest.*~~)
>   *It's* ***necessary to plan*** *carefully.* (NOT ~~*It's* ***necessary plan*** *carefully.*~~)

The infinitive with *to* is used after the modal verb *ought*.
>   *We* ***ought to see*** *if Pat's OK.*

1   Change the sentences as shown.

1   I couldn't understand the timetable. *(wasn't able)*
   I wasn't able to understand the timetable.
2   It's important to eat enough. *(You should)*
3   I'd like to go sailing this summer. *(I might)*
4   She will probably get married in June. *(She expects)*
5   I said I would help her. *(I agreed)*
6   It's necessary to make careful plans. *(We must)*
7   Perhaps he's ill. *(He seems)*
8   I want to change my job. *(I wish I could)*
9   I may come and see you next week. *(I hope)*
10   You don't need to apologise. *(You needn't)*
11   They will open a new branch in North London. *(They have decided)*
12   I will certainly pay you on Saturday. *(I promise)*
13   I couldn't find the ticket office. *(I didn't manage)*
14   I prefer to go by myself. *(I would rather)*
15   She said she wouldn't see him again. *(She refused)*
16   I can play chess. *(I've learnt)*

I don't want to etc

We can use **to** for the infinitive of a **repeated verb**, if the meaning is clear.

*'Are you moving?' 'We hope **to**.'* (= ... *'We hope **to move**.'*)
*'Come and dance.' 'I don't want **to**.'*
*I don't play tennis, but I used **to**.*
*'You made Ann cry.' 'I didn't mean **to**.'*

1 Put the beginnings and ends together.

BEGINNINGS	ENDS
'Ann really upset Granny.'	but we can't afford to.
'Are you enjoying your new job?'	'He seems to.'
'Can I see you home?'	'I don't really want to – it's too cold.'
'Can you mend this by Tuesday?'	'I intend to. They can't go on keeping
'Did you get my coat from the cleaner's?'	the whole street awake every night.'
'Do you collect stamps?'	'I'd like to, but I'm working late.'
'Do you think he knows what he's doing?'	'I'll try to, but I can't promise.'
'Do you want to come out with us tonight?'	'I'm sure she didn't mean to.'
'Does she think she'll win?'	'If you'd like to.'
'How would you and Sue like to spend the	'No, but I used to.'
weekend with us?'	'Sorry, I forgot to.'
'I think you ought to see the police about	'We don't need to – there's always
the people next door.'	plenty of room.'
'Shall we go swimming?'	'We'd love to.'
'Should we book seats in advance?'	'Well, I'm starting to.'
We'd like to move to a bigger house,	'Yes, she expects to.'

We cannot usually drop *to*.

*'Come and have a drink.' 'I'd **like to**.'* (NOT *'I'd ~~like.~~'*)

But we can drop *to* in the expressions *if you like/want*, *when you like/want*
and *as you like*.

*'Can I help?' '**If you like**.'*　　　*We'll stop **when you want**.*

'I can say we live in a fascist state if
I want to. It's a free country.'

infinitive of purpose

We can use an **infinitive** to say **why somebody does something**.

> *She sat down **to rest**.* (NOT *... ~~for rest~~*. OR *... ~~for resting~~.*)

In order to ... and *so as to ...* are common before *be*, *know* and *have*; and before other verbs in a more formal style.

> *I got up early **in order to be** ready to leave at eight.*
> *She studied English **in order to** have a better chance of getting a job.*
> *I came to Britain **so as to know** more about British culture.*

In order and *so as* are normal before *not to*.

> *I spoke quietly **so as not to** frighten her.* (NOT *~~I spoke quietly **not to** ...~~*)

1 **Write sentences to say why people go to some of the following places. Begin *You go* ...**

1 a library   *You go to a library to borrow books.*
2 a bookshop
3 a cinema
4 a theatre
5 a swimming pool
6 a gymnasium
7 a driving school
8 a station
9 an airport
10 a travel agent's
11 a church
12 a football stadium
13 a bank
14 a post office
15 a restaurant
16 a supermarket
17 a garage
18 a newsagent

'Please – I come here to forget my troubles.'

2 **Write a sentence to say why you are learning English. (To get a better job? To study something else? To travel? To ...?) If you can work with other students, find out why they are learning English.**

interested and **interesting** etc

Interested, *bored*, *excited* etc say **how people feel**.
Interesting, *boring*, *exciting* etc describe **the people or things** that cause
the feelings.

> *I was very **interested** in the lesson.* (NOT *I was very **interesting** ...*)
> *His lessons are always **interesting**.* (NOT *His lessons are ... **interested**.*)
> *Do you ever get **bored** at work?*
> *My job's pretty **boring**.*

1 Complete the words.

1 I was surpris____ to see Ann there.
2 It was surpris____ to see her.
3 I find this work very tir____.
4 It makes me tir____.
5 Her exam results were disappoint____.
6 She was pretty disappoint____.
7 She was excit____ about her new job.
8 It was an excit____ new challenge.
9 We were shock____ to hear about your brother.
10 The news was really shock____.
11 His explanations are confus____.
12 Listening to him, I got confus____.
13 I get annoy____ when people break promises.
14 It's annoy____ when that happens.

▲ 2 Look at the cartoon. Who is boring?

'No really, your husband's right, it is late and we must go.'

3 What are the people interested in? Make sentences. Example:

An astronomer is interested in the stars.

| astronomer | botanist | cook | doctor | explorer | fashion designer |
| geographer | historian | linguist | mathematician | zoologist | |

| animals | clothes | food | languages | medicine | numbers | places |
| plants | the past | the stars | travel | | | |

-ing forms as subjects, objects etc

We can use **-ing forms** as **subjects**, **objects** or **complements**.

> **Smoking** is bad for you. (subject)
> I hate **packing**. (object)
> My favourite activity is **reading**. (complement)

An -ing form can have its own object.

> **Smoking cigarettes** is bad for you.
> I hate **packing suitcases**.
> My favourite activity is **reading poetry**.

1   Complete the sentences with -ing forms of the verbs in the box.

answer	climb	drink	forget	hear	learn	lie
pay	say	ski	type	watch		

1   ____ too much alcohol is very bad for you.
2   I don't like ____ bills.
3   He really enjoys ____ his own voice.
4   What's wrong with ____ in bed all day?
5   Her favourite sports are ____ and ____ mountains.
6   ____ languages is hard work.
7   I hate ____ goodbye.
8   ____ is better than remembering.
9   ____ animals can teach you a lot.
10 'What's your job?' '____ the phone and ____ letters.'

2   If you can work with other students, find out what their favourite activities are. They should use ...ing in their answers.

That's not writing, that's typing.
Capote's criticism of Kerouac

Writing is nothing more than a guided dream.
J L Borges

Writing is easy; all you do is sit staring at a blank sheet of paper until the drops of blood form on your forehead.
Gene Fowler

First I write one sentence: then I write another. That's how I write. And so I go on. But I have a feeling writing ought to be like running through a field.
L Strachey

There are three rules for writing the novel. Unfortunately, no one knows what they are.
W Somerset Maugham

All good writing is swimming under water and holding your breath.
F Scott Fitzgerald

Writing a book of poetry is like dropping a rose petal down the Grand Canyon and waiting for the echo.
Don Marquis

We can use a **determiner (e.g. _the_, _this_, _my_)** or a **possessive _'s_** before an _-ing_ form.

> **_the rebuilding_** of the cathedral   _Do you mind_ **_my smoking?_**
> _I don't like_ **_his borrowing_** _my things without asking._
> _What's all_ **_this shouting?_**
> **_John's leaving_** _home upset everybody._

Object forms are possible instead of possessives, especially after a verb or preposition. They are less formal.

> _I don't like_ **_him borrowing_** _my things without asking._
> _She was upset about_ **_John leaving_** _home._

3   Make these sentences less formal.

1   Do you mind my asking you a question?
2   I do not appreciate your shouting at me.
3   I could not understand Pat's wanting to pay for everybody.
4   What is the use of their asking all these questions?
5   The delay was caused by Peter's needing to see a doctor.
6   I was astonished at your expecting us to give you a room.
7   The holiday was ruined by Ann's having to go home early.
8   She cannot stand my telling her what to do.

_No_ is often used with an **_-ing_ form** to say that something is **not allowed**.

> _NO SMOKING_   _NO PARKING_   _NO WAITING_

'Sorry sir, no smoking in the museum.'

For more about _-ing_ forms after verbs, nouns and adjectives, see pages 199–209.

preposition + -ing

We use **-ing forms after prepositions**.

*You can only live for a few days **without drinking**.*
     (NOT ... without ~~to drink~~.)

1   **Make ten or more sentences from the table. You can use the same**
    preposition in more than one sentence. Example:

Are you interested in coming to Greece with us?

Are you interested	about	answering that child's questions.
Do you feel	as well as	changing her job, but I don't think she will.
Do you have time to do	at	coming to Greece with us?
anything else	besides	convincing the police that she was not a
He insisted	for	burglar.
He passed his exams	in	cooking.
How	in spite of	disturbing you.
I apologise	instead of	eating.
I like walking	like	going out to a restaurant tonight?
I sometimes dream	of	having time to read all my books.
I'm fed up	on	helping me?
I'm not capable	with	looking after the children?
I'm tired	without	moving to Canada.
She succeeded		not doing any work.
She talked		paying for everything.
She's keen		playing football.
She's very good		seeing George next week.
Thank you		selling things.
We're excited		staying at home?
We're thinking		swimming and dancing.
Why don't you come out		telling me the truth.
with us		understanding this – it's too difficult.
You can't live		

2   **Complete this sentence in five or more different ways:**
    I couldn't live without _____ing (_____).

For *after, before, when, while* and *since + -ing*, see page 240. For *-ing* after the
preposition *to*, see page 198.

preposition + -ing: special cases

We use **by ...ing** to say **how** – by what **method** or **means** – we do something.
We use **for ...ing** to give the **purpose** of something – to say what it is used for.
On doing something (formal) means '**when / as soon as** you do something'.

You can find out somebody's phone number **by looking** in the directory.
He made his money **by buying** and selling houses.
I've bought some special glue **for mending** broken glass.
'What's that funny knife **for**?' '**Opening** letters.'
On hearing the fire alarm, go straight to the nearest exit.
On arriving at the office, she noticed that her secretary was absent.

1   **Find the answers in the box; write them with *by ...ing*.**

> look in a dictionary   oil it   play loud music   rob a bank
> stroke it   switch on the ignition   take an aspirin
> use an extinguisher

1   How do you make a cat happy?   *By stroking it.*
2   How can you annoy your neighbours?
3   How can you get money fast?
4   How do you stop a door squeaking?
5   How do you find out what a word means?
6   How can you cure a headache?
7   How can you put a fire out?
8   How do you start a car?

2   **Write sentences to say what these things are for. Example:**

A telephone is for talking to people who are a long way away.

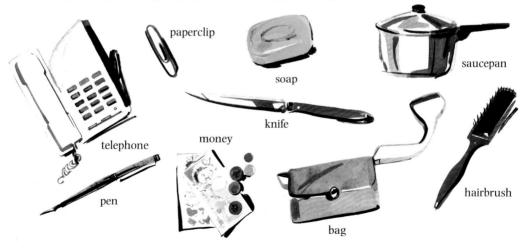

paperclip

soap

saucepan

knife

money

telephone

pen

hairbrush

bag

3   **Write a sentence beginning *On arriving home yesterday, I ...***

to ...ing

The **preposition *to*** is followed by an **-*ing* form**.

> I ***look forward to your letter / to hearing*** *from you.* (*To* is a
> preposition used after *look forward* – it can be followed by a noun
> or an -*ing* form.)
> **Compare**: *I **hope to hear** from you.* (*To* is part of the infinitive after
> *hope*, not a preposition – it couldn't be followed by a noun.)

Other expressions followed by *to* ...*ing*: *be/get used to, object to*.
> *If you come to England you'll soon **get used to driving** on the left.*
> *I **object to** people **trying** to sell me things over the telephone.*

DO IT YOURSELF

**1   Choose the best explanation of each expression. Check your
    answers in the key.**

1   I look forward to seeing you.
    A It gives me pleasure to think that I will see you.
    B I know I will see you.
    C I hope I will see you.
2   I'm used to driving in London.
    A I drive in London regularly.
    B In the past, I drove in London regularly.
    C I have driven in London so often that it seems easy and natural.
3   I object to paying good money for badly made products.
    A This often happens to me.
    B I am not pleased when this happens.
    C I try to stop this happening.

**2   Here are some sentences taken from real conversations. Can you
    put together the beginnings and ends, using *to* ...*ing*?**

BEGINNINGS	ENDS
Aren't you used (*walk*)	back to school.
Starting at half four's no problem –	difficult kids.
I look forward (*receive*)	I'm not used (*come*) this way.
I look forward (*see*) you again	I'm used (*get up*) early.
I object (*pay*) for it.	in six months' time.
I'll never get used (*sleep*)	It should be free.
I'm not looking forward (*go*)	it's hard to be without it.
I'm not sure where to turn.	on the floor.
If you're used (*have*) money,	this far?
Sean's used (*deal*) with	your comments.

For *used to* + infinitive (e.g. *I used to be shy when I was younger*), see page 128.

verb + infinitive or -ing form

Some **verbs** are followed by the **infinitives of other verbs**. Example: *want.*
Some **verbs** are followed by the *-ing* **forms of other verbs**. Example: *enjoy.*

DO IT YOURSELF

1 Do you know which verbs are followed by infinitives and which are followed by *-ing* forms? Make two lists; then check them in the key.

agree	avoid	can't help
dare	decide	deny expect
(can't) face	fail	fancy
feel like	finish	give up
happen	hope	imagine
keep (on)	manage	mean
mind	miss	offer postpone
practise	prepare	pretend
promise	put off	refuse
risk	seem	spend time
(can't) stand	suggest	wish

2 Put in the correct forms of the verbs.

1 You can't help *(like)* him.
2 We decided *(stay)* at home.
3 We expect *(hear)* from Ann soon.
4 Do you fancy *(go)* out tonight?
5 I don't feel like *(cook)*.
6 When do you finish *(study)*?
7 I've given up *(smoke)*.
8 Imagine *(be)* married to her!
9 I managed *(find)* a taxi.
10 Would you mind *(pass)* the bread?
11 I missed *(see)* the beginning of the film.
12 She pretended *(be)* ill.
13 Don't put off *(see)* the doctor.
14 He spends ages *(talk)* on the phone.
15 I want *(see)* the manager.
16 Do you enjoy *(watch)* football?

'I don't want to go to their party and have a good time. I don't enjoy having a good time.'

Some verbs are followed by **preposition + ...*ing***.

I'm ***thinking of changing*** my job. (NOT ~~I'm thinking to change my job.~~)

For verbs that can be followed by both infinitives and *-ing* forms, see page 204.

go ...ing

We often use **go ...ing** to talk about **sporting** and **leisure** activities.

*Let's **go climbing** next weekend.*   *Did you **go dancing** last Saturday?*

1   What can you do in these places?

1

2

3

4

5

6

7

For explanations of the words that we use to talk about grammar, see pages 298–302.

need ...ing

It *needs doing* means 'It **needs to be done**'.

*The car **needs washing**. (= ... needs **to be washed**.)*
*My shoes **need mending**.*

1   Look at the pictures. What needs doing in each one? Use the
    words in the box.

| clean   cook   cut   make   mend   paint   re-string |
| service |

1

2

3

4

5

6

7

8

verb + object + infinitive

Some verbs can be followed by **object + infinitive**. Examples: *want, prefer*.

He **wants me to wash** his socks. (NOT ~~He **wants that I wash** his socks.~~)
I **would prefer you to pay** now.

Other verbs that can be followed by **object + infinitive**:

advise   allow   ask   can't bear   cause   encourage
expect   forbid   force   get   help   invite   leave
mean   need   order   persuade   remind   teach
tell   warn

---

1   Make sentences about Mary, using ... *want(s) her to* ...   Example:

Everybody wants her to do something.

Everybody	Her boss	Her daughter	Her husband
Her mother	Her son	The butcher	The dog
The government	The vicar		

do something	buy her a car	buy him some new clothes
cook supper	go to church	leave her husband pay his bill
pay taxes	take him for a walk	work harder

---

2   Change the sentences. Example:

I told John 'I think you should stop smoking'. *(advise)*
I advised John to stop smoking.

1   They said we couldn't look at the house. *(didn't allow)*
2   I said to Jake, 'Please be more careful.' *(ask)*
3   She said to me, 'Do try the exam.' *(encourage)*
4   I think he'll come soon. *(expect)*
5   I went away, so he had to solve the problem. *(I left ...)*
6   Was it your idea that I should pay? *(Did you mean ...)*
7   The captain told the men, 'Attack!' *(order)*
8   'Don't forget to buy coffee,' I told Sue. *(remind)*
9   She gave me lessons in cooking. *(teach)*
10   She mustn't tell anybody. *(I don't want ...)*

---

3   Complete one or more of these sentences.

1   My parents want(ed) me to ____.
2   My parents don't/didn't want me to ____.
3   I would like my children to ____.

For explanations of the words that we use to talk about grammar, see pages 298–302.

4 Complete the cartoon caption with the correct structure.

'I'm not asking *(you serve)* me– just to include me in your conversation.'

Let and *make* are followed by **object + infinitive without *to*.**

> Don't ***let me forget*** to phone Jill.   You ***make me laugh***.

Passive structures with *make* have the infinitive with *to*.
> He ***was made to apologise***.

---

5 *Let* or *make*? **Make sentences beginning *Her parents let her* ... or *Her parents made her* ...**

1 stay up late	6 drink beer
2 do the washing up	7 clean up her room
3 read what she liked	8 go to church
4 iron her own clothes	9 have parties
5 do her homework	10 choose her own school

6 What did your parents let/make you do when you were small? Write three or more sentences. If possible, find out what other students' parents let/made them do.

For structures with *see*, *hear*, *watch* and *feel*, see page 205.

-ing form and **infinitive** both possible

Some verbs can be followed by **both -ing forms and infinitives**. There are often **important differences of meaning**.

Exercises 1–7: check your answers in the key.

1 *Remember*, *forget* and *regret*. **Look at the examples. Which structure is used to talk about *things people did*, and which is used to talk about *things people are/were supposed to do*?**

I still **remember buying** my first bicycle.
Remember to lock the garage door tonight.
I'll never **forget meeting** the President.
I **forgot to buy** the soap.
I **regret leaving** school at fourteen: it was a big mistake.
We **regret to say** that we are unable to help you.

2 *Go on*. **Look at the examples. Which structure is used for *a change to a new activity*, and which is used for *continuation of an activity*?**

She **went on talking** about her illness for hours.
Then she **went on to talk** about her other problems.

3 *Allow* and *permit*. **When do we use an -ing form and when do we use an infinitive?**

We don't **allow/permit smoking**.
We don't **allow/permit people to smoke**.

4 *Stop*. **One structure says that an *activity stops*; the other gives the *reason for stopping*. Which is which?**

I've **stopped smoking**!
I **stopped** for a few minutes **to rest**.

5 *Like*, *love*, *hate* and *prefer*. **Both structures can be used except – when?**

Do **you like dancing / to dance?**   **Would you like to dance?**
I don't get up on Sundays. I **prefer staying / to stay** in bed.
'Can I give you a lift?' 'No, thanks. I**'d prefer to walk.'**

6 ***Try* can be used to talk about *trying something difficult*, or about *trying an experiment* (to see if something works). Which structure(s) is/are used for each meaning?**

He **tried sending** her flowers and **writing** her letters, but it had no effect.
I **tried to change / changing** the wheel, but my hands were too cold.

7 ***See, hear, watch* and *feel*. These can be followed by *object + infinitive without to* or *object + -ing form*. One is used to talk about an *action going on*, the other about *a completed action*. Which is which?**

I **saw** her **pick up** the parcel, **open** it and **take** out a book.
I last **saw** him **walking** down the road towards the shops.
I **heard** her **play** Bach's A Minor concerto on the radio last night.
As we passed his house we **heard** him **practising** the violin.

8 **Choose the correct verb forms. (If two answers are possible, put both.)**

1 Do you remember *(meet)* her last year?
2 Sorry – I forgot *(post)* your letters.
3 I regret *(not visit)* her when she was ill.
4 We discussed the budget and then went on *(talk)* about sales.
5 Do you want to go on *(learn)* English?
6 He doesn't allow us *(make)* personal phone calls.
7 The hospital only allows *(visit)* at weekends.
8 I like *(watch)* TV in the evenings.
9 Would you like *(spend)* the weekend with us?
10 Thanks – I'd love *(come)*.
11 If nothing else works, try *(read)* the instructions.
12 I'll try *(repair)* your car tomorrow.
13 I saw John *(wait)* for a bus as I came home.
14 I heard you *(break)* something – what was it?
15 I can feel something *(crawl)* up my leg.
16 We'll have to stop *(get)* petrol.
17 He stopped *(work)* when he was sixty-five.
18 I regret *(tell)* you that you have failed your examination.

After some verbs (e.g. *begin, can't bear, continue, intend, propose, start*), both -*ing* forms and infinitives are possible without much difference of meaning.

  I ***began playing / to play*** *the piano when I was six.*
  We must ***continue looking / to look*** *for a new house.*

adjective + infinitive or -ing form

Many **adjectives** can be followed by **infinitives**. This is common when we are talking about **feelings and reactions**.

*She was very **pleased to see** me.*   *I'm **sorry to disturb** you.*

DO IT YOURSELF

1   **Thirteen of the adjectives in the box can be used in the sentence**
    ***I was ... to see her*. Which five cannot? Check your answers in the**
    key. Example:

    I was *afraid* to see her.

afraid	anxious	certain	fine	glad	happy
intelligent	lazy	likely	lucky	ready	right
shocked	surprised	unusual	well	willing	wrong

Some other adjectives are followed by **preposition + *-ing* form**.

▲ 2   **Choose the right prepositions and make sensible sentences.**
       Example:

       I'm annoyed at/about having to work tonight.

I'm	annoyed	about	studying.
	bad	at	breaking the speed limit.
	bored	of	listening to the children.
	capable	with	going for a long time without sleep.
	excited		seeing my family next weekend.
	fed up		having to work tonight.
	fond		getting up early.
	good		seeing the same faces every day.
	guilty		repairing cars.
	tired		dancing.

3   **Write sentences about three things you are good at doing, three**
    things you are bad at doing, and three things you are fed up with
    doing.

noun + infinitive or **-ing** form

Some **nouns** can be followed by **infinitives**; others can be followed by
preposition + ...*ing*.

*You were **a fool to agree**.   She has a terrible **fear of being** alone.*

DO IT YOURSELF

1 **Are these nouns normally followed by infinitives or by**
   preposition + ...*ing*? Make two lists; check your answer in the key.

decision	difficulty	hope	idea	need	plan
thought	time	wish			

2 **Choose the correct way of completing each sentence.**

1   Has she told you about her decision *(to go / of going?)*
2   I have difficulty *(to read / in reading)* quickly.
3   We have no hope *(to arrive / of arriving)* in time.
4   I hate the idea *(to leave / of leaving)* you.
5   Is there any need *(to tell / of telling)* Peter?
6   She has a plan *(to spend / of spending)* three years studying.
7   I won't get married: I dislike the thought *(to lose / of losing)* my freedom.
8   It's time *(to go / for going)* home.
9   I have no wish *(to meet / of meeting)* him again.

3 **Join the beginnings and ends. Put in prepositions where**
   necessary. Example:

Who had the idea of moving to Berlin?

BEGINNINGS	ENDS
Has he got any hope *(pass)*	*(buy)* that car.
He made a decision *(start)*	*(get)* angry.
Does your fear *(fly)*	*(get)* up!
Lucy has difficulty	*(keep)* her temper.
She hated the thought *(die)*	*(move)* to Berlin?
She was a fool	the exam?
There's no need	*(start)* a business.
They have a plan	a new life.
Time	stop you travelling?
Who had the idea	without seeing the world.

for ... to ... after **adjective/noun**

After an adjective or a noun, if an **infinitive** needs **its own subject** this is introduced by **for**. Compare:

> *Ann will be happy* **to help** *you.*
> *Ann will be happy* **for the children to help** *you.*

> *My idea was* **to learn** *Russian.*
> *My idea was* **for her to learn** *Russian.*

This structure is common after adjectives and nouns when we are talking about **possibility**, **necessity**, **importance** and **frequency**.

1   **Rewrite these sentences using the structure with *for ... to ...***
    Example:

> She can't come. ➡ *It's impossible for her to come.*

1   The meeting needn't start before eight. *(There's no need for the ...)*
2   The postman ought to come. *(It's time for ...)*
3   He's not usually late. *(It's unusual for ...)*
4   I want the children to go to a good school. *(I'm anxious for ...)*
5   John shouldn't go to Australia. *(It's a bad idea ...)*
6   Sue shouldn't change her job just now. *(It would be a mistake ...)*
7   Can Paul come to the meeting? *(Is it possible ...?)*
8   The car really should have regular services. *(It's important ...)*
9   He normally stays up late on Saturdays. *(It's normal ...)*
10   I'd be happy if you took a holiday. *(I'd be happy for ...)*

We can use *for* with the infinitive of *there is* – **for there to be**.

> *It's important* **for there to be** *enough jobs for everybody.*

2   **Imagine you are planning a new town. Rewrite the following sentences using *for there to be*.**

1   It's important that there should be public libraries.
2   It's vital that there should be a good public transport system.
3   It's important that there should be plenty of open spaces.
4   It's essential that there should be enough car parks.

    Now write five more sentences about the town using *for there to be*.

After some adjectives, we can use an **infinitive** to mean **'for people to ...'**.

*She's **easy to amuse**. (= She's **easy for people to amuse**.)*
*Just open the packet, and it's **ready to eat**.*

3   Make some sentences from the table.

English Chinese small children silver boiled eggs lobster maths modern music *etc*	is/are	easy hard difficult impossible nice (un)pleasant good interesting boring	to	please amuse understand clean listen to watch cook eat drink read learn *etc*

For *for ... to ...* after *too* and *enough*, see page 45.

questions

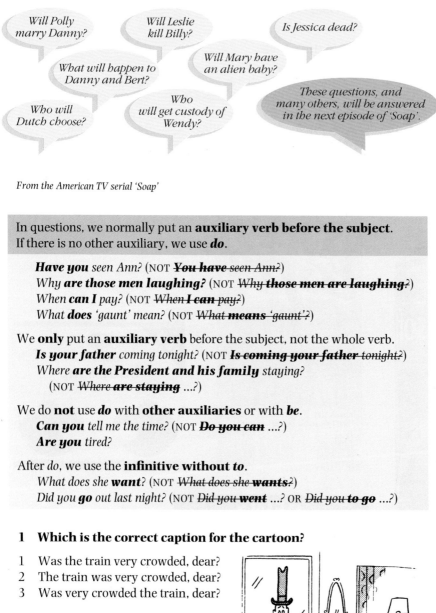

Will Polly marry Danny?

Will Leslie kill Billy?

Is Jessica dead?

What will happen to Danny and Bert?

Will Mary have an alien baby?

Who will Dutch choose?

Who will get custody of Wendy?

These questions, and many others, will be answered in the next episode of 'Soap'.

From the American TV serial 'Soap'

In questions, we normally put an **auxiliary verb before the subject**. If there is no other auxiliary, we use *do*.

> ***Have you*** seen Ann? (NOT ~~*You have seen Ann?*~~)
> *Why **are those men** laughing?* (NOT ~~*Why **those men are** laughing?*~~)
> *When **can I** pay?* (NOT ~~*When **I can** pay?*~~)
> *What **does** 'gaunt' mean?* (NOT ~~*What **means** 'gaunt'?*~~)

We **only** put an **auxiliary verb** before the subject, not the whole verb.
> ***Is your father*** coming tonight? (NOT ~~***Is coming your father** tonight?*~~)
> *Where **are the President and his family** staying?*
>   (NOT ~~*Where **are staying** ...?*~~)

We do **not** use *do* with **other auxiliaries** or with *be*.
> ***Can you*** tell me the time? (NOT ~~***Do you can** ...?*~~)
> ***Are you*** tired?

After *do*, we use the **infinitive without *to***.
> *What does she **want**?* (NOT ~~*What does she **wants**?*~~)
> *Did you **go** out last night?* (NOT ~~*Did you **went** ...?*~~ OR ~~*Did you **to go** ...?*~~)

1   Which is the correct caption for the cartoon?

1   Was the train very crowded, dear?
2   The train was very crowded, dear?
3   Was very crowded the train, dear?

2   Read the text, and then write questions for the answers. Example:

Two. ➜ *How many children have Joe and Pam got?*

In a small village in North Yorkshire, there's a big old farmhouse where three families live together: Alice and George and their three children, Joe and Pam and their two children, and Sue and her baby daughter. The adults divide up the work between them. George does the cooking, Joe and Sue do most of the housework, Pam looks after the shopping and does the repairs, and Alice takes care of the garden. Alice, George and Sue go out to work; Joe works at home designing computer systems, and Pam, who is a painter, looks after the baby during the day. Two of the children go to school in the village, but the three oldest ones go by bus to the secondary school in the nearest town, ten miles away.

The three families get on well, and enjoy their way of life. There are a few difficulties, of course. Their biggest worry at the moment is money – one of the cars needs replacing, and the roof needs some expensive repairs. But this isn't too serious – the bank has agreed to a loan, which they expect to be able to pay back in three years. And they all say they would much rather go on living in their old farmhouse than move to a luxury flat in a big city.

1	In North Yorkshire.	8	At home.
2	In a big old farmhouse.	9	Computer systems.
3	Three.	10	She's a painter.
4	Sue has.	11	Two of them.
5	The cooking.	12	By bus.
6	The housework.	13	In the nearest town.
7	The garden.	14	Ten miles.

We **do not** use *do* when the **subject** is a question word like ***who*** or ***what***.

Who opened *the window?* (NOT ~~Who **did** open~~ ...?)
What happened *to your arm?* (NOT ~~What **did** happen~~ ...?)
Which costs *more?* (NOT ~~Which **does** cost more?~~)

But we use *do* if the question word is the **object**.
Who do *you believe – him or me?*
What did *you have for supper?*
What does *'catalyst' mean?*

---

3   Look at the text again, and write questions for these answers.

1   George does.
2   Joe and Sue.
3   Pam does them.
4   Alice.
5   Money.
6   One of the cars.
7   The roof.

what ... like, what time, what sort etc

Note the difference between **how?** and **what ... like?**
We use **how?** to ask about things that **change** – e.g. moods, health, work.
We use **what ... like?** to ask about things that **don't change** – e.g. people's character and appearance. Compare:

> *'**How**'s Joe?' 'He's very well.'*
> *'**What**'s Joe **like**?' 'Tall, good-looking, a bit shy.'*

> *'**How** does she seem today?' 'Much happier.'*
> *'**What** does your sister look **like**?' 'Short, dark and cheerful-looking.'*

1 Make questions with *how* or *what ... like*.

1 *('your flat?')* 'Small but very comfortable.'
2 *('your mother?')* 'Fine, thanks.'
3 *('work going?')* 'Not very well at the moment.'
4 *('business?')* 'Terrible.'
5 *('Anne's boyfriend?')* 'Not very nice.'
6 *('School?')* 'Much better now.'

Other common expressions beginning with *what*: **what time, what sort of, what colour, what size, what make**. Note the way they are used in sentences.

> **What time** *does the film start?* (NOT USUALLY *At what time ...*)
> **What sort of** *music do you like?*
> **What size** *are your shoes?*   **What size** *shoes do you wear?*
> **What colour** *are her eyes?*   **What colour eyes** *has she got?*
> **What make** *is your car?*   **What make of car** *did you get?*

Ever can be used with a question word to express surprise.
> **Who ever** *gave you that necklace?*   **What ever** *does she see in him?*

2 Complete the questions with a suitable expression.

1	___ jeans do you wear?	7	___ food do you like?
2	___ is her hair?	8	___ are your gloves?
3	___ books do you read?	9	___ bike is the best?
4	___ is your TV?	10	___ did you find that coat?
5	___ is the concert?	11	___ told you you could sing?
6	___ does the train leave?	12	___ are you going to do?

For explanations of the words that we use to talk about grammar, see pages 298–302.

negative structures

To make **negative** verb forms, we put *not* **after an auxiliary verb** or *be*.
If there is no other auxiliary, we use *do*.

> We **have not** forgotten.   It **wasn't** raining.   She **can't** swim.
> That **isn't** right.   I **don't** like the soup. (NOT ~~I like not the soup.~~)

Do is followed by the **infinitive without** *to*.
> I didn't **think**. (NOT ~~I didn't to think / thinking / thought.~~)

Do is **not** used with **other auxiliary verbs** or (normally) with *be*.
> You **mustn't** worry. (NOT ~~You don't must worry.~~)   Tea **isn't** ready.

Do is not used with infinitives or *-ing* forms.
> It's important **not to worry**. (NOT ... ~~to don't worry.~~)
> It's nice sitting here and **not working**.

1 Correct these sentences by making them negative.

1 Marx discovered America. *Marx didn't discover America.*
2 Austrians speak Japanese.
3 Roses are green.
4 Cats can fly.
5 Shakespeare was French.
6 Fridges run on petrol.
7 The sun goes round the earth.
8 Telescopes make things smaller.
9 There are seventeen players in a rugby team.
10 Bananas grow in Scotland.

We do **not** use *do* with other negative words like *never* or *hardly*.

> He **never works**. (NOT ~~He does never work.~~)   It **hardly matters**.

'Leave it, Terry, I slept with him, but it didn't mean anything.'

negative questions

CONTRACTED (INFORMAL)	UNCONTRACTED (VERY FORMAL)
Isn't it ready yet?	**Is it not** ready yet?
Why **haven't you written** to Ann?	Why **have you not written** to Ann?
Can't she swim?	**Can she not** swim?

Note the different position of *n't/not* in contracted and uncontracted structures.

1   Write informal negative questions to ask somebody:

1   if she is not cold   4   if the shops are not closed
2   why she is not eating   5   if the postman has not come
3   if she does not speak French   6   if her mother is not at home

We often use negative questions to **confirm that something has happened, is true, etc**. The meaning is similar to '**It's true that ..., isn't it?**'

Didn't you go and see Helen yesterday? How is she?

We can use negative questions to make expressions of opinion less direct.
Wouldn't it be better to switch the light on?
(Less direct than *It would be better ...*)

2   Use negative questions to confirm the following ideas.

1   I think you went to Paris last week. → *Didn't you go ...?*
2   I think you speak German.
3   That looks like Pamela in the green dress.
4   I believe you studied at Cambridge.
5   Perhaps this is your coat.
6   I think your father is a doctor.
7   I thought Tony was going to come with us.
8   You'll be in Edinburgh next week, won't you?
9   I think you're making a mistake.
10   Perhaps it would be better to stop now.

Another use of negative questions is in **polite invitations**.

Won't you come in?   **Wouldn't you like** something to drink?

But we do **not** use negative questions to **ask people to do things for us**.
Can you help me?   **You couldn't** help me, could you?
BUT NOT ~~Can't you help me?~~ (This sounds like a criticism.)

We can also use negative questions to **check that something has not happened, is not true, etc**. The meaning is like **'Is it true that ... not ...?'**

Don't you feel well?   Oh dear. **Can't they come** this evening?

Negative questions can express **surprise** that **something has not happened**, is not happening, etc. This may sound **critical**.

Hasn't the postman come yet?   **Didn't she tell** you she was married?
Can't you read? It says 'closed'.   **Don't you** ever **listen** to what I say?

▲   **3   Use negative questions to confirm the following ideas.**

1   It looks as if she can't swim. ➡ *Can't she swim?*
2   Is it true that she didn't pass the exam?
3   I believe you may not have paid for your ticket.
4   I think perhaps you didn't lock the door.
5   It seems as if you can't understand English. I said 'No'.
6   I'm afraid you don't like my cooking.
7   Perhaps you didn't get the letter I sent.
8   So you didn't enjoy the film?
9   Is it true that you and John aren't going to get married?
10   It seems that you don't want any more potatoes.

In **answers** to negative questions, **'Yes'** goes with or suggests an **affirmative** verb, and **'No'** goes with or suggests a **negative** verb.

'Don't you like it?' **'Yes** (I do like it).'   'Aren't you ready?' **'No** (I'm not ready).'

4   Add *Yes* or *No* to the answers.

1   'Aren't you ready?' '*Yes*, I am.'
2   'Don't you like this?' 'I don't.'
3   'Can't you stop?' 'I can't.'
4   'Isn't this nice?' 'It is.'
5   'Haven't you paid?' 'I have.'
6   'Wasn't she at home?' 'She was.'
7   'Aren't you happy?' 'I'm not.'
8   'Didn't you get my letter?' 'I didn't.'

'Haven't you brought any vegetables with it?'

For negative questions in exclamations, see page 221.

not and **no**

We use **not** to make a **word**, **expression** or **clause negative**.

> **Not surprisingly**, we missed the train. (NOT ~~No surprisingly~~ ...)
> The students went on strike, but **not** the teachers.
>   (NOT ... ~~no the teachers.~~)
> I can see you tomorrow, but **not** on Thursday.
> I have **not** received his answer.

We **don't** usually put **not** with the **subject**. Instead, we use a structure with *it*.

> **It wasn't Bill** who phoned, it was Pete. (NOT ~~Not Bill phoned~~ ...)

We use **no** with a **noun** or **-ing** form to mean **'not any'** or **'not a/an'** (see page 35).

> **No teachers** went on strike. (= There were**n't any** teachers on strike.)
> I've got **no Thursdays** free this term. (= ... **not any** Thursdays ...)
> I telephoned, but there was **no** answer. (= ... **not an** answer.)
> *NO SMOKING*

1 Put in *not* or *no*.

1 I like most vegetables, but ＿＿ peppers.
2 She was ＿＿ able to understand him.
3 They had ＿＿ butter left in the shop.
4 They repaired my watch, but ＿＿ properly.
5 We've got ＿＿ time to talk now.
6 I can come round, but ＿＿ tonight.
7 They did ＿＿ want to help.
8 'Do you smoke?' '＿＿ usually.'
9 She's a woman with ＿＿ sense of humour.
10 'Shall I put some music on?' 'OK, but ＿＿ jazz.'

NO-MAN'S LAND

negatives: I don't think etc

We usually use **I don't think + affirmative verb**, not **I think + negative verb**.
The same is true with **believe**, **suppose**, **imagine** and similar verbs.

> I **don't think you know** Joe. (More usual than **I think you don't know** Joe.)
> I **don't believe she's** at home.
> I **don't suppose you can** lend me £5?

1   Change the sentences as in the example.

He's not at home. *(I think)* ➔ *I don't think he's at home.*

1   You're not right. *(I think)*
2   You haven't met my sister. *(I believe)*
3   You don't know where Ruth is. *(I suppose)*
4   We won't arrive before midnight. *(I imagine)*
5   They don't know what they're doing. *(I think)*
6   I didn't make myself clear. *(I think)*
7   You didn't remember to bring my book back. *(I suppose)*
8   I haven't got enough money. *(I believe)*

We use similar structures with **seem**, **expect** and **want**.

> He **doesn't seem to like** you. (Less formal than He **seems not to like** you.)
> I **don't expect to be** back before Monday. (Less formal than I **expect not** ...)
> I **never want to see** you again. (More natural than I **want never to see** ...)

2   Change the sentences as shown.

1   I don't think he's well. *(He doesn't seem ...)*
2   I probably won't be home late. *(I don't expect ...)*
3   I would hate to climb another mountain. *(I never want ...)*
4   It's not raining, apparently. *(It doesn't seem ...)*
5   I probably won't pass the exam. *(I don't expect ...)*
6   He is determined not to get married. *(He never wants ...)*

With *hope*, we make the following verb negative.

> I **hope it doesn't rain**. (NOT I ~~**don't hope it rains**~~.)

imperatives

We use **imperatives** to tell people what to do, advise them, encourage them etc.
Imperatives look the same as **infinitives without *to***.
Negative imperatives begin with **do not/don't**.

> **Look** in the mirror before you drive off.   **Try** again.
> **Have** some more tea.   **Cheer** up.
> Please **do not lean** out of the window.   **Don't worry**.

We can use **do** to make **emphatic imperatives**.
> **Do sit** down!   **Do stop** making that noise!

1   Read the text and put in the verbs from the box.

add   bake   don't use   mix   oil   put in   shape

Potato Pancake

| one pound of boiled potatoes |
| two tomatoes |
| butter |
| tablespoon flour |
| seasoning |
| parsley |
| one small finely chopped onion |

Mash the potatoes in butter. __1__ any milk. Season. __2__ the chopped onion, chopped tomato, flour, and a handful of chopped parsley. __3__ well. Lightly __4__ a flat baking dish and __5__ the potatoes. __6__ into a fairly thick circular cake. Brush lightly with melted butter and __7__ in a hot oven until brown on top.

Bruce Beeby: Father in the Kitchen

▲ **2   Can you write a recipe (instructions for cooking something), or instructions for doing something else?**

Note the position of **always** and **never**: before imperatives.

> **Always try** to tell the truth. (NOT ~~Try always~~ ...)
> **Never do** that again.

3   Put in *always* or *never*.

1   Add salt to potatoes when you cook them.
2   Check the tyres before you drive a car.
3   Cook chicken when it's frozen.
4   Wait more than fifteen minutes for somebody who's late.
5   Unplug electrical appliances before repairing them.
6   Count your change after buying something.
7   Put off till tomorrow what you can do today.
8   Say 'I will love you for ever'.
9   Pay bills the day you get them.
10 Apologise for things that are not your fault.

'No, no, always land buttered side down!'

In imperatives, **do** and **don't** can be used before **be**.

> **Do be** quiet!   **Don't be** silly.

4   Make sentences beginning *do be* or *don't be* for the following situations. Use the words and expressions in the box.

| angry | back by midnight | careful | frightened | greedy |
| jealous | on time | rude | stupid | |

1   You are a parent; your child is eating too much.
2   Your child is going to cycle to school through heavy traffic.
3   You are just going to tell somebody that you have damaged their car.
4   Your fourteen-year-old child is going out to a party.
5   You are going into a room where a nervous old lady is alone in the dark.
6   Your ten-year-old child has just told you she is going to leave home.
7   You are arranging to meet somebody who is usually late.
8   Your child has just told you to shut up.
9   Your boyfriend/girlfriend is upset because you went out with somebody else.

5   Write some advice for people visiting your country. Do this together with other students if possible.

let's

We can use **let's** (or *let us* – very formal) **+ infinitive without *to*** to make **suggestions** or give **orders** to a group that **includes the speaker**.

> **Let's have** a drink.   **Let's stay** in this evening.

The normal **negative** is **Let's not** ...; *Don't let's* ... is informal; *Let us not* is very formal.

> **Let's not tell** Granny what happened.

1   **Write the suggestions, using *Let's*. Examples:**

   1 *Let's go swimming.*   2 *Let's not go swimming.*

Note also the common expressions **let me see** and **let me think**.

> *So what time will I get there?* **Let me see** – *suppose I start at half past six ...*
> *What am I going to wear?* **Let me think** – *it's too cold for the black dress ...*

exclamations

Exclamations with *how* and *what* are constructed differently.

HOW **+** ADJECTIVE   WHAT (**+** ADJECTIVE) **+** NOUN
How beautiful!   *What a surprise!*
How strange!   *What strange people!*

We do not drop articles after *What*.
What a *stupid idea!* (NOT ~~What stupid idea!~~)

DO IT YOURSELF

1 **Look at the examples, and write a rule to say where the subject and verb come in an exclamation. Check your answer in the key.**

*How beautiful **she is**!* (NOT ~~How she is beautiful!~~)
*How hard **he works**!* (NOT ~~How he works hard!~~)
*What a lot of languages **your sister speaks**!*

2 **Change the sentences into exclamations with *how* or *what*.**

1   That's a strange picture.
    What a strange picture!
2   That's interesting.
3   That's a nuisance.
4   You've got big eyes, grandmother.
    (What big ...!)
5   That's disgusting.

6   Those children are noisy.
7   He cooks well.
8   We were wrong.
9   He talks a lot of nonsense.
10 She wears funny clothes.
11 She plays badly.
12 I was a fool.

We can use **negative questions** (see page 214) as **exclamations**.

Isn't she *beautiful!*   **Doesn't he** *work hard!*   **Wasn't it** *a surprise!*

3 **Change the sentences from Exercise 2 into exclamations with negative questions. Example:**

Isn't that a strange picture!

'How romantic! Breakfast in bed!'

there is

THE MOST COMMON STRUCTURES WITH INTRODUCTORY *THERE*		
there is/are	there was/were	there will be
there is/are going to be	there has/have been	there had been

Questions: is there, are there *etc*
Contraction: there's *(pronounced /ðəz/, like the beginning of 'the zoo')*

We use ***there is*** to say that **something exists** (or doesn't exist) somewhere.
It is is not used in this way.

> **There's** *a hole in my sock.* (NOT ~~It's a hole in my sock.~~)
> **There's** *snow on the mountains.*
> **There are** *two men at the door.*
> *Once upon a time* **there were** *three little pigs.*
> **There will be** *rain tonight.*
> **There has** *never* **been** *anybody like you.*

In an informal style we often use *there's* before a plural noun.

> **There's some grapes** *in the fridge.*

1 Put in the correct form of *there is(n't).*

1 ____ no water on the moon.
2 ____ no railways in the 18th century.
3 Once upon a time ____ a beautiful princess.
4 Tomorrow ____ snow.
5 ____ some soup, if you're hungry.
6 ____ any potatoes?
7 ____ wars all through history.
8 ____ many tigers left in the wild.
9 ____ an accident – can I phone?
10 I'm afraid ____ time to see Granny.

2 Put in *there's* or *it's*.

1 ____ a cat in your bedroom.
2 ____ hard to understand him.
3 ____ cold tonight.
4 ____ ice on the roads.
5 ____ nice to see you.
6 ____ somebody on the phone for you.
7 ____ a problem with the TV.
8 ____ too late to go out.
9 ____ a funny smell in the kitchen.
10 'What's that noise?' '____ the wind.'

There is introduces **indefinite** subjects. Compare:

> **There's a window** *open.*
> **The window's** *open.* (NOT ~~There's the window open.~~)

For explanations of the words that we use to talk about grammar, see pages 298–302.

More complicated structures:

there may/can/must *etc* be   there is likely to be
there is certain/sure to be   there is no sense/point/use in ...ing
there is no need to ...   there is something/anything/nothing
there seems/appears to be   wrong / the matter with ...

Infinitive: there to be
-ing form: there being
Use in tags (see page 226): There will be enough, **won't there?**

There can also be used with auxiliary *be.*
> ***There were*** *children **playing** in the garden. (= Children **were playing** ...)*

3   Put together the beginnings and ends.

BEGINNINGS	ENDS
According to the forecast,	'He says there's nothing wrong with
I can't see how to open the door.	me.'
I'm looking forward to the party.	'There seems to be something lying in
OK, children, now I don't want there to be	the road.'
That must be Jeff.	any noise while I'm on the phone.
There are too many people	but there may be some tomorrow.
There aren't any tickets now,	if you've got a headache – you won't
There's no need to hurry.	enjoy it.
There's no point in going out	it won't start.
There's something the matter with the car –	looking for too few jobs in this country.
'What did the doctor say?'	There are sure to be some nice people
'Why have we stopped?'	there.
	There can't be two people who look like
	that.
	There must be a keyhole somewhere.
	there's likely to be more snow tonight.
	We've got plenty of time.

'George, is there a mountain near here?'

dropping sentence-beginnings

In informal speech we often **drop unstressed beginnings** of sentences.
This happens mainly with **articles**, **possessives**, **personal pronouns**,
auxiliary verbs and **be**, **demonstratives** and introductory **there is**.

Car's running badly. (= The car's ...)   *Must dash. (= I must dash.)*
Won't work. (= It won't work.)   *Be four pounds fifty. (= That'll be ...)*

**1   Put back the words that have been dropped and write the
      complete sentences.**

1   Wife's on holiday.   6   Don't think so.
2   Couldn't understand a word.   7   Train's late again.
3   Seen Joe?   8   Know what I mean?
4   Careful what you say.   9   Got a pen?
5   Nobody at home.   10   Lost my glasses.

**2   Make these sentences more informal
      by dropping words from the beginning.**

1   I've changed my job.
2   She doesn't know what she's doing.
3   That'll cost you £10.
4   Be careful of the flowers.
5   There's no time to waste.
6   The bus is coming.
7   Do you speak English?
8   I haven't been there.
9   He thinks he's clever.
10   Have you got a light?

Got anywhere
where its
SAFE to
BREATHE?

TRAVEL

We only drop pronouns before stressed words.

Like *your tie.*   **Haven't** *seen him.*   **Can't** *swim.*
BUT NOT ~~Have seen him. Can swim.~~ (Affirmative auxiliaries are
    unstressed.)

We can drop auxiliary verbs before personal pronouns except *I* and *it*.
    You *coming?*   **She** *want something?*   BUT NOT ~~I late? It raining?~~

dropping words after **auxiliaries**

In informal speech, we often use just an **auxiliary verb instead of repeating a longer expression**.

*'Get up!' 'I **am**.'* (= *'I am getting up.'*)
*He said he'd write, but he **hasn't**.* (= *... he hasn't written.*)

If there is no auxiliary to repeat, we use *do*.
*She said she would phone, and she **did**.*

1   Make these conversations more natural by dropping unnecessary expressions after auxiliaries.

1   I can't see you today, but I can see you tomorrow.
2   I've bought one of those blouses, and Sue has bought one too.
3   'You wouldn't have won if I hadn't helped you.' 'Yes, I would have won.'
4   'That car needs cleaning.' 'It certainly does need cleaning.'
5   'You'd better phone Bill.' 'I have phoned Bill.'
6   'The photocopier isn't working.' 'Yes, it is working.'
7   She can't swim, but I can swim.
8   Phil doesn't want to go, and Celia doesn't want to go either.
9   She thinks I don't love her, but I do love her.

▲   **2   Read the text. What words have been dropped?**

'I came round because I really think the whole thing is too absurd.'
'So do I. I always did (1).'
'You can't have (2) half as much as I did (3). I mean really, when one comes to think of it. And after all these years.'
'Oh, I know. And I dare say if you hadn't (4), I should have (5) myself. I'm sure the last thing I want is to go on like this. Because, really, it's too absurd.'
'And if there's one thing I'm *not*, it's ready to take offence. I never have been (6), and I never shall be (7).'
'Very well, dear. Nobody wants to quarrel less than I do (8).'
'When a thing is over, let it *be* over, is what I always say. I don't want to say any more about anything at all. The only thing I must say is that when you say I said that everybody said that about your spoiling that child, it simply isn't what I said. That's all. And I don't want to say another thing about it.'
'Well, certainly I don't (9). There's only one thing I simply can't help saying ...'

Adapted from a piece by E M Delafield

question tags: basic rules

Question tags often **follow sentences** in speech and informal writing.
They are used to **check** whether something is true, or to **ask for
agreement**.

> *You haven't seen Joe, **have you**?*   *This tea isn't very nice, **is it**?*

Negative tags are usually contracted. The contracted tag for *I am* is *aren't I*?
> *Nice day, **isn't it**?*   *I'm late, **aren't I**?*

We most often put **negative tags after affirmative sentences**, and **non-
negative tags after negative sentences**. We do not put tags after
questions.

> *It's cold, **isn't it**?*   *It's not warm, **is it**?*   BUT NOT *~~Is it cold, isn't it?~~*

If the main sentence has an auxiliary verb or *be*, this is used in the tag. If
not, *do* is used. *There* can be used as a subject in tags.
> *She **can** swim, **can't** she?*   *You **wouldn't** like a puppy, **would** you?*
> *He **gave** you a cheque, **didn't** he?*   *There's a problem, **isn't there**?*

1   **These are sentences from real conversations. Put in the question tags.**

1   I'm cooking tonight, ____?
2   We're going to Mum's, then, ____?
3   Your brothers are not being kind to
    you today, ____?
4   I'm not quite myself, ____?
5   They weren't ready, ____?
6   She's not a baby now, ____?
7   That's the law, ____?
8   He's a lovely little boy, ____?
9   That fireman can see them, ____,
    Dave?
10 It must be a year now, ____?
11 It'll be all right, ____?
12 They look like big candles, ____?
13 They won't have bulbs, ____?
14 There's a light out there, ____?
15 Cathy's still got curly hair, ____?
16 She doesn't look well, ____?
17 They've been really horrible, ____?
18 I was first really, ____?

'It's always poor you, isn't it, Albert?'

Drawing by C Barsotti; © 1995
The New Yorker Magazine, Inc.

question tags: advanced points

We use ***they*** to refer to ***nobody***, ***somebody*** and ***everybody*** (and ***no one*** etc).
We use **non-negative tags** after ***never***, ***no***, ***nobody***, ***hardly***, ***scarcely***, ***little***.
We use ***it*** in question tags to refer to ***nothing***.

> ***Nobody*** *phoned, did* ***they?***   *It's* ***hardly*** *rained all summer,* ***has it?***
> *She* ***never*** *smiles,* ***does she?*** (NOT ... ~~***doesn't she?***~~)
> *It's* ***no*** *good,* ***is it?***   ***Nothing*** *can happen, can* ***it?***

▲ **1 Put in suitable tags.**

1 Everybody's here, aren't ____?
2 You're never happy, ____?
3 There's no milk, ____?
4 Nothing matters, ____?
5 Nobody likes her, do ____?

6 She hardly spoke, ____?
7 Somebody's forgotten their coat, ____?
8 There's scarcely enough time, ____?
9 You never wrote, ____?

Informal questions/requests often use **negative sentence + question tag.**
After imperatives, we can use ***won't you?*** to invite people to do things, and ***will/would/can/can't/could you?*** (informal) to **tell** or **ask** people to do things.
After a **negative imperative** we use ***will you?*** After ***Let's*** we use ***shall we?***

> *You* ***can't*** *lend me £5,* ***can you?***   *Do sit down,* ***won't you?***
> *Give me a hand,* ***will you?***   *Shut up,* ***can't you?***
> *Don't forget,* ***will you?***   *Let's have a party,* ***shall we?***

▲ **2 Put together the sentences and tags.**

Do have some more tea	Don't drive too fast	Let's start again
Pass me the newspaper	You couldn't tell me the time	

could you?	shall we?	will you?	won't you?	would you?

If a tag is a **real question**, it is pronounced with a **rising intonation**.
If the tag only **asks for agreement**, it is pronounced with a **falling intonation**.

> *The meeting's at four o'clock, isn't it?*   *Nice day, isn't it?*

short answers and attention signals

In conversation, we often give **short answers** using
pronoun + auxiliary verb.

> *'Can he swim?' 'Yes, **he can**.'*
> *'Has the rain stopped?' 'No, **it hasn't**.'*
> *'Don't forget to phone.' '**I won't**.'*
> *'She likes cakes.' '**She** certainly **does**.'*

1   Write short answers for these sentences.

1   'Are you ready?'   6   'Have you seen Les?'
2   'Do you speak English?'   7   'Can you understand him?'
3   'It's too hot.'   8   'He plays well.'
4   'Don't be late.'   9   'She sounded tired.'
5   'Send me a postcard.'   10   'Say hello to Linda for me.'

Interrogative short answers using **auxiliary verb + pronoun** (like
question tags) can express **attention**, **interest** or **surprise**.

> *'It was a terrible party.' '**Was it?**' 'Yes, ...'*
> *'We had a lovely holiday.' '**Did you?**' 'Yes, we went ...'*
> *'I've got a headache.' '**Have you**, dear? I'll get you an aspirin.'*
> *'John likes that girl next door.' 'Oh, **does he?**'*
> *'I don't understand.' 'Oh, **don't you?** I'm sorry.'*

Negative replies to affirmative sentences can express emphatic agreement.
> *'It was a lovely concert.' 'Yes, **wasn't it!** I did enjoy it.'*
> *'She's lost a lot of weight.' 'Yes, **hasn't she?**'*

▲   **2   Rewrite this as a conversation, putting in interrogative short
    answers. Example:**

> *'It was a lovely wedding.' 'Was it?' 'Yes. Though ...'*

It was a lovely wedding. Though I didn't think much of Maggie's dress.
That colour doesn't suit her at all. Anyway, I don't really go for church
weddings. The service went on for ages. And I was sitting right at the back,
so I couldn't hear the vicar. The music was nice, though. They played that
hymn about sheep. Lovely. I must say I didn't enjoy the reception much.
The food wasn't very good. And the bride's father made such a stupid
speech. And I got one of my headaches. Champagne always gives me a
headache. And I was sitting next to that Mrs Foster from down the road.
I can't stand that woman. She's always criticising. Anyway, I must go.
Nice to talk to you. It really was a lovely wedding.

I (don't) think so etc

We often use **so** in answers, instead of a *that*-clause. This is common after **be afraid**, **hope**, **suppose**, **think**.

'Did you lose?' I**'m afraid so.***
'Do you think we'll have good weather?' *'Yes, I* **hope so.***
  (NOT *'Yes, I hope.'*)
'Are you ready?' *'I* **suppose so.***' (unwilling agreement)
'Is Alex here?' *'I* **think so.***' (NOT *'I think it.'* OR *'I think.'*)

1 **Here are some exchanges taken from recorded conversations. See if you can guess which of the following expressions was used in each exchange:** *I'm afraid so, I hope so, I suppose so* **or** *I think so.*

1 'Is it working?' 'Yes, ____.'
2 'Dead, aren't they?' '____.'
3 'Do we want it?' 'Not sure. ____.'
4 'Is that when she said it?' '____.'
5 'It should be warmer in April.' '____.'
6 'Did he know who you were?' 'Oh, yes, ____.'
7 'When is it? Tomorrow?' 'Yes, ____.'
8 'You're mean, aren't you?' '____.'
9 'It should be quite easy, though.' '____.'
10 'I could borrow one of your dresses, couldn't I?' '____.'

Negatives are: **I'm afraid not, I hope not, I suppose not** and (usually) **I don't think so**.

2 **Complete the negative answers.**

1 'Did you find out?' '*(afraid)*.'
2 'Will you be home late?' 'No, *(think)*.'
3 'We're not having lunch too early, are we?' '*(hope)*.'
4 'It's not a good idea, is it?' 'No, *(suppose)*.'
5 'Do they serve tea here?' '*(afraid)*.'
6 'I think she's got a new boyfriend?' '*(hope)*.'
7 'We won't be in time for the train.' '*(suppose)*.'
8 'Is this where she lives?' '*(think)*.'

so am I etc

> *So am I* means **'I am too'**; *so does he* means 'he does too'; and so on.
> *Neither/Nor am I* means **'I'm not either'**, and so on.
>
> She's from Scotland, and **so am I**.   I was tired, and **so were the others**.
> *'I've lost their address.'* **'So have I.'**   I like dancing, and **so does he**.
> I can't swim, and **neither can Bill**.   *'She didn't understand.'* **'Nor did I.'**

1   Complete the sentences with *so am I* etc or *neither/nor am I* etc.

1   He's tall, and _____ his sister.
2   'I haven't paid.' '_____ I.'
3   Penguins can't fly, and _____ ostriches.
4   'I love this music.' '_____ I.'
5   'I lost my passport.' '_____ Nicola.'
6   I don't like her, and _____ my friends.
7   The food was bad, and _____ the wine.
8   Sue won't be there, and _____ her mother.
9   'Pete looks ill.' '_____ you.'
10 'I wasn't surprised.' '_____ I.'

**2   If possible, work with another student and find five or more
things that you have got in common. Write sentences. Example:**

She likes tennis, and so do I.

**3   Look at the pictures, and make sentences about pairs of things
using *so is* etc or *neither/nor is* etc. Examples:**

The bike has got two wheels, and so has the motorbike.
The Sphinx is not alive, and neither is the pyramid.

it: preparatory subject and object

When the subject of a sentence is an infinitive or a clause, we generally use **it** as a **preparatory subject**, and put the **infinitive or clause later**.

*It's nice **to talk** to you.* (More natural than ***To talk** to you is nice.*)
*It was surprising **that she didn't come back**.*

Note also the structure ***It looks as if/though**...*
*It **looks as if** she's going to win.*
*It **looks as though** we'll miss the train.*

1   Rewrite these sentences with *It* ... to make them more natural.

1   To book early is important. *It is important to book early.*
2   To hear her talk like that annoys me.
3   To get from here to York takes four hours.
4   To get upset about small things is silly.
5   To get up in the morning is nice, but to stay in bed is nicer.
6   To watch him makes me tired.
7   To hear her complaining upsets me.
8   To say no to people is hard.

2   Put the sentences together using *It* ...

1   He wasn't there. This surprised me.
    It surprised me that he wasn't there.
2   She's got some money saved. This is a good thing.
3   He's got long hair. This doesn't bother me.
4   John never talked to her. This worried her.
5   She should be told immediately.
    This is essential.
6   He didn't remember my name.
    This was strange.
7   He can't come. This is a pity.
8   The children should get to bed early.
    This is important.
9   Wolves attack people. This is not true.
10 She stole money. This shocked me.

'Can't I plead with you, Helen? It isn't my wish that our marriage should end like this.'

3 Put the beginnings and ends together.

BEGINNINGS	ENDS
It doesn't interest me	as if we're going to have trouble with Ann again.
It looks	how many unhappy marriages there are.
It seems	if we have to ask her to leave.
It will be a pity	that everybody should have a chance to speak.
It's exciting	that he forgot to buy the tickets.
It's important	that we'll be a little late.
It's probable	what you think.
It's surprising	when a baby starts talking.

We can also use *it* as a **preparatory subject** for an *-ing* **form**.
This is especially common in the structures *it's worth* ... and *it's no use* ...

   It's worth visiting the Lake District.   *It's no use trying* to explain.

**4 Write five or more sentences about places in your country,
    beginning *It's (not) worth visiting ..., because ...***

We can also use *it* as a **preparatory object**.

   I find *it* difficult **to talk to you**.

5 Put the beginnings and ends together.

BEGINNINGS	ENDS
He made it difficult	a problem to walk.
His bad leg made it	that she hadn't written.
I thought it strange	what he wanted.
He made it clear	to hear her stories.
I find it interesting	to like him.

When it is not necessary to change, it is necessary not to change.
Lucius Cary

It's easy to see the faults in people I know; it's hardest to see the good, especially when the good isn't there.
Will Cuppy

It is impossible to enjoy idling thoroughly unless one has plenty of work to do.
Jerome K Jerome

It was such a lovely day I thought it was a pity to get up.
W Somerset Maugham

Anybody who has ever struggled with poverty knows how extremely expensive it is to be poor.
James Baldwin

emphasis with it, what etc

We can **emphasise** a part of a sentence by using the structure *It is/was ... that*. Compare:

> *The secretary sent Jake the photos yesterday.*
> *It was the secretary that/who sent Jake the photos yesterday.*
>   (not the boss)
> *It was Jake that the secretary sent the photos to yesterday.* (not Bill)
> *It was the photos that the secretary sent Jake yesterday.*
>   (not the drawings)
> *It was yesterday that the secretary sent Jake the photos.* (not last week)

▲ 1 **Change these sentences to emphasise each part in turn.**

1 The baby put marmalade on Dad's trousers this morning.
2 Maria gave her old bicycle to Pat last week.
3 Carl broke the kitchen window with a ladder today.
4 Mark met Cathy in Germany in 1992.

▲ 2 **Change these sentences as shown.**

1 I don't want tea, I want coffee.
   It's not tea I want, it's coffee.
2 I don't love you, I love Peter.
3 Carol isn't the boss, Sandra is.
4 I don't hate the music, I hate the words.
5 I didn't lose my glasses, I lost my keys.
6 Bob isn't getting married, Clive is.
7 I didn't see Judy, I saw Jill.
8 He's not studying maths, he's studying physics.
9 Max isn't crazy, you are.
10 You don't need a nail, you need a screw.

Note the use of pronouns in this structure in formal and informal styles.

FORMAL	INFORMAL
*It is **I who am** responsible.*	*It's **me that's** responsible.*
*It is **you who are** in the wrong.*	*It's **you that's** in the wrong.*

'It's not the fighting I hate, it's the washing-up!'

Another way of emphasising is to use a structure with **what**
(= 'the thing(s) that'). Compare:

> **The wind** keeps me awake.   **What** keeps me awake **is the wind**.
> I need **a change**.   **A change is what** I need.

We can use **all (that)** (meaning **'the only thing that'**) in the same way
as *what*.

> **All** I need is a home somewhere.   **All** I did was touch him.

▲ **3**   **Change the sentences so as to emphasise the words *in italics*.**

1   He wants *a motorbike*.
     What he wants is a motorbike.
2   I need *a drink*.
3   I like *her sense of humour*.
4   I hate *his jealousy*.
5   *Cycling* keeps me fit.
6   *The travelling* makes the job interesting.
7   I only want *five minutes' rest*. (*All I want is ...*)
8   I found *something very strange*.
9   *The weather* stopped us.
10 I don't understand *why she stays with him*.

4   **Complete these sentences.**

1   All I need is ____.
2   What I really like is ____.
3   What I really hate is ____.
4   What I want to know is ____.

conjunctions

Conjunctions join clauses into sentences.
Examples: **but**, **because**, **while**, **if**.

> She was poor **but** she was honest.
> I went to bed **because** I was tired.
> Can you watch the kids **while** I'm out?
> I'll do it **if** I can.

DO IT YOURSELF

1   **Six of these words cannot be used as conjunctions. (For example, they could not come just before the clause ...** *she went home.***) Which six? Check your answers in the key.**

after	all	although	and	as	at	because
before	by	if	or	since	so	that	this
under	unless	until	when	whether	with	

One conjunction is enough to join **two clauses** – we do not normally use two.

> **Although** she was tired, she went to work.
> She was tired, **but** she went to work.
> BUT NOT **Although** ~~she was tired,~~ **but** ~~she went to work.~~

> **As** you know, I work very hard.
> You know **that** I work very hard.
> BUT NOT **As** ~~you know,~~ **that** ~~I work very hard.~~

2   **Put the beginnings and ends together.**

BEGINNINGS	ENDS
Although he was very bad-tempered,	after you have a meal.
Always brush your teeth	and I'll hit you.
Always wash your hands	before you have a meal.
As Liz told you,	but everybody liked him.
Because I knew her family,	he had lots of friends.
Talk to me like that again	I did what I could for her.
Don't do that again	her mother left for Berlin last Friday.
He had a terrible temper,	or I'll hit you.
Liz explained to you	so I tried to help her.
I was sorry for her,	that her mother went back home last week.
If you do that again,	unless you stop that.
There'll be trouble	you'll be sorry.

conjunctions and **clauses**: position

Some conjunctions and their clauses can go either **first** or **last** in a sentence.

> *If you need help*, come and see me.
> Come and see me *if you need help*.

We often use a comma (,) when the conjunction and its clause are first in the sentence.

1 **Write the sentences with the clauses *in italics* first, when this is possible.**

1 I'll come round to your place *after I've finished work.*
2 Let's have a weekend in the country *when the weather gets better.*
3 You ought to see Paula *before you go back to Canada.*
4 I enjoyed the lecture, *although I didn't understand everything.*
5 Your train leaves in half an hour, *so you'd better hurry.*
6 We won't know what's happening *until Sean phones.*
7 I'm going to buy some new jeans, *as we're going out tonight.*
8 Somebody broke into the house *while they were asleep.*
9 He hasn't looked at another woman *since he met Julie.*
10 I'm quite sure *that she's telling the truth.*
11 I'd like to know *whether my photos are ready.*
12 He didn't understand the policeman *because he was deaf.*

Note the order of events with ***before*** and ***after***.

> He worked as a salesman ***before he got married***.
> ***Before he got married***, he worked as a salesman.
>   (Both sentences say that he worked as a salesman first.)
> *She went to China **after she finished school***.
> ***After she finished school***, she went to China.
>   (Both sentences say that she finished school first.)

2 **Underline or write down the verb for the thing that happened first.**

1 He did military service before he went to university.
2 I phoned Sarah after I spoke to Bill.
3 Before the rain stopped, he went out shopping.
4 After she gave up her job at the bank, she left her husband.
5 I felt really depressed before you turned up.
6 Things were quite different after Susie left.

using **conjunctions**

Do you know how to use these conjunctions: **so that** (purpose or result), **as long as / provided**, **while** (contrast), **until**, **as if/though**?

*Let's start now, **so that** we're sure to have enough time.*
*She spoke very quietly, **so that** nobody could hear a word.*
*You can go out **as long as** (OR **provided**) you tell us where you're going.*
*The summers here are wet, **while** the winters are very dry.*
*I'll look after the kids **until** you get back.*
*I feel **as if** (OR **as though**) I'm getting a cold.*

In a formal style, *whereas* can be used in the same way as *while*.
  *Sound travels at 330 metres per second, **whereas** light travels at 300,000*
    kilometres per second.

1   Put in suitable conjunctions.

1   You can have my bike _____ you bring it back tomorrow.
2   I'm staying here _____ I get my money back.
3   It was very dark in the passage, _____ I couldn't see where I was going.
4   Joe was short and dark, _____ his sister was the exact opposite.
5   You look _____ you've seen a ghost.
6   He won't get any money _____ he finishes the work properly.
7   It looks _____ it's going to rain.
8   You can cancel the ticket _____ you tell the airline 48 hours in advance.
9   I'm going to the bank now, _____ I'll have enough money for shopping.
10 _____ I think his novels are good, his poetry isn't up to much.

2   Join the beginnings and ends with *so that* or *as long as*.

BEGINNINGS	ENDS
He went to Switzerland	he could learn French.
I don't mind you singing	it doesn't rain.
We moved the piano	that's OK with you.
We took some blankets	there would be room for the Christmas tree.
We'll come back this afternoon	we would be warm enough.
We'll play tennis	you do it quietly.

3   Rewrite these sentences, beginning *While* ...

1   It was sunny, but there was a cold wind.
While it was sunny, there was a cold wind.
2   She's very clever, but she's got no common sense at all.
3   I know how you feel, but I think you're making a mistake.
4   The job's well paid, but it's deadly boring.
5   I'm interested in economics, but I wouldn't want to work in a bank.
6   The hotel was nice, but it was a long way from the beach.

**4   Write sentences about the pictures, beginning *He/She/It looks
as if* ... Use expressions from the box to help you.**

been painting	going swimming	going to rain	got a cold
had bad news	had good news	lost something	seen a ghost

Compare ***because*** and ***because of***, and ***(al)though*** and ***in spite of***.

*She lost her job **because she was ill**.*
*She lost her job **because of her illness**.*

Although/Though it was raining, *we went out for a walk.*
In spite of the rain, *we went out for a walk.*

conjunctions with -ing forms

Some conjunctions can introduce clauses made with *-ing* forms. This is common with *after*, *before*, *when*, *while* and *since*.

After talking to you I felt better.
Look in the mirror *before driving off*.

1 Put in a suitable conjunction.

1   I usually have a snack ____ going to bed.
2   He had a heart attack ____ watching a video.
3   ____ spending all that money on CDs I'd better not buy anything else.
4   Use damp string ____ tying up parcels; when it dries it shrinks and gets tight.
5   How many jobs have you had ____ leaving school?
6   We went for a walk ____ leaving for the airport.
7   Put this on ____ shaving and you'll smell wonderful.
8   I haven't heard anything from her ____ getting that letter last month.
9   I often listen to music ____ working.
10 Always wear goggles ____ working with metal.

2 Put the sentences together, using conjunction + ...*ing*.

BEGINNINGS	ENDS
Don't go swimming	before (*talk*) to Eric.
Have a rest every hour or so	before (*go*) on stage.
He has been terribly depressed	he began to feel ill.
I had a word with Janet	immediately after (*eat*).
I often solve problems in my head	since (*fail*) the exam.
She always gets nervous	we haven't even had time to unpack.
Since (*come*) back from America	when (*drive*) long distances.
A few days after (*return*) from holiday	while (*run*).

A few conjunctions (e.g. *until*, *when*, *if*) can be used with past participles.

*Leave in oven **until cooked**.*
***When questioned**, he denied everything.*
*I can usually remember names and faces **if given** enough time.*

-ing clauses without **conjunctions**

It is possible to have *-ing* and *-ed* clauses without **conjunctions**. These are usually rather formal, and are most common in written English.

> *Having failed to persuade John*, I tried his brother.
> (= *As I had failed ...*)
> *Used economically*, a tin will last for weeks.
> (= *If it is used economically ...*)
> *Putting down my newspaper*, I went over to the phone.
> It rained for two weeks on end, *completely ruining our holiday*.

▲ **1 Rewrite the sentences, using *-ing* or *-ed* clauses without conjunctions.**

1 As he had left school at twelve, he had no qualifications.
2 It tastes delicious if it is fried in butter and sprinkled with lemon juice.
3 She walked over to her desk and picked up a paper.
4 The water came into the houses, and flooded the downstairs rooms.
5 As I knew his tastes, I took him a large box of expensive chocolates.
6 He put on his coat and went out.
7 A lorry broke down in Bond Street, and caused a massive traffic jam.
8 As I didn't want to frighten her, I phoned before I went round.
9 If it is sent first class, it should arrive tomorrow.
10 At 3 a.m. Simon came in, and woke everybody in the house.

▲ **2 Complete the text with words from the box.**

dreaming	getting	sacrificing	staring	thinking
thrown				

Then they quarrelled, and Micky, __1__ his head was getting too hot for his tongue, went out to the dunes and stood in the wind __2__ at the sea. Why was he tied to this weak and fretful man? For three years since the end of the war he had looked after Charlie, __3__ him out of hospital and into a nursing home, then to houses in the country, __4__ a lot of his own desire to have a good time before he returned to Canada, in order to get his brother back to health. Micky's money would not last for ever; soon he would have to go, and then what would happen?

But when he returned with cooler head, the problem carelessly __5__ off, he was kind to his brother. They sat in eased silence before the fire, the dog __6__ at their feet, and to Charlie there returned the calm of the world.

V S Pritchett: The Two Brothers

both ... and; neither ... nor

These expressions can **join nouns**, **verbs** or **other** kinds of expression.

*She plays **both** tennis **and** badminton.*
*He **both** sings **and** dances.*
*That's **neither** interesting **nor** true.*
***Neither** Sue **nor** Ann was there.*
*The place **both** depressed me **and** made me want to go home.*

1   Join the sentences with *both ... and* or *neither ... nor*.

1   He repairs cars. He repairs motorbikes. *(He repairs both ...)*
2   He doesn't speak English. He doesn't speak French.
3   I don't like her. I don't dislike her.
4   I admire him. I distrust him.
5   Paul is on holiday. Sally is on holiday.
6   The secretary did not have the file. The accountant did not have the file.
7   The play was funny. The play was shocking.
8   He collects paintings. He collects jewellery.
9   You're not right. You're not wrong.
10   She didn't look at me. She didn't say anything.

2   Write sentences using *both ... and* or *neither ... nor*. Example:

Neither Julius Caesar nor Cinderella had a TV.

Queen Victoria

Dickens

Helen of Troy

Kennedy

Sitting Bull   Cinderella   Shakespeare

Julius Caesar

**3   Make sentences about yourself and another person, using
      both ... and or *neither ... nor*.**

leaving out **that**

We often **leave out** the conjunction *that* in an informal style. This happens mostly **after very common verbs and adjectives**.

> She **knew (that)** I was right.   I'm **glad (that)** you're better.

1   Put the beginnings and ends together.

BEGINNINGS	ENDS
Did you know	he didn't say hello to you.
He suggested	I phoned you?
I believe	I wouldn't forget your birthday.
I expect	she wasn't angry with me.
I heard	there were mice in the cellar?
I thought	this is your coat.
I was surprised	we might like to go skiing with him.
I'm glad	we've had this talk.
It's funny	you love me.
Tell me	you'd get lost.
Were you surprised	you'd got a new job.
You knew	you've seen this already.

We can also leave out *that*, in an informal style, after **so**, **such**, **now**, **provided**.

> Come in quietly **so (that)** she doesn't hear you.

▲ **2   Put in the right conjunction, with *that* if the sentence is formal, and without *that* if it is informal.**

1   He may use the firm's car ____ he pays for all petrol used.
2   I left the bedroom door open ____ I'd hear the phone.
3   ____ she's sixteen she thinks she can do what she likes.
4   It was ____ a serious operation ____ she was not expected to live.
5   Closed-circuit television was installed ____ everybody would be able to watch the performance.
6   You can go out ____ you're back in time to give me a hand with the cooking.
7   ____ the new managers have taken over we expect the company to become profitable in the very near future.

tenses after conjunctions

If the exact time is shown once in a sentence, this may be enough. So **tenses** are **simplified** after many **conjunctions**.
For example, we often use **present tenses** instead of **will** ...

*This discovery will mean **that** we **spend** less on food.*
*I will be delighted **if** he **wins**.*

We use a **present perfect** (instead of a future perfect) to express **completion**.
*I'll tell you **when** I've finished.*

1 Complete these sentences using *will* once and a present tense once.

1   You *(find)* hamburgers wherever you *(go)*.
2   When I *(have)* time, I *(write)* to her.
3   *(you stay)* here until the plane *(take)* off?
4   It *(be)* interesting to see whether he *(recognise)* you.
5   I *(go)* where you *(go)*.
6   He *(give)* £5 to anybody who *(find)* his pen.
7   One day the government *(ask)* people what they *(want)*.
8   You *(find)* all the shops *(be)* closed tomorrow.
9   Whether I *(win)* or not, I *(have)* a good time.
10 As soon as I *(arrive)* I *(phone)* you.

'I'll call you back in twenty minutes when the restaurant is crowded.'

After conjunctions, we often use **simple past tenses** instead of **would**.

> *He would never do anything **that made** her unhappy.*
> *It would be nice **if** she **asked before** she **borrowed** things.*

▲ **2 Complete these sentences, using *would* ... once in each.**

1 In a perfect world, you *(be able)* to say exactly what you *(think)*.
2 I *(always try)* to help anybody who *(be)* in trouble, whether I *(know)* them or not.
3 He *(never do)* anything that *(go)* against his conscience.
4 It *(be)* nice if everybody *(have)* what they *(want)*.
5 I *(hit)* anybody who *(talk)* to me like that.
6 In your position, I *(tell)* the boss what I *(think)*.
7 I *(be)* happier if I *(can)* live where I *(like)*.
8 I knew he *(not give)* me what I *(ask)* for.
9 If we lived in London, it *(mean)* that we *(spend)* less time travelling.

We sometimes use **simple tenses** instead of **perfect** or **progressive**.

> *I hadn't understood **what** she **said**.*
> *He's working. But at the same time **as he works**, he's exercising.*

▲ **3 Complete these sentences.**

1 I *(be)* sorry that I *(not help)* her when she *(need)* it. *(simple past twice, past perfect once)*
2 It *(be)* a good time while it *(last)*. *(simple past and present perfect)*
3 I *(usually like)* the people I *(work)* with. *(simple past and present perfect)*
4 For the previous thirty years, he *(do)* no more than he *(need)* to. *(simple past and past perfect)*
5 Usually when she *(talk)* to you she *(think)* about something else. *(simple present and present progressive)*

▲ **4 Complete these sentences in any way you like.**

1 I would never _____ a person who _____.
2 It would be nice if _____.
3 In a perfect world, you would be able to _____ when _____.
4 I would be happier if _____ what _____.

'Nobody calls me stupid. Meet me
outside when the big hand and the
little hand are on the 12.'

indirect speech: why things change

1 **Look at the text, and write down all the words and expressions that are different in Bill's and Peter's sentences.**

BILL (on Saturday evening): 'I don't like this party. I want to go home now.'

PETER (on Sunday morning): 'Bill said that he didn't like the party, and he wanted to go home right away.'

DO IT YOURSELF

2 **Which do you think is the best explanation for the differences? Check your answer in the key.**

1 After verbs like *said*, you change tenses and pronouns in English.
2 The time, place and speakers are different.
3 If the main verb is past, the other verbs have to be past too.

3 **Read the dialogue. Imagine that Bill talks to a friend the next day and tells him about the conversation, using indirect speech structures ('I said/told her that ...; so she asked if ...'). Write down ten or more words in the conversation that would have to be changed in Bill's report.**

BILL: You're looking good today.
ANN: Oh, thanks, Bill. You are sweet.
BILL: OK. If you sit down I'll get you a drink.
ANN: There's nowhere to sit.
BILL: Yes, there is. Over there in the corner.
ANN: I don't want to sit there. It's too dark. I'll sit here.
BILL: You can't. These seats are taken.
ANN: No, they aren't.
BILL: Really, Ann. Why do you always have to argue? They're taken.
ANN: Excuse me. Are these seats taken?
JOE: Well, this one is, but the other one's free.
ANN: OK. I'll sit here, then. Thanks.
JOE: You're welcome. What's your name?
BILL: Hey, what about me?
ANN: Ann. What's yours?
JOE: I'm Joe Parsons. Can I get you a drink?
ANN: That's very kind. Can I have a bitter lemon?
BILL: I'm getting her a drink.
JOE: No, you're not, mate. I am.
BILL: I don't believe this. Ann, what are you playing at?
ANN: Really, Bill, I don't know what's wrong with you today. I'll see you around, OK?

indirect speech: 'here' and 'now'

Some words may be changed in indirect speech, because **the original speaker's 'here' and 'now' are not the same** as the reporter's.

DO IT YOURSELF

1 **The following sentence was said in England in November 1994:**
'I've been in this part of the world since March this year.'
Does the first or second 'this' have to be changed if the sentence is reported:

a in England a week later?   c in Holland a week later?
b in England a year later?   d in Holland a year later?

Check your answer in the key.

2 **Match the direct and indirect speech expressions. Example:**

here – there

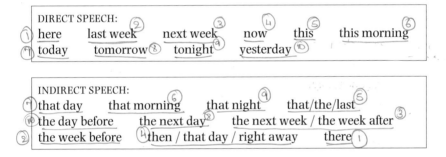

3 **Imagine these sentences were reported in another place a month later. Put in the 'here' and 'now' words.**

1 'I'll see you tomorrow.' She said she'd see me *the next day.*
2 'I'll phone you this evening.' He said he'd phone ~~that~~ evening.
3 'Do you like it here?' She asked if I liked it ~~there~~.
4 'My uncle died last week.' He told me his uncle had died ~~the~~ week before
5 'This meat tastes funny.' She said ~~that~~ meat tasted funny.
6 'I'm leaving now.' He told us he was leaving right away
7 'I overslept this morning.' She told him she'd overslept ~~that~~ morning
8 'The train leaves at 11.00 tonight.' I was told the train left at 11.00 ~~that~~ night.
9 'Pete phoned me yesterday.' He said Pete had phoned him ~~the day~~ before
10 'My brother's arriving here today.' She said her brother was arriving ~~that~~ day

indirect speech: tenses

After reporting expressions like *he said*, *I asked*, *she thought*, **tenses** are usually **different** from those in the original words (because the reporter's time is different from the original speaker's time). Verbs become **more past**.

ORIGINAL WORDS (DIRECT SPEECH)	REPORTED WORDS (INDIRECT SPEECH)
You **look** nice.	I told her she **looked** nice.
	(NOT ~~I told her she **looks** nice.~~)
I **can't** swim.	He pretended he **couldn't** swim.
I**'m learning** French.	She said she **was learning** French.
Has he **forgotten**?	I wondered if he **had forgotten**.
John **phoned**.	She told me that John **had phoned**.
Will you marry me?	I asked him if he **would** marry me.
	(NOT ... ~~if he **will** marry me.~~)

DO IT YOURSELF

1 Complete the table. Check your answers in the key.

DIRECT SPEECH	INDIRECT SPEECH
simple present	*simple past.*
present progressive	past progressive
present perfect	*past perfect*
simple past	*past perfect*
will.	would ...

2 Complete the reported sentences with the correct tenses.

1 'I'm tired.' She said she _was_ tired.
2 'You play very well.' He told me I _played_ very well.
3 'Can you help us?' They asked if I _could_ help them.
4 'We're leaving.' They told us they _were leaving_.
5 'She hasn't brushed her hair.' I noticed that she _hadn't brushed_ her hair.
6 'John's had an accident.' Pam rang to say that John _had an_ accident.
7 'I left school at fifteen.' Her letter said that she _left_ school at fifteen.
8 'She won't say anything.' I knew she _would not say_ anything.
9 'Nobody will know.' I thought nobody _would know_.
10 'This letter has been opened.' I could see that the letter _was opened_.

For explanations of the words that we use to talk about grammar, see pages 298–302.

3   Put in the right tenses.

> I've never met anybody like you before.

> What do you do for a living?

> I'm moving around all the time.

> Why do you want to take me to America?

> We're meant for each other, and nobody is going to stand in our way.

> Do you want a lift home?

> I'm doing some undercover work for the CIA.

> I'll call you tomorrow.

> I think I'm falling in love with you.

I had a really funny evening yesterday, Mary. I got talking to this boy in the pub, very nice-looking he was, and I could see he (1 *fancy*) me. He said he (2 *never meet*) anybody like me before, and he felt I (3 *have*) a very unusual kind of beauty. Oh, yes? I said. Then he asked me if I (4 *want*) a lift home, so I said no, I (5 *be*) hungry, so we went out for a curry.

I asked him what he (6 *do*) for a living, and he said he (7 *do*) some undercover work for the CIA at the moment. He said he (8 *can not*) give me his address because he (9 *move*) around all the time. So I asked him why he (10 *think*) I (11 *want*) his address. Then he asked if he (12 *can*) have my phone number. He said he (13 *call*) me today to fix for me to go to America with him. So I asked him why he (14 *want*) to take me to America, and he said he (15 *think*) he (16 *fall*) in love with me. I knew he (17 *lie*), but it was kind of fun. Anyway, I told him I (18 *have*) got a boyfriend already, but he said that (19 *not matter*). We (20 *be*) meant for each other, he said, and nobody (21 *go*) to stand in our way, because our lives (22 *be*) written in the stars.

Then he borrowed £20 from me to pay the bill because he said he (23 *leave*) his wallet at home, and he went off to the toilet, and I never saw him again.

Tenses don't change after present or future reporting verbs, because there is no important change of time.

He **says** he **doesn't** want to play any more. ('I **don't** want ...')
I**'ll tell** her your idea **is** great.

Tenses do not usually change after present perfect reporting verbs, either.
The government **has announced** that taxes **will be** raised.

indirect speech: present situations

Situations that have not changed: if the original speaker was talking about a **present or future situation that is still present or future** when the words are reported, **the tenses may not change** after a past reporting verb.

DIRECT SPEECH	INDIRECT SPEECH
The earth **is** round.	He proved that the earth **is/was** round.
'How old **are** you?' 'What?'	'I asked how old you **are/were**.'
Where **does** she **work**?	I've often wondered where she **works/worked**.
It **will** be windy tomorrow.	They said it **will/would** be windy tomorrow.

1   Imagine these sentences were reported soon after they were said: change them to indirect speech in two different ways.

1   What day is it?   *I asked what day it is.   I asked what day it was.*
2   What's the dark-haired child's name? *(I asked)* what was the dark-haired child name?
3   I'm utterly fed up! *(Are you deaf? I said)* I was utterly fed up
4   It's raining. *(I told you)* it was raining.
5   You'll get your money. *(I said)*
6   The weather is changing. *(This article I was reading said)*
7   The repairs will cost £5,000. *(Al told me)*
8   Is Jane coming to see us? *(I asked)*
9   You're going to the north. *(Pat told me that)*
10 You won't pass your exam. *(I bet George £5 yesterday that)* he wouldn't pass his exam.
11 He hasn't got much sense of humour. *(See – I told you)* he hadn't got much sense of humous.
12 They're getting married next week. *(Sue rang this morning, and she said)* they were getting married next week.

We do not keep the original speaker's tenses if we **do not agree** with what he/she said, or if we want to show that **the ideas do not come from us**.

*They were certain that the gods **lived** in the sky.*
*Did you hear that? She said she **was** fourteen!*
*He announced that profits **were** higher than forecast.*
*I didn't know she **was** ill.*

'Ed Roxey! I didn't know you were dead!'

Drawing by Joseph Farris; © 1994
The New Yorker Magazine, Inc.

indirect speech: questions

Indirect questions normally have the **subject before the verb**.

> *He wanted to know when **I could start**.* (NOT ... ~~when could I start.~~)
> *I asked where **the president and his wife were staying**.*

Do** is **not used in indirect questions, and question marks are not used.

> *I wondered how **they felt**.* (NOT ... ~~how did they feel?~~)

The same structure is used to report the answers to questions.

> *I **knew how they felt**.*
> *Nobody told me **why I had to sign the paper**.*

1   Turn these into indirect questions, beginning *I asked*.

1   What's Peter's address?
2   When's the new manager coming?
3   How does she know my name?
4   Why are all the windows open?
5   How many books does he want?
6   Where do they keep the money?
7   What time is the meeting?
8   When does the last train leave?
9   How does the photocopier work?
10   How often does Ann go shopping?

Yes/no questions are reported with ***if*** or ***whether***.

> *The driver asked **if/whether** I wanted the town centre.*

We prefer ***whether*** before ***or***, especially in a formal style.

> *I enquired **whether** she was coming by road **or** by air.*

2   Turn these into indirect questions, beginning *I wondered*.

1   Do they like me?
2   Will I be ready in time?
3   Is there any food in the house?
4   Is service included or not?
5   Can I pay by cheque?
6   Does my hair look funny?
7   Has the postman been?
8   Do they speak English?
9   Am I doing the right thing?
10   Is the meeting on Tuesday or Wednesday?

indirect speech: infinitives

We use **infinitives** to report sentences about future actions – for example
promises, **agreements**, **orders**, **offers**, **advice**, **suggestions**, **requests**.

*He promised **to write**.*	*She agreed **to wait** for me.*
*I told Andrew **to be** careful.*	*Ann has offered **to baby-sit** tonight.*
*I advise you **to think** again.*	*She asked us **not to be** late.*

The structure **question word + infinitive** is common.
*He asked her **how to make** a white sauce.*
*Don't tell me **what to do**.*

1 Change the sentences as shown.

1   I won't tell anybody. *(He promised)*
    He promised not to tell anybody.
2   I'll cook supper. *(She offered)*
3   Leave early. *(He advised me)*
4   Please close the door. *(She asked me)*
5   I'll stop smoking. *(She promised)*
6   Why don't I do the shopping? *(He offered)*
7   You ought to tell the police. *(She advised me)*
8   Wait outside. *(I told her)*
9   OK, I'll pay half. *(He agreed)*
10 Park round the corner. *(She told me)*
11 How do I find the house? *(I asked him)*
12 Phone me before nine. *(She told me when)*
13 Say you're ill. *(I told him what)*
14 We'll pay for the tickets. *(We offered)*

'I told him to choose his
weapons and be here at six.'

This structure is **not** used after **suggest** or **say**.

*He **suggested trying** somewhere else.* (NOT *He suggested to try* ...)
*The policeman **said I musn't** park there.* (NOT ... *said me not to park* ...)

For explanations of the words that we use to talk about grammar, see pages 298–302.

tell and **say**

Tell and **say** are similar, but there are **differences**. Look at the examples and try to see what they are.

> *I told the assistant that I wanted size 8.* (NOT ~~I told that I wanted size 8.~~)
> *I said that I wanted size 8.*
> *I said to the assistant that I wanted size 8.* (NOT ~~I said the assistant that~~ ...)
>
> *I said to her 'What are you doing?'* (NOT ~~I told her 'What are you doing?'~~)
> *I said 'hello'.* (NOT ~~I told him hello.~~)
>
> *I told him to hurry up.* (NOT ~~I said him to hurry up.~~)

DO IT YOURSELF

1 Choose the correct forms of the rules. Check them in the key.

1 After *(say/tell)*, we normally say **who** is spoken to. We do not put 'to' before the object.
2 After *(say/tell)*, we don't have to say **who** is spoken to. If we do, we put 'to' before the object.
3 *(Say/Tell)* means 'inform' or 'instruct'. It can't introduce questions.
4 *(Say/Tell)* can't normally be used before an infinitive.

2 Put in the correct forms of *say* or *tell*.

1 I _said_ that I wasn't ready.
2 _Tell_ me what you need.
3 Have you _told_ the doctor about it?
4 Did you _say_ something to me?
5 He doesn't _tell_ me anything.
6 Mary _told_ her mother she was going to the office.
7 Why didn't she _say_ goodbye?
8 _Tell_ him to be quiet.
9 Who _said_ that?
10 _Say_ that you won't forget me.

'I did say something, but that was yesterday.'

Tell can be used without a personal object in a few expressions like *tell a lie, tell the truth, tell a story, tell the time.*

indirect speech: special cases

Past tenses are changed to **past perfect** tenses after past reporting verbs, but only if this is necessary in order to make the time relations clear. Compare:

DIRECT SPEECH	INDIRECT SPEECH
I **saw** Penny a couple of days ago.	In his letter, he said he**'d seen** Penny a couple of days before.
Dinosaurs **were** around for 250 million years.	This guy on TV said dinosaurs **were** around for 250 million years.

▲ 1 **Change these to indirect speech.**

1 I saw him once before in London. *(I knew)*
2 Shakespeare didn't speak French. *(The professor said)*
3 He died two years ago. *(When I got there, I found out)*
4 Three thousand years ago there were tigers in England.
   (It said on this TV programme)
5 Somebody threw a bomb at the Prime Minister.
   (It said on this morning's news)
6 The ancient Romans suffered from lead poisoning. *(I read in a magazine)*

Usually unchanged after past reporting verbs: **past perfect**, **had better**, **would**, **could**, **should**, **ought**, **might**, **must**.

DIRECT SPEECH	INDIRECT SPEECH
I **hadn't seen** him before.	She said she **hadn't seen** him before.
You**'d better** go.	He said I**'d better** go.

▲ 2 **Change these to indirect speech.**

1 Would you like a drink? *(She asked me)*
2 I couldn't help it. *(I said)*
3 We should be home about six. *(They thought)*
4 It might rain. *(The forecast said)*
5 She must be joking. *(Everybody said)*
6 I hadn't seen the notice. *(I explained)*

'I thought you'd like to know that the day after you died you won a $22.5 million lottery.'

revision of **indirect speech**

1 Change these sentences to indirect speech (reported some time later).

1 He's ill. *(She thought)*
2 I'll be back tomorrow. *(He said)* He said he ~ would be back the next day.
3 I don't like this music. *(She said)*
4 Where's the bus station? *(She asked me)*
5 Have you finished? *(I asked him)*
6 Nobody loves me. *(I felt)*
7 Do you want tea or coffee? *(He asked her)*
8 I'll clean the flat. *(She offered)*
9 When is the car going to be ready? *(I asked)*
10 What am I doing here? *(I wondered)*
11 The earth is not flat. *(He proved)*
12 These figures can't be right. *(I knew)*
13 Her cat understands everything she says. *(She thought)*
14 What does the boss want? *(I asked)*
15 Did Mary phone back? *(I wondered)*
16 Did dinosaurs lay eggs? *(I wondered)*
17 You ought to see the doctor. *(He advised me)*
18 Would you like a drink? *(She asked him)*

2 Choose the correct forms of the cartoon captions.

'Don't ask me – I thought they *(are / were / would be)* yours.'

DONEGAN

DONEGAN

'Well, now, Swinnerton, no doubt you're wondering *(why did I send / why I sent / why I did send)* for you.'

if: ordinary tense-use

If can be used with **the same tenses as most conjunctions**.

> **If** you **didn't** do much maths at school, you**'ll find** economics difficult.
> **If** that **was** Mary, why **didn't** she **stop** and say hello?
> Oil **floats** if you **pour** it on water.

An *if*-clause can come at the beginning or end of a sentence. When it comes first, it is often separated by a comma (,).

1   Join the beginnings and ends, putting in *if*.

BEGINNINGS	ENDS
anybody asks you what you're doing,	I'll take it back to the shop.
How can you make decisions	you're not feeling up to it.
I buy three kilos,	say you're with me.
I don't get up till nine,	that'll do for a few weeks.
I can't fix the video,	I never get anything done.
I'll go with you	we can catch the early train.
The shops are easy to get to	you want to learn a musical instrument.
We don't have to go out	you don't know what's going on?
you're ready before eight,	you like.
You have to practise	you park near the station.

Note the difference between **if** and **when**.
If: something may happen. **When**: something definitely happens.

2   *If* or *when*?

1 ____ I become President
2 ____ it gets dark
3 ____ the film finishes
4 ____ she passes her exam
5 ____ it doesn't rain tomorrow
6 ____ I wake up tomorrow
7 ____ you change your mind
8 ____ his parents die
9 ____ the bus stops

10   'But are you absolutely sure you saw him take something, because ____ you're wrong ...'

In an ***if*-clause**, we normally use a **present tense** to talk about the **future**. (This happens after most conjunctions – see page 244.)

> ***If*** I **have** *enough time tomorrow, I'll come and see you.*
> (NOT ~~*If I* **will have** ...~~)
> *I'll give her your love* **if** *I* **see** *her.* (NOT ... ~~*if I* **will see** *her.*~~)
> *If it's fine tomorrow, I'm going to paint the windows.*

For cases when we use *will* after *if*, see page 137.

3   Choose the correct tenses (present or *will* ...).

1   If you *(say)* that again, I *(scream)*.
2   I *(be)* surprised if she *(manage)* to sell that car.
3   If the boys *(come)* to supper, I *(cook)* chicken breasts.
4   I *(need)* some money if we *(go)* out tonight.
5   I *(miss)* you if we *(move)* to Wales.
6   If you *(wash)* up, I *(dry)*.
7   Ann *(be)* sorry if Helen *(not come)*.
8   If you *(get)* lonely, I hope you *(phone)* me – any time.
9   If you *(look)* in the top drawer, you *(find)* your passport.
10 It *(be)* funny if Norman *(get)* the job.

4   Complete these sentences any way you like.

1   I'll be surprised if _____.
2   I'll be very happy if _____.
3   I'll be sorry if _____.

▲ **5   Here are a fortune-teller's predictions for a race. Who does she think will win?**

Jake will come first if Howard comes third.
If Howard comes third, Pete will come second.
Pete won't come second if Jake comes first.
Howard will come first if Pete comes third.
Pete will not come third if Jake comes second.
If Jake comes third, Pete will come first.
Howard will come second if Jake comes third.

We sometimes use ***if* ... *then*** to emphasise that one thing depends on another. (Note that we do **not** use ***if* ... *so*** in this way.)

> ***If*** *she can't come to us,* **then** *we'll have to go and see her.*
> (NOT ... ~~**so** *we'll have to go and see her.*~~)

if: special tense-use

With *if*, we can use ***would*** and **past** tenses to 'distance' our language from reality, when we talk about present or future **unreal situations**.

MAIN CLAUSE: WOULD … ('D)	IF- CLAUSE: PAST TENSE

I **would tell** you her name
   (NOT I **will tell** you her name)
	if I **knew** it.
	   (NOT if I **would know** it.)

She**'d be** perfectly happy	if she **had** a car.
What **would** you **do**	if you **lost** your job?

After *I* and *we*, *should* is possible instead of *would*. (*Would* is more common.)
The *if*-clause can come first in the sentence.
> **If I knew her name**, I **should** tell you.

This structure can make a suggestion sound less definite (and so more polite).
> It **would be** nice if you **helped** me a bit with the housework.
> **Would** you **mind** if I **came** round about seven tomorrow?

1   Put in the correct verb forms.

1   The kitchen *(look)* better if we *(have)* red curtains.
2   I *(be)* sorry if we *(not see)* her again.
3   It *(be)* a pity if Andy *(not get)* the job.
4   If I *(know)* his address, I *(go)* round and see him.
5   What *(you do)* if you *(win)* the lottery?
6   It *(be)* quicker if you *(use)* a computer.
7   If you *(not be)* so busy, I *(show)* you how to play.
8   If we *(have)* some eggs, I *(make)* you a cake.
9   If you really *(love)* me, you *(buy)* me those diamonds.
10   I'm sure Moira *(help)* you if you *(ask)* her.
11   If it *(not be)* so cold, I *(tidy)* up the garden.
12   If I *(have)* the keys, I *(show)* you the cellar.
13   If I *(have)* children like hers, I *(send)* them to boarding school.
14   Where *(you go)* if you *(need)* to buy a picture frame?
15   *(you mind)* if I *(go)* first?
16   If all of us *(come)*, *(you have)* room in your car?
17   It *(be)* nice if you *(spend)* some time with the children.
18   I *(not do)* this if I *(not have)* to.

2 What would you do if ...? Here are some people's answers. Can you write the sentences? Example:

1 *If I spoke Chinese, I would go to China.*   2

3   4

5   6

3 If you can work with other students, do drawings like the ones in Exercise 2, and see if they can write the sentences.

> As well as *would*, we can use ***could*** (= 'would be able to') and ***might*** (= 'would perhaps').
>
> *I **could** lend you my car if you wanted.*
> *He **might** change his mind if we talked to him.*

4 Complete these sentences using *could* or *might*.

1 If it wasn't raining, we *(play)* tennis.
2 If she asked me politely, I *(feel)* like helping her.
3 If he wasn't so bad-tempered, I *(go)* out with him.
4 If I had more money, I *(get)* a small flat.
5 If you spoke more slowly, I *(understand)* you better.
6 If you cooked it in butter, it *(taste)* better.

if I go and if I went: the difference

The difference between, for example, *if I go ... I will* and *if I went ... I would* or between *if I speak ...* and *if I spoke ...*, is **not** a difference of **time**. They can both refer to the present or future.
The **past** tense (and *would*) usually suggests that the situation is **less probable**, or **less definite**, or **impossible**, or **imaginary**. Compare:

> *If I **become** President, I'll ...* (said by a candidate in an election)
> *If I **became** President, I'd ...* (said by a schoolgirl)

> *If I **win** this race, I'll ...* (said by the fastest runner)
> *If I **won** this race, I'd ...* (said by the slowest runner)

> *Is it all right if I **invite** John to supper?* (direct request)
> *Would it be all right if I **invited** John to supper?* (polite request)

1   Choose the correct verb forms.

1   If she *(comes/came)* late again, she'll lose her job.
2   I'll let you know if I *(find/found)* out what's happening.
3   If we *(live/lived)* in a town, life would be easier.
4   I'm sure he wouldn't mind if we *(arrive/arrived)* early.
5   *(We'll/We'd)* phone you if we have time.
6   If I won the lottery, I *(will/would)* give you half the money.
7   It *(will/would)* be a pity if she married Fred.
8   If I'm free on Saturday, I *(will/would)* go to the mountains.
9   She *(will/would)* have a nervous breakdown if she goes on like this.
10   I know I'll feel better if I *(stop/stopped)* smoking.

2   Choose the most sensible verb form.

1   If I *(live/lived)* to be 70 ...
2   If I *(live/lived)* to be 150 ...
3   If I *(am/were)* better looking ...
4   If I *(wake/woke)* up early tomorrow ...
5   If Scotland *(declares/declared)* war on Switzerland ...
6   If we *(have/had)* the same government in five years' time ...
7   If everybody *(gives/gave)* ten per cent of their income to charity ...
8   If everybody *(thinks/thought)* like me ...
9   If there *(is/was)* nothing good on TV tonight ...
10   If my English *(is/was)* better next year ...
11   If the government *(bans/banned)* cars from city centres next year ...
12   If I *(have/had)* bad dreams tonight ...

if I were

After *if*, we often use ***were* instead of *was***. In a formal style, *were* is considered more correct.

*If I **were** rich, I would spend all my time travelling.*

1 Put the beginnings and ends together, using *if ... were*. Example:

If he were a better dancer, her feet wouldn't hurt.

BEGINNINGS	ENDS
he / a better dancer	her feet wouldn't hurt.
I / a rabbit	I wouldn't be working.
I / forty years younger	I'd be quite pretty.
I / Moroccan	I'd give everybody ten weeks' holiday.
I / the manager	I'd go dancing all night.
it / not so cold	I'd go for a walk.
it / Sunday	I'd live in a hole.
my nose / shorter	I'd speak Arabic.
people / more sensible	life in the office would be easier.
she / better-tempered	there wouldn't be any wars.

We often use the structure ***I should(n't) ... if I were you*** to **give advice**.

I shouldn't *worry* ***if I were you***.
If I were you, ***I'd*** *get that car serviced.*

2 Write some sentences beginning *If I were you* ... to: other students / your teacher / your mother / your father / your child / the President / the Pope / ...

'Look, I should sit down if I were you. Have you got a drink? Now it's nothing to worry about, really it isn't ...'

if: unreal past situations

With *if*, we use **would have ...** and **past perfect** tenses to 'distance' our language from reality, when we talk about **unreal situations** in the past.

MAIN CLAUSE: WOULD HAVE + PAST PARTICIPLE	IF-CLAUSE: PAST PERFECT TENSE
I **would have been** in bad trouble You **would have passed** your exam	if Jane **hadn't helped** me. if you **had worked** harder. (NOT *If you **would have** worked* ...)

The *if*-clause can come first.

> *If Jane hadn't helped me, I would have been in bad trouble.*

1 Put in the correct verb forms.

1 If I *(know)* you were coming, I *(invite)* some friends in.
2 He *(go)* to university if his father *(not be)* ill.
3 If you *(say)* you weren't hungry, I *(not cook)* such a big meal.
4 The team *(win)* if Jones *(play)* better.
5 If they *(not cut)* off the electricity, I *(finish)* my work.
6 If Bell *(not invent)* the telephone, somebody else *(do)* it.
7 If you *(not spend)* so much time making up, we *(not be)* late.
8 The burglars *(not get)* in if you *(remember)* to lock the door.
9 If he *(not be)* a film star, he *(not become)* President.
10 If she *(have)* more sense, she *(sell)* her car years ago.
11 If he *(not spend)* so much on his holiday, he *(have)* enough to pay for the house repairs.
12 You *(not catch)* cold if you *(take)* your coat.
13 You *(win)* if you *(run)* a bit faster.
14 We *(get)* better tickets if we *(book)* earlier.
15 It *(be)* better if you *(ask)* me for help.
16 'If Cleopatra's nose *(be)* shorter, the whole history of the world *(be)* different.'   *(Pascal)*

Instead of *would have ...*, we can use **could have ...** (= 'would have been able to') and **might have ...** (= 'would perhaps have ...').

> *If he'd run a bit faster, he **could have won**.*
> *If I hadn't been so tired, I **might have realised** what was happening.*

2   Write sentence chains with *if* to show how things could have been different. Example:

1   *If he hadn't worked so hard, he wouldn't have passed his exams. If he hadn't passed his exams, he wouldn't have gone to university. If he hadn't gone to university, ...*

1   He worked hard → passed exams → went to university → studied languages → learnt Chinese → went to China → went climbing in Tibet → tried to climb Everest → disappeared in a snowstorm

2   He bought a bicycle → went for ride in country → fell off → woke up in hospital → met beautiful nurse → wrote bestselling novel about her → got rich → married beautiful nurse and had three charming children → lived happily ever after   *If he hadn't bought a bicycle, ...*

3   Mary's mother went out that evening → Mary cooked for herself → got interested in cooking → opened very successful restaurant → had Prime Minister as customer → PM ordered mussels → mussels poisoned PM → PM died → Mary went to prison for life

3   If you can work with other students, make a sentence chain for them.

This structure is sometimes used to talk about **present and future situations** which are **no longer possible** because of the way things have turned out.

> *If my mother had been alive,* **she would have been eighty next year.**
> (OR *If my mother were alive, she would be ...*)
> *If my mother hadn't knocked my father off his bicycle thirty years ago,*
> **I wouldn't have been here now.** (OR *... I wouldn't be here now.*)

'Just think, I'd have been an old man by now if I'd ever grown up.'

unless

> **Unless** means **'if not'**, in the sense of **'except if'**.
>
> Come tonight **unless** I phone.
>   (= ... **if** I do**n't** phone / ... **except if** I phone.)
> I'll take the job **unless** the pay is too low.
>
> Note that after *unless* we use a present tense to talk about the future.

1   **Join the beginnings and ends together, using *unless* instead of *if not*. Example:**

I'll be back tomorrow unless there's a strike.

BEGINNINGS	ENDS
I'll be back tomorrow	if he doesn't start working.
He'll get thrown out of school	if I don't phone to say I can't come.
I always watch TV in the evenings	if I don't go out.
Let's have dinner out	if it doesn't rain.
I'll see you at ten	if the children don't want it.
I'll tell you a good joke	if there isn't a change of government.
Things will go on getting worse	if there isn't a strike.
We're going to have a picnic	– if you're not too tired.
You can have the last sausage	if you don't know the code.
You can't open the door	– if you haven't heard it before.

> **Unless** is **only** used to mean **'except if'**.
>
> My wife will be upset **if** I do**n't** get back tomorrow.
>   (NOT ~~My wife will be upset unless I get back tomorrow.~~ 'If not' doesn't
>   mean 'except if' here.)

2   **Which of these sentences can be rewritten with *unless*?**

1   I'll be surprised if he doesn't have an accident soon.
2   It will be better if we don't tell her anything.
3   You can have the car tonight if Harriet doesn't need it.
4   I'll tell you if I can't come.
5   I'm going to dig the garden this afternoon if it doesn't rain.
6   She'd look nicer if she didn't wear so much make-up.

in case

We use *in case* to talk about **precautions** – things we do to be **ready for what might happen**. After *in case* we use a **present tense** to talk about the **future**.

> *I've bought a chicken **in case your mother stays to lunch**.*
> *I wrote down her address **in case I forgot it**.*

We can use *should ...* after *in case* – this gives the idea of 'by chance'. *Should* is common in sentences about the past.

> *I've bought a chicken in case your mother **should** stay to lunch.*
> *I wrote down her address in case I **should** forget it.*

1 A woman is packing to go on holiday in Austria. Make sentences:

SHE'S PACKING:
a German phrase book   a pack of cards   a racket
a thick sweater   a swimsuit   aspirins   binoculars
her address book   some books   walking boots

IN CASE:
she decides to send postcards   she has time to read
she meets people who play bridge   she wants to go walking
the hotel has a heated pool   the hotel staff don't speak English
the sun gives her a headache   the weather is cold
there is a tennis court   she wants to go bird-watching

In case is **not** the same as *if*. Compare:

> *I'll buy a bottle of wine (now) **in case** Roger comes (later).*
> *I'll buy a bottle of wine (later) **if** Roger comes (and if he doesn't come I won't).*

2 *If* or *in case*?

1 I'm taking my umbrella with me ____ it rains.
2 I'll open the umbrella ____ it rains.
3 People phone the fire brigade ____ their houses catch fire.
4 People insure their houses ____ they catch fire.
5 We have a burglar alarm ____ somebody tries to break in.
6 The burglar alarm will go off ____ somebody tries to break in.
7 I'll let you know ____ I need help.
8 I'll take the mobile phone ____ I need to phone you.

it's time, **would rather**: structures

Infinitives are possible after ***it's time*** and ***would rather***
(= 'would prefer').
Would rather is followed by an infinitive **without** *to*.

> ***It's time to buy*** *a new car.*   ***It's time*** *for him* ***to go*** *to bed.*
> *She doesn't want to go out.* ***She'd rather stay*** *at home.*

1   **Put the expressions together to make conversations. Example:**

'It's time to go out.' 'I'd rather stay at home.'

IT'S TIME TO

go out.   clean the car.   cook supper.   get a new fridge.
get your hair cut.   go home.   invite the Harrises.
plan our trip to Scotland.   see the dentist.
start work on the garden.

I'D RATHER

stay at home.   go on using the old one for a bit.
have something cold.   invite the Johnsons.   keep it long.
not clean it today.   go to Wales.   see her next year.
start next week.   stay here for a bit longer.

'I'm afraid we've done all we can do. Now it's time to play golf.'

'I often say, Mrs Dent, I'd rather have your little Christopher in my class than all the bright, clever ones!'

In clauses after ***it's time*** and ***would rather***, a **past** tense has a **present** or **future** meaning.

> ***It's time*** *he* **went** *to bed.*   ***It's time*** *you* **washed** *those trousers.*
> *'Shall I open a window?'* ***'I'd rather*** *you* **didn't**.'
> *Don't come today.* ***We'd rather*** *you* **came** *tomorrow.*

2 Write sentences using *It's time you/he/etc.*

1 You ought to clean that car.
 It's time you cleaned that car.
2 She should get her hair cut.
3 We ought to have a holiday.
4 You need to cut the grass.
5 You should wash that sweater.
6 You ought to stop smoking.
7 He ought to grow up.
8 We ought to paint the kitchen.
9 He needs a new car.
10 That team hasn't won a match for ages.

3 Rewrite the *second* **sentence in each conversation, starting with** *I'd rather we/you/etc.*

1 'You'd better phone Judy.' 'No, you phone her.'
 I'd rather you phoned her.
2 'Let's talk things over.' 'No, let's talk tomorrow.'
3 'Shall I come at nine?' 'Ten would be better.'
4 'I'll phone Sue.' 'No, don't.'
5 'Can she work with you?' 'Why doesn't she work with Maggie?'
6 'I'll cook tomorrow.' 'Tonight would be better.'
7 'Ask that policeman.' 'You ask him.'
8 'Mark wants to go out.' 'I'd prefer him to stay in.'
9 'Can they use our sheets?' 'It would be more convenient if they brought their own.'
10 'The government wants to cut taxes.' 'It would be better if they did something about the homeless.'

4 Write a sentence beginning *It's time the government did something for/about* ...

5 The government is planning to build ten new motorways. Write a sentence beginning *I'd rather they spent the money on* ...

wish, **if only**: structures

Wish and **if only** can be used with **would** and **past tenses** (like *if* – see page 258).
These structures express **regrets**, and wishes for **unlikely** or **impossible** things.
If only is more emphatic.
Past tenses are used to talk about the **present**.

> I **wish** I **was** better looking.   I **wish** I **spoke** French.
> Don't you **wish** you **could** fly?   **If only** I **knew** more people!

Were can be used instead of *was*, especially in a formal style.
> He wishes he **were** better looking.

1   Write sentences beginning *I wish* ... or *If only* ...

1	He smokes.	6	I don't like dancing.
	I wish he didn't smoke.	7	It rains all the time.
2	I don't speak Russian.	8	She works on Sundays.
3	I haven't got a car.	9	I can't eat eggs.
4	I'm not hard-working.	10	The radio doesn't work.
5	I'm bad at sport.		

We use **would** ... to talk about things that we **would like people (not) to do**. This often expresses dissatisfaction or annoyance: it can sound **critical**.

> I wish you **would go** home.   If only the postman **would come**!

We can use this structure to talk about things as well as people.
> I wish this damned car **would start**.   If only it **would stop** raining!

2   Write sentences beginning *I wish* ... *would* ...

1   Somebody won't stop talking.
    I wish he would stop talking.
2   It's not snowing.
3   The phone keeps ringing.
4   The baby won't stop crying.
5   The kettle won't boil.
6   The traffic lights won't go green.
7   Your mother hasn't written.
8   Pat hasn't found a job.
9   The exam results haven't come.
10   Spring hasn't come.

3   Write some sentences beginning:

I wish I had ...
If only I could ...
I wish I spoke ...
I wish I knew ...
If only I was ...
I wish I wasn't ...

> We use a **past perfect** tense to express **regrets about the past**.
>
> I wish you **hadn't said** that.
> Now she wishes she **had gone** to university.
> If only she **hadn't told** the police, everything would be all right.

4   Put the beginnings and ends together, using *I wish* + past perfect. Example:

I wish I'd been nicer to my sister when we were kids.

BEGINNINGS	ENDS
(be) nicer to my sister	a better school.
(choose)	a different career.
(do) more travelling	harder at university.
(go) to	last night.
(go) to bed earlier	my teeth.
(not get married)	the truth.
(not tell) him	when I had the chance.
(save) money	when I was eighteen.
(study)	when I was earning a good salary.
(take better care of)	when we were kids.

I WISH I WAS EIGHTEEN AGAIN (1978) (wm) Sonny Throckmorton (P)George Burns.

I WISH I WERE ALADDIN (1935) (wm) Mack Gordon – Harry Revel (I)Film: *Two For Tonight*, by Bing Crosby. (P)Bing Crosby.

I WISH I WERE IN LOVE AGAIN (1937) (w) Lorenz Hart (m) Richard Rogers (I)Musical: *Babes In Arms*, by Grace McDonald and Rolly Pickert. (R)1948 Film: *Words And Music*, by Judy Garland and Mickey Rooney.

I WISH I WERE TWINS (SO I COULD LOVE YOU TWICE AS MUCH) (1934) (w) Frank Loesser – Eddie De Lange (m) Joseph Meyer (P)Fats Waller

I WISH IT WOULD RAIN (1968) (wm) Barrett Strong – Roger Penzabene – Norman Whitefield (P)The Temptations. (CR) Gladys Knight and The Pips.

I WISH IT WOULD RAIN DOWN (1990) (wm) Phil Collins (P)Phil Collins.

I WISH THAT WE WERE MARRIED (1962) (wm) Marion Weiss – Edna Lewis (P) Ronnie and the Hi-Lites.

D and H Jacobs: Who wrote that song?

relative **who**, **which** and **that**

We often join sentences by putting **who** or **which** ('relative pronouns') in place of *he, she, it* or *they*. We use **who** for **people** and **which** for **things**.

> *I've got a friend.* ***He*** *collects stamps.* → *I've got a friend* **who** *collects stamps.*
>   (NOT *...* **who he** *collects stamps.*)
> *There's a problem.* ***It*** *worries me.* → *There's a problem* **which** *worries me.*

1   Join the sentences with *who* or *which*.

BEGINNINGS	ENDS
Do you know a shop?	He lives next door.
I know somebody.	He stole my car.
I want some plates.	He/She deals with exports.
I was at school with the man.	It isn't working.
I'd like to speak to the person.	It needs to be eaten.
She's got friendly with a boy.	It sells good coffee.
The police haven't found the man.	They last for years.
There's some cheese in the fridge.	She could mend that chair.
We've got some light bulbs.	They can go in the microwave.
This is the switch.	He is driving that taxi.

We often use **that** instead of *which*, and instead of *who* in an informal style.

> *There's a problem* **that** *you don't understand.*
> *I know some people* **that** *could help you.* (informal)

2   Rewrite four or more of the sentences from Exercise 1 using *that*.

In place of *him, her, it* and *them* (objects), we can use **who(m)**, **which** or **that**. *Who* is very informal as an object; *whom* is more formal.

> *Where's that nurse? I saw* ***her*** *last time.* → *Where's that nurse* **who(m)/**
>   **that** *I saw last time?* (NOT *...* **who(m) I saw her** *last time.*)
> *These are problems. You don't have* ***them***. → *These are problems* **which/**
>   **that** *you don't have.* (NOT *...* **which you don't have them.**)

For explanations of the words that we use to talk about grammar, see pages 298–302.

3 Do you know the English words for nationalities and languages? Complete the sentences; use a dictionary to help you.

1   The people who live in _Greece_ ____ speak Greek.
2   The language that people speak in Hungary is called ____.
3   The language ____ people speak in China is called ____.
4   The people who live in _Italy_ speak Italian.
5   The ____ live in ____ _Turkey_ Turkish.
6   The language ____ Algeria is called Arabic.
7   The language _Scottish_ ____ Scots Gaelic.
8   The people _of_ ____ Holland _speak Holland_ ____.
9   The language ____ Irish.
10 The people ____ Portugal ____.
11 ____ Welsh.
12 _Japan_ Japan _Japanese_.

4 Write five more sentences like the ones in Exercise 3.

We normally use **that**, not *which*, after **all**, **everything**, **nothing**, **the only** ... and **superlatives**. We do **not** use **what** in these cases.

*I've told you **all that** I know.* (NOT ... ~~**all what** I know.~~)
***The only thing that** matters to me is your happiness.*

5 Join the beginnings and ends.

BEGINNINGS	ENDS
All the poetry	that happened.
At school I learnt nothing	that he wrote was destroyed in a fire.
I've told you everything	that she said made any difference.
Nothing	that was ever made.
It's the best western film	that I could get.
The most useful thing	that was useful to me.
This is the only hire car	that you can do is leave now.
You can have everything	that you want.

After words for **time** and **place**, we can use **when** and **where** as relatives.

*I'll never forget **the day when** I first met you.* (= ... the day **on which** ...)
*Do you know **a shop where** I can find sandals?* (= ... a shop **at which** ...)

leaving out **relative pronouns**

We can **leave out object** pronouns *who(m)*, *which* and *that*.

Where's that nurse I saw last time?
These are problems you don't have.

DO IT YOURSELF

1   In which three sentences do you feel the relative pronoun can be left out?

1   The job **that** he got wasn't very interesting.
2   A woman **who(m)** my sister knows has just bought the house next door.
3   The doctor **who** treated me didn't know what he was doing.
4   I'm sorry for people **who** haven't got a sense of humour.
5   Have you got anything **that** will clean this carpet?
6   Have you got a typewriter **that** I can use?

Which rule is correct? Check your answer in the key.

We can leave out a relative pronoun:
1 when it refers to a person.
2 when it refers to a thing.
3 when it is the subject in its clause.
4 when it is the object in its clause.

▲   **2   Is the relative pronoun the subject or object in these clauses?**

1   That's the woman who lives next door.
2   Our doctor is a person whom I really respect.
3   He had a simple idea which changed the world.
4   I've lost that nice ring which Bill gave me.
5   It's a book that everybody talks about and nobody reads.
6   Once there were three rabbits that lived near a river.
7   That's the man who I wanted to see.
8   An orphan is a child who hasn't got any parents.
9   He keeps telling you things which you already know.
10   They never thanked me for the money that I sent them.

▲   **3   Look again at Exercise 2. Take the sentences in which the relative pronoun is the object, and rewrite them without *who(m)/which/that*.**

For explanations of the words that we use to talk about grammar, see pages 298–302.

▲ **4 Make each pair of sentences into one sentence without using who(m)/which/that.**

1 You asked me to get you a paper. Here's the paper. *(Here's ...)*
2 You recommended a film. We went to see the film, but we didn't think much of it. *(We went ...)*
3 My sister bought a new car last month. The car has broken down four times already. *(The car ...)*
4 You didn't recognise an actor on television last night. The actor was Kiefer Sutherland. *(The actor ...)*
5 Jane had some friends at school. Only a very few of the friends went on to university. *(Only ...)*
6 My father had an operation for his heart problem. The operation was only a partial success. *(The operation ...)*
7 Mark wrote an essay while we were on holiday. The essay has won a prize in the school competition. *(The essay ...)*
8 My daughter brings friends home. Some of the friends look as though they never wash. *(Some of ...)*

'It's really very simple, Miss Everhart. Now you just move the cursor across the screen to the area of the world you wish to destroy.'

Women have their faults
Men have only two:
Everything they say,
Everything they do.

Traditional

Everything I like is either illegal,
immoral or fattening.

Traditional

For relative clauses ending in prepositions (e.g. *That's the girl I told you **about**), see page 290.

what = 'the thing that' etc

We can use **what** to mean **'the thing(s) that'** or **'the stuff that'**.
What is like a **noun + relative pronoun** together.

    What *she said made me angry.*   *I gave him* ***what*** *he needed.*

We don't use *what* after *all*, *everything* or *nothing* (see page 271).
    Everything that *I have is yours.* (NOT ~~*Everything what* ...~~)

1 Join the beginnings and ends using *what*. Examples:

    I'll pay for what I broke.   *What I need is a drink.*

BEGINNINGS	ENDS
I'll pay for	happened to poor Harry?
I need	I broke.
Did you read about	I don't eat.
He just teaches you	I expected.
I want to know	I meant.
The dog can have	is a drink.
The holiday wasn't at all	made me very happy.
They hadn't got	she asked for.
You misunderstood – that isn't	is where's my car gone?
you said	you already know.

'I've already met the tall, dark man. What I'd like to know is, where is he now?'

For emphasising uses of *what*, see page 235.

relative **whose**

We can join sentences by putting **whose** in place of **his**, **her** or **its**. This structure is rather formal.

*I saw a girl. **Her** beauty took my breath away. → I saw a girl **whose** beauty took my breath away.*

*He went to a meeting. He didn't understand **its** purpose. → He went to a meeting **whose** purpose he didn't understand.*

▲ **1 Make sentences with *whose*.**

1 A good builder is *one whose houses don't fall down.*
2 A good parent is one whose _____.
3 A good gardener _____.
4 A good doctor _____.
5 A good writer _____.
6 A good teacher _____.
7 A good tourist guide _____.
8 A good cook _____.

▲ **2 In the Alpine village of Fernalm, everybody is related to everybody else. Can you sort out the four sentences, putting in *whose* where necessary, so as to make everything clear? Example:**

1 Anton, whose brother Fritz ...

1 • Anton,
   • sister Anneliese also helps out in the sports shop
   • brother Fritz helps him run the sports shop
   • lives with Marika
2 • girlfriend Heidrun is an instructor at the ski school
   • Anneliese has a younger brother Max
   • wife Paula works in the restaurant run by Anton's other brother Toni
3 • daughter Liesl runs the pizzeria
   • wife Monika works part-time for the baker down the road, Karsten
   • The person in charge of the ski school at the moment is Klaus
4 • wife Christiane was national ice-dancing champion in her younger days
   • Monika also helps in the bar, the 'Happy Skier', which is run by Erwin
   • uncle Erich runs a hotel, in partnership with Klaus's brother Paul

non-identifying **relative clauses**

> Some relative clauses **identify** – they say **which** person or thing, or **what kind of** person or thing, you are talking about. Others **do not identify**.

1 Look at the following pairs of sentences. Which relative clauses identify – the ones in the 'a' sentences or those in the 'b' sentences? Check your answers in the key.

1 a The woman **who/that does my hair** has just had a baby.
   b Dorothy, **who does my hair,** has just had a baby.
2 a She married a man **(that/who/whom) she met on a bus**.
   b She married a nice architect from Belfast, **whom she met on a bus**.
3 a Have you got a book **that's really easy to read**?
   b I lent him *The Old Man and the Sea*, **which is really easy to read**.
4 a What did you think of the wine **(that) we drank last night**?
   b I poured him a glass of wine, **which he drank at once**.

2 Look at Exercise 1 again and answer the questions. Check your answers in the key.

1 Without the relative clauses, which make more sense – the 'a' sentences or the 'b' sentences?
2 Non-identifying relative clauses (in the 'b' sentences) have commas (,,). Why do you think this is?
3 In which kind of clause can we use *that* instead of *who(m)* or *which*?
4 In which kind of clause can we leave out a relative pronoun when it is the object?
5 Do you think non-identifying clauses are more common in a formal or an informal style?

▲ **3 Change *who/whom/which* to *that*, or leave it out, if possible.**

1 This is Peter Taylor, who works with my sister.
2 People who don't answer letters annoy me.
3 What happened to the oranges which I bought yesterday?
4 This room, which isn't used any more, belonged to our eldest son.
5 My Uncle Sebastian, who has always been a bit of a traveller, has just gone off to Thailand.
6 We live in a village called Netherwold, which has 150 inhabitants.
7 I like a film which has a beginning, a middle and an end – in that order.
8 I've had a card from Sally, who used to live next door.

9 Do you remember those people who we met in Corfu?

10 We had some good advice from Mr Blenkinsop, whom we consulted about investments.

11 She took twelve aspirins, which is six times the normal dose.

12 He published a book called *Asleep in the Bath*, which nobody ever read.

Note the use of **which** to refer to a whole clause. Compare:

> The dentist pulled out **the teeth which/that** were causing the trouble.
> ('Which/that' just refers to 'the teeth'.)
> **The dentist had to pull out two of my teeth, which** was a real pity.
> ('Which' refers to the whole clause before: 'The dentist ... teeth'.)

Note that *what* cannot be used in this way.

> He got the job, **which** surprised us all. (NOT ... **what** surprised us all.)

▲ **4 Put in *which* or *what*.**

1 She cycles to work every day, ____ keeps her healthy.

2 I very much liked ____ you said at the meeting.

3 They gave me ____ I asked for.

4 The lights suddenly went out, ____ frightened Granny terribly.

5 This is ____ I need.

6 Everybody arrived late, ____ didn't surprise me in the least.

7 The door was locked, ____ was a nuisance.

8 He wouldn't tell me ____ I wanted to know.

9 She let me borrow one of her dresses, ____ was very kind of her.

10 We're going to have to repair the roof, ____ will cost a fortune.

AUGUST 5 1950

The women's Channel swim record was broken today by an American woman, who cut an hour off the time set 24 years ago. Florence Chadwick had

---

September 9 1971

GEOFFREY JACKSON, the 56-year-old British Ambasador to Uruguay, who has been held captive for eight months by the left-wing Tupamaros guerrillas, was released tonight.

January 16 1979

THE SHAH of Iran fled from his capital today, driven into exile by supporters of Ayatollah Khomeini, who has master-minded the downfall of the 'Peacock Throne' from his own exile in Paris.

JANUARY 25 1971

PRESIDENT MILTON OBOTE of Uganda, who has been attending the Commonwealth conference in Singapore, has been overthrown by his army commander, General Idi Amin, who accused Obote of

---

December 8 1980

JOHN LENNON, who as one of the Beatles helped shape the music and philosophies of a generation, was shot dead late tonight outside the Dakota Building, his home in New York.

reduced **relative clauses**

We sometimes **leave out *who/which/that* + *is/are/was/were***.

*Do you know that man **standing near the door?***
    (= ... **who is standing** ...)
*The man **accused of the killing** said that he was at the cinema at the time.*
    (= The man **who was accused** ...)
*Letters **posted before twelve noon** will usually be delivered by the
    next day.*

▲ **1 Change the sentences as shown in the examples.**

Paper that is made from rice is sometimes used for stationery.
Paper made from rice is sometimes used for stationery.

1   Who's that good-looking man who is talking to Alison?
2   Luggage that is left unattended will be taken away by police.
3   Left-handed children who are forced to write with their right hands often
    develop psychological problems.
4   The nurse who is looking after my aunt is very kind to her.
5   All the rubbish that is floating in the sea is a real danger to health.
6   Ham which is made in the traditional way costs more, but tastes better.
7   Women tourists who are wearing trousers are not allowed in the temple.
8   James thought that the man who was with his girlfriend was her brother.
9   The man who was bitten by my neighbour's dog was her husband's boss.

▲ **2 Join the sentences without using *who/which/that*. Example:**

There was a man. The man was seen running from the burning
building.
There was a man seen running from the burning building.

1   I keep having a dream in which there's a woman. The woman is
    standing with her back to me.
2   James says he heard a shot. The shot was fired in the street.
3   Are those your trousers? The trousers are hanging over the balcony.
4   They live in a beautiful old house. The house was built 300 years ago.
5   The Navajo are famous for beautiful jewellery. The jewellery is made of
    silver and turquoise.
6   Passengers are asked to keep behind the yellow line. The passengers are
    standing on Platform 2.
7   Pauline has a very strange old painting of a woman. The woman is
    holding a small dog.

relatives: revision

1   Put in *which*, *what* or *that*.

1   He spoke very fast, _which_ made it hard to understand him.
2   Thanks, but that's not _____ I wanted.
3   I'll tell you something _____ will surprise you.
4   I did _____ I could.
5   I did everything _____ I could.
6   She kept falling over, _____ made everybody laugh.
7   He's a university professor, _____ is hard to believe.
8   You can have anything _____ you want.
9   Her sense of humour – that's _____ attracts people to her.
10 He said nothing _____ made sense.

▲ **2   (a) Put in nothing at all, or (b) if that is not possible, put in *that*, or (c) if that is not possible, put in *who(m)* or *which*.**

1   This is Ann Hargreaves, _who_ runs the bookshop.
2   Have you heard about the problems _(that)_ Joe's having at work?
3   Never buy yourself anything _that_ eats.
4   I don't like people _____ can't laugh at themselves.
5   We took the M4 motorway, _____ goes straight to Bristol.
6   I'll never forget the first film _____ I saw.
7   Harry Potter, _____ writes detective stories, lives in our street.
8   I think this is the best holiday _____ we've ever had.
9   I'm looking for something _____ will clean leather.
10 We planted some birch trees, _____ grow tall very quickly.

3   Put the quotations together.

'I'll discuss it with you,' she said, in a voice	borrow your watch and tell you what time it is, then walk off with your watch. *Robert Townsend*
A politician is a statesman	can be taught. *Oscar Wilde*
Any man who hates dogs and babies	can't be all bad. *L Rosten on W C Fields*
Anyone who has been to an English public school	that could have been used to defrost her refrigerator. *Rex Stout*
Consultants are people who	what he never had. *Izaak Walton*
No man can lose	who approaches every question with an open mouth. *Adlai Stevenson*
Nothing that is worth knowing	will feel comparatively at home in prison. *Evelyn Waugh*

reading **relative clauses**

Relative clauses can make sentences **more difficult to read**.

*A 36-year-old teacher **who was arrested in Cardiff after trying to set
fire to a school** is said to have seriously injured two policemen.*
*The financial problems **which some of the company's branches have
been facing over the last eighteen months** are mainly caused by
increased foreign competition.*

DO IT YOURSELF

**1   Why do the relative clauses make the above sentences harder to
read? Check your answer in the key.**

1   They separate the subject from the object.
2   They separate the subject from the verb.
3   They separate the verb from the object.

When **relative pronouns are left out**, this can make reading difficult.

*The woman Barbara was out shopping with that Tuesday afternoon was her
stepmother. (= The woman **that** Barbara was out shopping with ...)*

▲   **2   Make these sentences easier to read by adding
who(m)/which/that.**

1   The earrings he gave her for Christmas must have cost at least £500.
2   The fax he got that morning was addressed to someone else.
3   The sofa we bought last year is falling to pieces already.
4   The people he had hoped to introduce Lee to were not there.
5   The flat the terrorists hid the guns in was owned by an MP.
6   The song she could not remember the name of was *Rambling Boy*.

Relative clauses can put together **nouns and verbs that do not belong
together**.

*The hair of the young woman sitting next to me on **the park bench was
purple**. (It was not the park bench that was purple.)*
*The picture that I put in **Helen's room needs cleaning**.*
  (It's not the room that needs cleaning.)

▲ 3   **Read the sentences and answer the questions.**

1   The rosebush Sue gave to my little sister is growing beautifully.
    (Who or what is growing?)
2   The two tall men we saw with Duncan and Jack were their nephews.
    (Who are the uncles and who are the nephews?)
3   The man my mother was working for before she met my father was very
    intelligent, but also very disorganised. *(Who was disorganised?)*
4   A woman who lives near my sister has just won the national lottery.
    (Has my sister won the lottery?)
5   The newspaper which first made contact with the kidnappers telephoned
    the police immediately. *(Who telephoned?)*
6   Police called to a house in Aston, Hampshire, after neighbours reported
    cries for help found 18-year-old J... E... stuck in a cat-flap after being
    locked out of his home. *(Who found him?)*

▲ 4   **Here are the ends of some sentences. Find the beginnings in
      the box.**

1   Spain taught me things about myself I had never suspected.
2   my wedding was bought in a little shop in Bath.
3   my parents' home was the nicest place I've ever lived in.
4   the airport in Memphis was going to Italy to collect a tiger for a zoo.
5   my little cousin Pam had crazy plans for an expedition to the North Pole.

> A very ordinary-looking woman I got talking to at
> A man I met by chance on a business trip to
> Some Polish people I was introduced to by
> The dress my sister wore to
> The little flat that I rented just after I left

▲ 5   **Can you write some beginnings for these endings?**

1   _____ my brother had rain coming through the roof.
2   _____ the green armchair is Emma's boyfriend.
3   _____ me doesn't work.

> **Reduced relative clauses** (see page 278) can be hard to read. Some
> examples:
>
> *Most of **the people arrested** had been in trouble before.*
>   (= ... ***the people who were arrested** ...*)
> *Three quarters of **those questioned** wanted more money.*
>   (= ... ***those who were questioned** ...*)
> ***Three children found** sleeping in Abbey Park late last night were taken to a*
>   *foster home by social workers.*
>   (= ... ***children who were found** ...*)
> *A lot of **the buildings designed** by architects don't take young children.*

whoever, no matter who etc

We can use **whoever** to mean **'it doesn't matter who'**, 'anybody who' or 'the person who'.

> **Whoever** told you that was lying.
> **Whoever** comes to the door, tell them I'm out.
> I'm not opening the door, **whoever** you are.

Whatever, whichever, whenever, wherever and however are used in similar ways. Present tenses are used to talk about the future after these words.
> **Whatever** you do, I'll always love you. (NOT ~~Whatever you'll do~~ ...)
> **Whichever** of them you marry, you'll have problems.
> I try to see Vicky **whenever** I go to London.
> **Wherever** he **goes**, he'll find friends.
> **However** much he eats, he never gets fat.

1 Put in *whoever, whatever* etc.

1 _____ you marry, make sure he can cook.
2 Keep calm, _____ happens.
3 You'll be very welcome, _____ day you come.
4 The people in Canada were friendly _____ we went.
5 You can stay with us _____ you like.
6 _____ many times you say that, I won't believe you.
7 I'll marry _____ I like.
8 _____ you explain it to her, she's still going to be angry.
9 It's certain to be a good game, _____ wins.
10 _____ I try to talk to her she goes out of the room.

'Well, wherever he is, he's just dug up two dozen snowdrops!'

▲ **2 Rewrite the following sentences using *whoever*, *whatever* etc.
Example:**

I don't know who directed this film, but it's not much good.
Whoever directed this film, it's not much good.

1 Send it to the person who pays the bills.
2 The thing that is in that box is making a very funny noise.
3 People always want more, it doesn't matter how rich they are.
4 It doesn't matter how you travel, it'll take you at least three days.
5 You can say what you like, I don't think he's the right man for you.
6 Use which room you like, but make sure you clean it up afterwards.
7 It doesn't matter what problems you have, you can always come to me
   for advice.
8 The person who phoned just now was very polite.
9 Any time I see you I feel nervous.
10 It doesn't matter what you do; I'll love you.

We can use ***no matter who/what/when*** etc in the same way as
whoever etc.

> ***No matter*** who comes to the door, tell them I'm out.

---

3 Put in *no matter who/what/etc.*

1 _____ you do, I'll always believe in you.
2 _____ he goes, he'll find friends.
3 _____ hard he tries, he always gets everything wrong.
4 _____ you say, I know I'm right.
5 _____ we go away, Paul won't be able to come with us.
6 _____ many times I tell them, they forget.

Whether ... or ... can be used to mean 'It doesn't matter whether ... or ...'.

> ***Whether*** we go by bus ***or*** train, it'll take at least six hours.
> I'm staying ***whether*** you like it ***or*** not.

---

4 Put the sentences together.

Whether he's lying	or an expert,	it's a wonderful story.
Whether we tell her now	or cross-country,	she's not going to be pleased.
Whether you're a beginner	or dislike her,	the equipment costs a lot.
Whether you ski downhill	or later,	you have to admire her.
Whether you like her	or telling the truth,	you'll learn something from the course.

prepositions with verbs, nouns etc

1 **Test yourself. See if you know what preposition is needed with each of these words. (Write '–' if no preposition is used.)**

1 Don't **approach** ____ the dog.
2 I **arrived** ____ the station at six.
3 If you don't know, **ask** ____ John.
4 She's very **good** ____ languages.
5 **Congratulations** ____ your success.
6 The bus **crashed** ____ a tree.
7 It all **depends** ____ the weather.
8 I'd like **details** ____ your courses.
9 Let's **discuss** ____ your plans.
10 I **divided** the cake ____ three parts.
11 Why is she **dressed** ____ black?
12 Nobody **entered** ____ the room.
13 This is an **example** ____ his work.
14 There is no **increase** ____ prices.
15 I'm **interested** ____ most sports.
16 He was very **kind** ____ her.
17 The soup **lacks** ____ salt.
18 I'm **looking** ____ a place to live.
19 He has to **look** ____ his mother.
20 My sister is **married** ____ a builder.
21 She **married** ____ him last year.
22 He wasn't very **nice** ____ me.
23 Have you **paid** ____ the drinks?
24 We need **proof** ____ his story.
25 What's the **reason** ____ the change?
26 You **remind** me ____ your brother.
27 Who's **responsible** ____ security?
28 I didn't **take part** ____ the meeting.
29 Could you **translate** this ____ Greek?
30 That's just **typical** ____ you.
31 I'm reading a novel ____ **Dickens**.
32 ____ **my opinion** you're wrong.
33 Who's the man ____ **the picture**?
34 I love walking ____ **the rain**.
35 Don't talk ____ that silly **voice**.
36 The answer's ____ **page 29**.

DO IT YOURSELF

2 **Look at the examples and complete the rule for the use of *at*, *in* and *on* to talk about time. Check your answers in the key.**

in 1976   in June
in the morning   at 4.15
at lunchtime   on Sunday
on Monday afternoon
at Christmas   at the weekend

Rule

____ + clock time
____ + part of a day
____ + part of a particular day
____ + particular day
____ + weekend, public holiday
____ + longer period

3 **Only one of these expressions has a preposition. Which one?**

1 I'll see you ____ next Monday.
2 I'm not free ____ this Thursday.
3 Tell me ____ what time it starts.
4 The exam's ____ my birthday.
5 Let's meet ____ one weekend.
6 I train ____ every day.
7 She phoned ____ this evening.

4 **Put in *at*, *in*, *on* or – .**

1 ____ Easter
2 ____ Tuesday
3 ____ 1994
4 ____ the evening
5 ____ Friday evening
6 ____ May
7 ____ next Wednesday
8 I don't know ____ what time
9 ____ supper time
10 ____ this Sunday
11 ____ that afternoon
12 ____ Sunday afternoon

at/in and **to**

1 **Look at the examples, and complete the rule with words from the box. Check your answers in the key.**

*I met her **at** a concert.*   *Let's go **to** a concert.*
*He's **in** London.*   *I sent it **to** London yesterday.*

Rule
At and *in* are used for ____.   *To* is used for ____.

distance	experience	intentions	movement
position	time		

If we say **what we do** in a place **before** we say **where we go**, we use **at/in** with the place. Compare:

*Let's **go to Marcel's** for coffee.*
*Let's go and **have coffee at Marcel's**.* (NOT *... **to Marcel's.***)

2 **Do you know which of these verbs can be followed by *at + person*?**

ask	call	laugh	look	phone	point	shoot
smile	speak	talk	walk	wave	write	

You can *shout at* or *to* somebody; you can *throw something at* or *to* somebody. Do you know the difference?

3 **Put in the correct preposition.**

1 I've spent the day ____ York.
2 Why don't you take Joe ____ the cinema?
3 Your key's ____ the reception desk.
4 We usually meet ____ the pub.
5 They're delivering the furniture ____ my flat on Tuesday.
6 What's the easiest way to get ____ Bristol?
7 Stop shouting ____ me.
8 Throw the keys down ____ me and I'll let myself in.
9 Let's throw snowballs ____ Mrs Anderson.
10 Can you shout ____ Paul and tell him it's supper time?
11 When you smile ____ me like that I'll do anything for you.
12 Promise you'll write ____ me every day.
13 I went ____ Canada to see my father.
14 I went to see my father ____ Canada.

by and **until**

1 Look at the examples, and put together the best explanations of how to use *by* and *until*. Check your answers in the key.

> *'Can you repair my watch if I leave it **until** Saturday?'*
> *'No, but we can do it **by** next Tuesday.'*
> *You can have the car **until** this evening.*
> *But you must bring it back **by** six o'clock at the latest.*

By is used ***Until*** is used	1 to say that **a situation will continue up to** a certain moment. 2 to say that **something will happen around** a certain time. 3 to say that **something will happen at or before** a certain moment.

In an informal style we often use ***till*** instead of *until*.

2 Complete the sentences with *by* or *until*.

1 'Can I stay ＿＿ the weekend?'
2 'Yes, but you'll have to leave ＿＿ Monday midday at the latest.'
3 This form must be returned ＿＿ April 17.
4 We'll just have to wait ＿＿ he's ready to see us.
5 The books have got to go back to the library ＿＿ Tuesday.
6 Do you think you can finish the painting ＿＿ Easter?
7 'Can I borrow your raincoat?' '＿＿ when?'
8 You ought to use this meat ＿＿ tomorrow.
9 There won't be any trees left ＿＿ the year 2050.
10 She went on screaming ＿＿ somebody came.

Before a **verb**, we can use ***by the time***. (For *until* before a verb, see p. 238.)

> *He'll be gone **by the time** we get home.*

'And returned by one o'clock.
I go to lunch then.'

for and **during**

1 **Look at the examples. Which word tells you *how long* and which word tells you *when*? Check your answers in the key.**

> *My father was in hospital **for** six weeks **during** the summer.*
>   (NOT ... ***during*** *six weeks* ...)
> *It rained **during** the night **for** two or three hours.*

2 **Put in *for* or *during*.**

1 Drinks will be served _____ the interval.
2 I'll come and see you _____ a few minutes _____ the afternoon.
3 They met _____ the war.
4 He said nothing _____ a long time.
5 I woke up several times _____ the night.
6 She studied in America _____ two years.

opposite and **in front of**

1 **Look at the picture. Which is *opposite* the house – the bus stop or the car? Which is *in front of* the house? Check your answers in the key.**

2 **Put in *opposite* or *in front of*.**

1 There's a supermarket _____ my house.
2 _____ me in the queue there was a very strange-looking woman.
3 I can't see the TV if you stand _____ it.
4 The lifts are directly _____ the reception desk.
5 Somebody's parked _____ my garage door, and I can't get my car out.
6 She sat down _____ me and started talking to me.

between and among

1 Look at the examples and complete the rules. Check these in the key.

> *She was standing **between** Alice and Mary.*
> *Our house is **between** the woods, the river and the village.*
> *His house is hidden **among** the trees.*
> *We were in a little valley **between** high mountains.*

RULES
We say _____ a group, crowd or mass of things that are not seen separately.
We say _____ two or more clearly separate people or things.
We say _____ things on two sides.

2 Look at the diagrams. Is X *between* or *among* the other things?

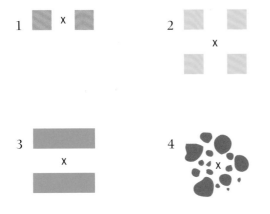

3 Put in *between* or *among*.

1 I saw something _____ the wheels of the car.
2 She was standing _____ a crowd of children.
3 We'll come and see you some time _____ Christmas and Easter.
4 I found the letter hidden away _____ some old photographs.
5 This is just one problem _____ many.
6 Switzerland lies _____ France, Germany, Austria and Italy.
7 I couldn't see Lily _____ the visitors.
8 The ball hit him directly _____ the eyes.
9 The lift got stuck _____ two floors of the hotel.
10 She stood there _____ piles of suitcases looking for a taxi.

prepositions at the **end of questions**

> **Prepositions** often come **at the end of questions**.
> *With whom ...?, For what ...?* etc are unusual and very formal.
> We usually prefer **Who ... with?**, **What ... for?** etc.

1   **Write questions for these answers, using 'Who ...?' or 'What ...?'**
      Example:

   'I went with my sister.'   *'Who did you go with?'*

   1   'I'm thinking about my exams.'   6   'She hit him with her shoe.'
   2   'I bought it from Janice.'   7   'My father works for Shell Oil.'
   3   'She sent it to the police.'   8   'I made it for you.'
   4   'I'll carry it in a paper bag.'   9   'The book's about Egypt.'
   5   'You can eat it with a spoon.'   10   'I was talking to Patrick.'

2   **Write questions for these answers, using 'Who ...?' or 'What ...?'**
      Example:

   'Soup.' *(start)*   *'What are we starting with?'*

   1   'A bus.' *(wait)*   6   'A strange bird.' *(look)*
   2   'The future.' *(worried)*   7   'My keys.' *(look)*
   3   'Films.' *(talking)*   8   'Travel and music.' *(interested)*
   4   'The manager.' *(speak)*   9   'My mother.' *(write)*
   5   'Universal Export.' *(work)*   10   'Life.' *(think)*

3   **Make questions with some of these words and expressions, using**
      'What ... you ...?' or 'Who ... you ...?'. Example:

   What/Who are you looking at?   OR   *... looking for?*

looking   waiting   listening   play tennis   country
letter   get it   have lunch   buy that car   in love
change your job   studying English

> Note the common structure **Where ... to/from?**
>
> **Where** *should I send it* **to?**
> *'***Where** *do you come* **from?** */* **Where** *are you* **from?**' *'Canada.'*

prepositions in relative clauses

In relative clauses (after *who, whom, which, that*), **verb + preposition** combinations usually **stay together**. This means that prepositions can be separated from their relative pronoun objects.

	OBJECT		VERB + PREPOSITION
something	*(that)*	*you can*	**write with**
the girl	*(whom)*	*I was*	**talking about**
the music	*(which)*	*we*	**listened to**

Prepositions can also go before their objects, but this is usually very formal.
*something **with which** you write   the girl **about whom** I was talking*
*the music **to which** she listened*

1 Join the beginnings and ends to make sensible sentences.

BEGINNINGS	ENDS
A cup is	something that a child plays with.
A picture is	something that water comes out of.
A tap is	something that you can look at.
A toy is	something that you can look through.
A vase is	something that you drink out of.
A window is	something that you put flowers in.

2 Put the words in order. Which description goes with which picture?

1 bite you with things that
2 in something you sleep that
3 on you that something put things
4 valuables in you that put something
5 teeth with you that thing a your clean
6 on a thing hang that clothes you
7 with liquid dishes you wash that
8 can a fire start with you that something

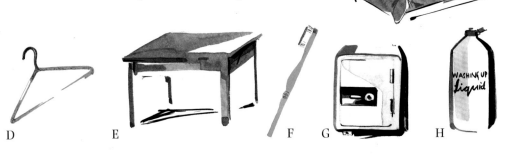

3   Make up similar descriptions for six or more of these things.

a key	a purse	a chair	a fridge	soap
furniture polish	olive oil	a knife	a razor	a gun
a notebook	a cooker	money		

4   Make these expressions less formal.

1   the people with whom we went on holiday
    the people we ...   OR   *the people that we ...*
2   a man with whom I sometimes play chess
    a man I ...   OR   *a man that I ...*
3   somebody for whom I have great respect
4   the girl to whom I was writing
5   the problem about which I was worried
6   a car for which I paid too much

**5   Look at the table, and then write some descriptions ending in
     prepositions. Examples:**

John is the man that Bill plays chess with.
Sue is the woman Ron is married to.

NAME	PLAYS CHESS WITH	IS MARRIED TO	WORKS WITH
Bill	John	Alice	Anne
Ron	Anne	Sue	Mary
Peter	Alice	Anne	Sue
Sally	Mary	John	Alice

'We're planning a small dinner party. Do you have
any vegetables no one's heard of yet?'

prepositions in passive clauses

In passive structures, **verb + preposition** groups **stay together**. Compare:

ACTIVE: *The doctors **operated on** her yesterday morning.*
PASSIVE: *She was **operated on** yesterday morning.*

1 Take words from each box to complete the sentences. More than one answer may be possible.

heard	looked	operated	paid	played	sat	slept
spoken	talked					

about	at	for	from	in	of	on	to	with

1 She was taken into hospital today, and she's going to be ＿＿ tomorrow.
2 I don't like being ＿＿ behind my back.
3 The new secretary's working very badly. He'll have to be ＿＿.
4 I don't think he came home last night. His bed hasn't been ＿＿.
5 That antique chair's not really meant to be ＿＿.
6 It's not really our house yet. It hasn't been ＿＿.
7 He left for America in 1980, and he hasn't been ＿＿ since.
8 The cat loves being ＿＿.
9 He's so shy: it even upsets him to be ＿＿.

2 Make three or more questions from the following table.

Who was	America Australia the novel *Anna Karenina* *Hamlet* *Happy Birthday to You* penicillin radio television electricity the film *The Birds* the Eiffel Tower the Taj Mahal the Mona Lisa ('La Gioconda')	built composed directed discovered invented painted written	by?

3 If you are in a class, write more questions like the ones in Exercise 2 and ask other students.

For explanations of the words that we use to talk about grammar, see pages 298–302.

preposition after **adjective** + **infinitive**

Prepositions come **after infinitives** in structures like:

*She's **easy to work with**.   He's **interesting to talk to**.*

1 **Change the sentences. Example:**

It's easy to work with Jane. ➜ *Jane's easy to work with.*

1   It's nice to talk to her.
2   It's difficult to live with him.
3   It's impossible to argue with my brother.
4   It's not very pleasant to travel in those old trains.
5   It's not easy to drive on ice.
6   It was difficult to swim across the river.
7   It's hard to get to her village.
8   It's very easy to get on with him.
9   It's difficult to paint with water-colours.
10   It's interesting to work with her.

2 **Join beginnings, middles and ends to make six or more sentences.**

BEGINNINGS	MIDDLES	ENDS
A broken cup is	boring	to listen to.
A broken fork is	comfortable	to sit on.
A cushion is	difficult	to eat with.
A small hard chair is	hard	to talk about.
A warm bath is	interesting	to drink out of.
Baby animals are	nice	to listen to.
Classical music is	uncomfortable	to talk to.
Family problems can be		to lie in.
Lectures are often		to play with.
People who travel a lot can be		to sit on.

3 **Using this structure, what can you say about the following?**

a very small spoon   shoes that are too small
a hard bed   a noisy hotel room   a broken pencil

numbers

A *hundred*, **a** *thousand* etc are less formal than **one** *hundred* etc. Compare:

> *I'll let you have it for* **a hundred** *pounds.*
> *We are prepared to sell the item for a sum of* **one hundred** *pounds.*

We use *one hundred* etc when we wish to sound precise.
> *It costs exactly* **one hundred** *dollars.*

We use *one*, not *a*, just before another number or inside a larger number.
> 1,300: **one** *thousand, three hundred* (NOT ~~a thousand, three hundred~~)
> £1.70: **one** *pound seventy*
> *six thousand,* **one** *hundred and eleven* (NOT ~~six thousand, a hundred~~ ...)

1   Write the figures in words.

1   We drove about 100 miles.
2   He wants £1,450 for the car.
3   'What's the population of your village?' 'Oh, 1,000, I suppose.'
4   3,144
5   $1.85
6   *(on a cheque):* Pay G S Hallam £1,000 only

Dozen, **hundred**, **thousand** and **million** have **no -s** after a number, *few* or *several*.

> *three* **dozen** *bottles* (NOT ~~three dozens (of) bottles~~)
> *a few* **hundred** *times*
> *six* **thousand** *miles*
> *several* **million** *pounds*

In other cases we use *dozens (of)*, *hundreds (of)* etc.
> *We've got* **dozens of** *bottles.*
> *He's done it* **hundreds of** *times.*
> *She made* **millions** *in the property market.*

2   Put in *dozen(s) (of)*, *hundred(s) (of)*, *thousand(s) (of)* or *million(s) (of)*.

1   He had to sign his name five ____ times. *(hundred)*
2   We export 40 ____ tons a year. *(million)*
3   I just need to borrow a few ____ pounds. *(hundred)*
4   I've told you ____ times. *(million)*
5   ____ refugees are flooding into the country. *(thousand)*
6   Could I have two ____ eggs? *(dozen)*

3   Do you know how to spell ordinal numbers? Write these in words.

1st *first*   2nd   3rd   4th   5th   6th   7th   8th
9th   10th   12th   16th   20th   21st   30th
100th   1000th

We use **ordinal numbers** to say the names of **Kings**, **Queens** and **popes**.

Henry the **Eighth**   *Elizabeth the* **Second**   *Pius the* **Twelfth**

'I'm afraid you've got the wrong number. This is Louis XV.'

WRITING DATES: 30 March 1995; 10 June 1980
SAYING DATES: *the thirtieth of March / March the thirtieth, nineteen ninety-five*
                   the tenth of June / June the tenth, nineteen eighty

---

4   Change these from written to spoken or from spoken to written form.

1   the tenth of April, nineteen ninety-six   4   16 May 1970
2   September the seventeenth, nineteen eleven   5   12 March 1993
3   the sixteenth of June, nineteen seventy-nine   6   14 January 1986

Telephone numbers are usually said one number at a time.

3174522: *three one seven four five two two* (OR *... double two*)
20645: *two oh* (OR *zero*) *six four five*

---

5   Write the following all in words:

1   your telephone number
2   your date of birth
3   the approximate population of your home village/town and your country

contractions

Contractions like **she's**, **isn't** represent the pronunciation of informal speech.
They are common and correct in **informal writing**, but unusual in formal writing.

AFFIRMATIVE CONTRACTIONS: PRONOUN+ 'M, 'RE, 'S, 'VE, 'D, 'LL	NEGATIVE CONTRACTIONS: AUXILIARY VERB / BE + N'T	
I am → I'm	are not → aren't	shall not → shan't
we are → we're	is not → isn't	would not → wouldn't
she is → she's	have not → haven't	should not → shouldn't
he has → he's	has not → hasn't	cannot → can't
I have → I've	had not → hadn't	could not → couldn't
you had → you'd	do not → don't	might not → mightn't
you would → you'd	does not → doesn't	must not → mustn't
they will → they'll	did not → didn't	ought not → oughtn't
	will not → won't	need not → needn't

With *be*, two negative forms are common: *you're not* or *you aren't*, *she's not*
or *she isn't* etc. With other verbs, the forms with *n't* are more common.
Am not is contracted to **aren't** only in questions.
  I'm late, **aren't** *I?* BUT *I'm not ready.* (NOT ~~I aren't ready.~~)

The contraction **'s** (= *is* or *has*) can be written after pronouns, nouns,
question words, *there* and *here*.
  It's *late.*   *Your* **father's** *gone home.*   **How's** *everything?*
  There's *the phone.*   **Here's** *your money.*

The contractions *'re, 've, 'd* and *'ll* are normally only written after pronouns.

1 Rewrite these sentences using contractions.

1	I am tired.	10	My car has broken down.
2	She is French.	11	You need not worry.
3	She has forgotten.	12	I cannot swim.
4	They have finished.	13	The door will not close.
5	I thought you had left.	14	It does not matter.
6	We will tell you tomorrow.	15	I have not forgotten.
7	I wish he would stop.	16	I am not sorry.
8	How is your mother?	17	Why are you not in bed?
9	Nobody is perfect.	18	Do you not like this?

For explanations of the words that we use to talk about grammar, see pages 298–302.

Affirmative contractions are **not usually stressed**. When an affirmative auxiliary verb is stressed (for example at the end of a sentence) we don't use a contraction. Compare:

'**You're** late.' 'Yes, **we are**.' (NOT ~~'Yes, **we're**.'~~)
'**He's** forgotten.' 'I think **he has**.' (NOT ~~'I think **he's**.'~~)

Negative contractions can be stressed, and are possible in any position.
'It **isn't** true.' 'No, it **isn't**.'

2   Rewrite the sentences only if contractions are possible.

1   Can you tell me where she is staying?
2   'Remember to take your medicine.' 'Yes, I will.'
3   Do you know where she is?
4   'Have you paid?' 'No, I have not.'
5   'It is not true.'
6   'On the contrary, it is true.'
7   'Would you like another cup?' 'Yes, I would.'
8   I do not believe they are fresh.
9   Telephone if you cannot come.
10 'Can you help me?' 'No, I cannot just at the moment.'

3   Complete the poem by putting in the contracted forms of the verbs in the box.

cannot	he has	he would	I will	that is	there is
we have	you have				

Mother, __1__ a strange man
Waiting at the door
With a familiar sort of face
You feel __2__ seen before.

Says his name is Jesus
Can we spare a couple of bob*
Says __3__ been made redundant
And now __4__ find a job.

Yes I think he is a foreigner
Egyptian or a Jew
Oh aye, and that reminds me
__5__ like some water too.

Well shall I give him what he wants
Or send him on his way?
OK __6__ give him 5p
Say __7__ all __8__ got today.

From *Roger McGough: Three Rusty Nails*

* a couple of bob (shillings): a little money

grammar: useful words

It will be easier to use this book if you know the words in the boxes. If you don't know them, we suggest you read the explanations and do the exercises.

---

noun   singular   plural   countable   uncountable

Nouns are mostly **names of things**, e.g. *cat, idea, money, oil, reason, strength.*

Singular nouns: *cat, idea, reason*; **plural nouns**: *cats, ideas, reasons.*

Countable nouns (e.g. *cat*) can be singular or plural; **uncountable nouns** (e.g. *oil, happiness*) are only singular, and cannot come after *a/an.*

---

adjective   comparative   superlative

Adjectives describe things, e.g. *old, big, strange, ready, famous, impossible.*

Comparative adjectives: *older, more famous.*

Superlative adjectives: *oldest, most famous.*

---

determiner   article   possessive   demonstrative

Determiners go before (adjectives and) nouns. They include **articles** (*a, the*), **possessives** (e.g. *my, your*), **demonstratives** (e.g. *this, that*) and **quantifiers** (e.g. *some, any, few, much, several, enough*).

---

1   Look at the expressions in the box and write down:

1   all the **nouns**, and say whether they are **uncountable**, **singular countable** or **plural**

2   all the **adjectives**, and say whether they are **ordinary**, **comparative** or **superlative**

3   all the **determiners**, and say whether they are **articles**, **possessives**, **demonstratives** or **quantifiers**.

a few small potatoes	some cold soup	this stupid suggestion
my best suit	a more interesting book	the cheapest petrol
his older brother	those high buildings	our worst problem
many younger people	these new rules	no dry wood

| pronoun | personal | possessive | reflexive | relative |

Pronouns replace nouns. They include **personal pronouns** (e.g. *I*, *she*, *us*, *you*), **possessive pronouns** (e.g. *mine*, *yours*), **reflexive pronouns** (e.g. *myself*, *oneself*) and **relative pronouns** (e.g. *who*, *whose*, *which*, *that*).

2 **Write down (a) three more personal pronouns; (b) three more possessive pronouns; (c) three more reflexive pronouns.**

| verb | auxiliary verb | modal auxiliary verb | | | | |
| tense | future | present | past | simple | progressive | perfect |

Verbs mostly refer to **actions**, **events** or **situations**, e.g. *run, turn, stop, seem*.

The **auxiliary verbs** *be, have* and *do* are used with other verbs to make tenses, questions, negatives and passives.

Modal auxiliary verbs are a small group of verbs (*can, may, must* etc – see page 106) which add meanings like possibility or obligation.

Tenses are forms of verbs which show **time relations**. There are **future**, **present** and **past** tenses. These can be **simple** (e.g. *will work, works, worked*), **progressive** (e.g. *will be working, is working, was working*) or **perfect** (e.g. *will have worked, has worked, had worked*).

3 **Read these sentences and write down the verbs.**

She lost her temper.	It never rains there.	Open the door.
This fish tastes funny.	Our team won.	I got a letter from Dave.

4 **Look at these verbs, and say whether they are *future*, *present* or *past* and whether they are *simple*, *progressive* or *perfect*. Which are the auxiliary verbs?**

1 will rain
2 is working
3 had forgotten
4 sits
5 came
6 will be seeing
7 was running
8 will have finished
9 has stopped
10 did not answer

| conditional | -ing form | infinitive | perfect infinitive | |
| past participle | imperative | active | passive | |

Conditionals: forms made with *would*, e.g. *I **would like** a drink.*

-ing forms: *smoking, waiting* etc

Infinitives: *I want **to go**; We must **stop*** etc

Perfect infinitives: *She must **have arrived*** etc

Past participles: *stolen, gone* etc

Imperatives: *Please **sit** down; **Go** away* etc

Active verbs: *Anne **invited** George; We **make** cars* etc

Passive verbs: *George **was invited** by Anne; Cars **are made** in our factory* etc

5   **Find a conditional, an *-ing* form, an infinitive, a perfect infinitive, a past participle, an imperative and an active and passive verb in this text, and write them down.**

I smoke too much, and I would certainly stop smoking if I could, but when my friends talk about it I just say, 'Shut up and leave me alone'. I don't actually think I'll stop unless I'm ordered to by a doctor. I suppose I should never have started.

| preposition | adverb | adverb particle |

Prepositions help nouns and pronouns to fit into sentences, e.g. *She ran **down** the road; I hate the idea **of** death; I'm glad **about** your new job.*

Adverbs say more about verbs, adjectives or other parts of a sentence, e.g. *We **really** tried; I **often** see her; **terribly** cold; **right** down the road; I start **today**.*

Adverb particles are small adverbs that follow verbs; they look like prepositions, but are not (see page 184), e.g. *Sit **down**; Let's go **on**.*

6   **Find the prepositions and adverbs and write them down. What sort of word is *out* in *walked out*? Can you write down five more prepositions and five more adverbs?**

Rob usually sits at the back with Ann, but yesterday he suddenly decided to sit at the front by Karen for a change. Ann got terribly upset and started shouting at Rob as loud as she could, so then Rob got upset and walked out in a temper.

subject   object   direct/indirect   complement

The **subject** usually comes before the verb, and most often says who or what **does something**, e.g. ***My father*** *drives fast cars*; ***She*** *sings well*.

The **(direct) object** usually comes after the verb; it often says who or what **something happens to**, e.g. *My father drives **fast cars**; I broke **a cup***.

Some verbs have two objects; the **indirect object** says who something is given to, done for etc, e.g. *She sent **the manager** a dozen roses*.

7   Write down the subjects, direct objects and indirect objects from these sentences.

1   Jake writes songs.
2   I gave Monica my address.
3   Can you tell me the time?
4   What sort of books do you like?
5   Write me a postcard when you have time.

> After *be, seem* and some other verbs, we can describe the subject with a noun or adjective **complement**, e.g. *He's **a doctor**; She seems **nervous***.

8   What are the complements in these sentences?

1   You're pretty.
2   He looks tired.
3   Are you a student?
4   When I saw him I felt sorry.

sentence   clause   main/subordinate clause   relative clause
indirect speech   conjunction   tag   affirmative
interrogative   negative

A **sentence** begins with a capital letter and ends with a full stop, a question mark or an exclamation mark.

Some sentences have more than one **clause** (e.g. *[I'll phone] [when I get home]*).

Subordinate clauses are introduced by conjunctions (e.g. ***when** I get home*).

Some **conjunctions**: *if, when, because, while, after, although.*

Main clauses (e.g. *I'll phone*) do not need conjunctions.

Affirmative verbs/sentences make statements (e.g. *You're late*).

Interrogative verbs/sentences ask questions (e.g. *Am I late?*).

Negative verbs/sentences are made with *not* (e.g. *I'm not late*).

9 **Write down the conjunctions and subordinate clauses from these sentences. Which sentences have interrogative main clauses? Which have affirmative main clauses? Which have negative main clauses?**

1   She talks all the time while I'm trying to work.
2   I don't mind if you stay out late.
3   Did you tell Alice where you were staying?
4   When I get back I'll explain everything.
5   Before you went out, did you switch the lights off?
6   Although it was snowing, it wasn't very cold.

Relative clauses are introduced by relative pronouns, e.g. *This is the switch* ***which turns on the heating***.

In **indirect speech**, we use subordinate clauses to report things that are said or thought, e.g. *She said* ***that I was wrong***; *I wondered* ***if they were lost***.

Tags are short **auxiliary + pronoun** expressions that are added to sentences, e.g. *It's getting warmer,* ***isn't it?***

consonant	vowel	(un)contracted	stress(ed)		intonation
expression	formal	informal	emphatic		

Consonants: *b, c, f, g, h* etc. **Vowels**: *a, e, i, o, u.*

Uncontracted forms: *I will, is not* etc. **Contractions / Contracted forms**: *I'll, isn't* etc.

Stress: pronouncing one part of a word, or one word, more strongly than others. In ***bett****er*, we stress *bett*; in *re****turn***, we stress *turn*; in *It's* ***late***, we stress *late*.

Intonation: the 'musical' movement of the voice up and down. Questions often end with a rising intonation.

Expression: a group of words that belong together, e.g. *out of work; on Monday.*

Informal language is used, for example, in friendly conversations; **formal** language, for example, in business letters. *We've got a suggestion* is informal; *We have a suggestion* is formal.

Emphatic: expressing something strongly. *We had no money at all* is more emphatic than *We didn't have any money.*

Answers to exercises

17   **1**   (*a* and *an*)   1 an   2 a   3 an   4 a   5 a   6 an   7 a   8 a   9 a   10 an
           11 an   12 a   13 a   14 an   15 a   16 a   17 an   18 a

      1   (*a/an* and *one*)   1 One   2 a   3 an   4 one/an   5 a   6 one   7 a   8 a   9 one

18–19   **1**   2 is a doctor   3 is a teacher   4 is a scientist   5 is a musician
           6 is a painter / an artist   7 is a photographer   8 is a secretary   9 is a builder
           10 is a hairdresser   11 is an electrician   12 is a butcher   13 is a mechanic
           14 is a cook   15 is a gardener   16 is a (lorry/truck) driver

      2   A curtain is a thing that you put across a window.
          A dictionary is a thing used for finding the meanings of words.
          A dentist is a person who helps people to keep their teeth healthy.
          A lawyer is a person who helps people with legal problems.
          A mechanic is a person who services and repairs cars.
          A tap is a thing that water comes out of.
          A teacher is a person who helps people to learn things.
          A telephone is a thing used for talking to people who are far away.

20   **1**   (*Examples of possible answers*)
          1's got a long nose / a small mouth.   7's got a short beard / a round face.
          2's got a round face / a nice smile.   8's got a big mouth / a loud voice.
          3's got a long neck / a small beard.   9's got a big moustache / a long nose.
          4's got an oval face / a long nose.   10's got a small mouth / an oval face.
          5's got a small nose / a big mouth.   11's got a small moustache / a nice smile.
          6's got a long beard / a bad temper.   12's got a long beard / a square face.

21   **1**   1 the   2 the   3 a   4 a   5 the; the   6 the; the   7 the; the   8 a; a; the; the
          9 the   10 the

      2   1 the   2 the   3 an   4 the   5 a   6 the   7 the   8 A   9 a   10 the   11 the
          12 the

22–23   **1**   1 –   2 –   3 –   4 –   5 –   6 the   7 the   8 the   9 the   10 –

      3   1 the wheel   2 the novel   3 the computer   4 The violin   5 the ballpoint pen
          6 The fax machine   7 the whale   8 The X-ray machine

24–25   **1**   1 to town; on foot / by bus; by bus / by car   2 at work; to bed   3 to school
          4 at Christmas / at Easter / in summer; at home   5 in the evening; at night
          6 at university; in hospital

      2   'He's from Texas.'

      3   (*Examples of possible answers*)
          B   We met the King at dinner in Oxford Prison.
          C   Paul went home by car.
          D   Anna goes to college in Sydney by bus.
          E   All of us met at Boston Airport.
          F   It's easy to get to Oxford station on foot.
          G   Anna flew to the Hague from Ottawa Airport.
          H   All of us went to Oxford Town Hall on foot.
          I   Anna flew a plane from Stirling to Lake Huron.
          J   I saw Paul at dinner in Stirling yesterday.
          K   The King has just come home from Sydney.
          L   Can you go by train from the Alps to the North Sea?

M All of us are going to try and climb Everest.
N I travel from home to work by bike.
O It's easy to get from Ottawa to Boston by train.
P The King was in prison in Cardiff.

26–27 **1**   1 a; a; the   2 a; the   3 –; –; –   4 an; a; the   5 an; a   6 an; the   7 –; –
8 –; a   9 –; a; –   10 –; –; –; –   11 –; the   12 –   13 –; a; a   14 a; the
15 a; the; the   16 –; a   17 the; the   18 a; a   19 a; the   20 a; a   21 a; an; the
22 a; an   23 –; –

2   1 –; a (B)   2 the (D)   3 –; –; –; –; –; – (C)   4 the; a; an; –; a (A)

28–29 **1**   **DIY**   This belongs to **me**.   This is **my** coat.   This is **mine**.
This belongs to **you**.   This is **your** money.   This is **yours**.
This belongs to **him**.   This is **his** car.   This is **his**.
This belongs to **her**.   This is **her** office.   This is **hers**.
This belongs to **us**.   This is **our** house.   This is **ours**.
This belongs to **them**.   This is **their** dog.   This is **theirs**.
Who does this belong to?   **Whose** bike is this?   **Whose** is this bike?

2   1 yours; hers   2 Whose; ours   3 your; Its   4 his; her   5 their   6 our; theirs
7 my; mine

3   2 that unemployed brother of hers   8 a beautiful cousin of hers
3 another good friend of mine   9 this wonderful news of yours
4 a brilliant idea of mine   10 that lazy son of ours
5 these stupid plans of his   11 those impossible children of theirs
6 those old books of yours   12 these silly cats of ours
7 some distant relations of his

4   1 his jacket/raincoat   2 her foot/mouth   3 its foot/tail/mouth   4 their coats
5 my raincoat/jacket   6 your mouth

5   'No, he's not ours! ...'

30 **2**   **DIY**   With *this/these*: happening now; just about to start; here; near
With *that/those*: finished; said before; over there; distant; unwanted

3   1 this   2 that   3 these   4 that   5 those   6 this   7 this   8 that   9 that
10 That   11 that   12 that   13 this; that

4   this

31 **1**   1 which   2 What   3 Which   4 Which (*or* What)   5 What   6 Which   7 What
8 Which   9 Which   10 Which   11 What

32–33 **1**   1 refuses   2 doubt   3 hardly   4 never   5 seldom   6 without

2   1 any; some   2 some   3 anything   4 any   5 some   6 somebody

3   1 anybody   2 some   3 some   4 any   5 anything   6 somebody   7 any

4   1 any   2 something   3 anything   4 something/anything   5 Some
6 something   7 any   8 any   9 any   10 some; some   11 anything   12 any
13 some/any   14 anything   15 anyone/someone   16 any   17 any   18 some

5   "... anywhere with anybody at any time ..."

34 **1**   1 any   2 –   3 some   4 –; –   5 –   6 some   7 –   8 some   9 some   10 –
11 –   12 any   13 some   14 –

2   some children

35 **1** 1 no   2 Nobody   3 No   4 none   5 No   6 None   7 no   8 nobody   9 None
10 no; no; no

2 *(Examples of possible answers)*
2 Nobody in my family speaks French.   7 There's nothing good on at the cinema.
3 Nobody speaks seventy-six languages.   8 I had no money.
4 There's nothing to eat at home.   9 I had nothing to say.
5 I'm afraid I've got no coffee.   10 None of them.
6 There's nobody at home just now.

36 **1** 1 Any   2 No   3 anything   4 nothing   5 can't hear   6 any   7 nobody
8 anybody

2 *(Examples of possible answers)*
1 any garage; any supermarket; any post office; any sports shop; any bookshop
2 any English teacher; any lawyer; any accountant; any photographer; any farmer

37 **1** A There's no place for women in the church.
B I suppose you've brought me here to tell me you haven't got any money.
C It's your birthday? Cook anything you want for supper.
D I'm sorry, he's not seeing anybody/anyone today.

38 **1** 1 All   2 everything   3 everything   4 everything   5 all   6 everything
7 everything   8 everything   9 all

2 1 All   2 everybody   3 All   4 all; everybody   5 everybody   6 all

39 **1** a whole family   all the islands   the whole road system   the whole of South Africa
all the children   the whole country   all the traffic   the whole of Asia   a whole week
all the vegetables   the whole political party   all the students   all the luggage
all the meat   all the MPs   a whole class

40–41 **2** 1 very much / so much   2 as many   3 too much   4 very much / so much
5 very much / so much   6 as many / so many   7 so many / too many   8 as many

3 1 little   2 little   3 few   4 few   5 little   6 little   7 few; few   8 few

4 1 little   2 a little   3 Few   4 a few   5 a few   6 a little; a little   7 little   8 few
1 It is not much use ...   3 Only a few teenagers ...
7 Nadia didn't drink much coffee, or any alcohol / ... and she didn't drink (any)
alcohol.
8 Unfortunately, he hadn't got / didn't have many friends.

42 **1** 1 the least; the fewest   2 Fewer (*or* Less); less   3 fewer (*or* less); less   4 less; less
5 the least   6 the fewest

2 *(Examples of possible answers)*
1 less confident   2 the least optimistic   3 less fluently   4 less prosperous
5 less politely   6 the least dangerous

43 **1** 1 others   2 other   3 others   4 others   5 other   6 other   7 others   8 others
9 other   10 other

2 more clothes   more friends   another child   another three pages / three more pages
another hour   another mile   more sleep   more job possibilities
another few days / a few more days   another hundred pounds   more money
more time   more freedom   more holidays   another problem
another twenty miles / twenty more miles

44–45 **1** **DIY** *Enough* normally comes after an adjective or adverb, and before a noun.

2   2 enough money; enough time   3 big enough   4 enough friends   5 old enough
6 enough champagne   7 hard enough   8 clever enough; enough confidence

3   *(Examples of possible answers)*
2 There were too many people for one car.   3 She was too busy.
4 It is too expensive.   5 There's too much traffic.   6 I wrote too slowly.
7 There's too much noise in here.   8 No, he's talking/speaking too quickly.

4   *(Examples of possible answers)*
2 not enough people   3 not enough water   4 too much water
5 too much work   6 too many cats   7 not enough food   8 too much food

5   2 old enough to take   3 too quietly for me to hear
4 clean enough for people to swim in   5 well enough to decide
6 too muddy for them to see   7 too tired to understand   8 well enough to listen
9 too fast for the police to catch

46–47 **1** 1 of 2 of 3 – 4 – 5 – 6 of 7 of 8 – 9 of 10 of 11 – 12 –
13 – 14 –

2   1 Most people   2 Most of the people   3 most of the people   4 Most people
5 most people   6 Most of the people   7 most people   8 Most of the people

3   … enough disorder; … A little less noise …

48–49 **1** 1 me 2 me 3 he; him 4 Me 5 me; him 6 he; her 7 him
8 me/him/her 9 me 10 her

2   1 Anne has (got) the same car as I have.   6 We're not / We aren't as old as them.
2 They have been here longer than we   7 He had a bigger meal than me.
have.   8 I'm not as quick as her.
3 I am much taller than he is.   9 'We're from York.' 'Me too.'
4 'He is going to Mexico.' 'So am I.'   10 'Who wants a drink?' 'Me.'
5 'Who said that?' 'She did.'

3   1 She 2 it 3 It's 4 it/her 5 it 6 Who 7 It 8 it 9 who 10 it

50–51 **1** 1 herself 2 himself 3 itself 4 ourselves 5 him 6 yourself 7 herself; her
8 you/us/her/him 9 me

2   1 ourselves 2 herself 3 himself 4 themselves 5 myself 6 itself

3   1 each other 2 themselves 3 each other 4 yourselves 5 each other
6 ourselves

4   1 ourselves 2 him 3 each other 4 myself 5 her 6 me/him/her/us/them
7 myself 8 each other 9 itself 10 themselves 11 yourself 12 you; them

52–53 **1** *(Examples of possible sentences)*
1 One needs / You need a passport to get into the US.
2 One needs / You need a ticket to travel by train.
3 Can one/you fly directly from Gdansk to Prague?
4 One has / You have to be good at maths to be a physicist.
5 One needs / You need a warm climate to grow oranges.
6 One/You can't get a driving licence until one is / you're seventeen.
7 One/You can't eat soup with a fork.
8 One has / You have to get up early to see animals in the forest.

2   1 They 2 they 3 they 4 They 5 You 6 you 7 your 8 you 9 you
10 they 11 you 12 them

3   1 they   2 their   3 their   4 they; them   5 them   6 her   7 theirs   8 they
9 them   10 her

54   **1**   2 red woollen one / big grey leather one   3 unsweetened   4 tall ones
5 new ones   6 long sunny one   7 Chinese   8 solid practical ones   9 sharp one
10 big grey leather one

2   1 One   2 one   3 Mine   4 some   5 one   6 any   7 hers   8 some

55   **1**   '... We love you because you're ours, like the car.'
'You sold my what to who?'
'Could you tell me if my glasses are ready yet?'
'Have you seen a lady without me?'
'Yes, of course it's important enough to disturb him.'
'Have you any "Do It Herself" books?'

56   **1**   **uncountable:** dust; flour; happiness; knowledge; love; milk; meat; music; oil; rain;
snow
countable: book; cup; flower; mountain; piano; river; song; table; wall

2   1 a glass   2 glass   3 wood   4 a wood   5 pity   6 a pity   7 Time   8 times
9 beers   10 Beer   11 experience   12 an experience   13 a chicken   14 chicken

57   **1**   accommodation – flat   baggage – suitcase   bread – loaf   furniture – table
information – fact   money – banknote   publicity – advertisement
traffic – cars   travel – journey   work – job

2   a flash of lightning; a stroke of luck; a clap of thunder

3   'A word of advice, Arthur ...'   '... Our baggage has been sent ...'

58   **1**   **DIY**   1 By adding -*s*.   2 By changing -*y* to -*ies*.   3 By adding -*s*.   4 *s, z, sh, ch, x*
5 *echoes, heroes, potatoes, tomatoes.*

2   addresses   boxes   brushes   computers   desks   faces   guys   lists   losses
messes   patches   peaches   plays   poppies   replies   toys   trees   videos
witches   worries

59   **1**   1 crisis – crises; means   2 aircraft; sheep   3 dozen; thousand   4 shelf; wolf
5 mouse; tooth   6 mathematics; news   7 police; scissors

60–61   **1**   1a school has   1b school have   2a club have   2b club has   3a staff do
3b staff does   4a class is   4b class are   5a orchestra are   5b orchestra is

2   '... Shall I tell them ...'

3   1 have   2 have   3 is   4 is   5 have; are   6 is   7 are   8 has   9 are
10 has   11 is   12 are   13 are   14 has   15 was   16 were   17 Is   18 have

62   **1**   (*Examples of possible answers*)
Ann and Pat's car   our dog's nose   most people's health   Jonathan's education
those women's legs   Katie's fear of heights   Simon and Jill's car   doctors' ideas

2   1 ✓   2 Are you Al's daughter?   3 ✓   4 Here's Barry's address.   5 ✓   6 ✓
7 ✓   8 ✓   9 It's a crazy idea of Alice's.   10 Where is that brother of Carol's?

63   **1**   1g; 2b; 3h; 4a; 5j; 6c; 7e; 8i; 9d; 10f

2   1 a music shop   2 a Birmingham man   3 a picture frame   4 mint tea
5 the station clock   6 a space rocket   7 a biscuit factory   8 soap powder

3   antique shop / bicycle shop   bicycle race   bus station   cowboy film   kitchen door
grape juice   road map   newspaper publisher

64 **1** 1 a chocolate cake   3 a kitchen cupboard   4 a matchbox   5 toothpaste
7 the kitchen door   8 a wine bottle   9 a train timetable   11 garden chairs

65 **1** 1 a bus station   2 a toy shop   3 the teacher's office   4 computer disks
5 my mother's chair   6 car papers   7 Tom's plan   8 a telephone box
9 the dog's toy   10 a horse race   11 vegetable soup   12 China's history
13 a cowboy film   14 street lamps   15 the firm's office   16 a bath towel
17 that cat's tail   18 a teacher trainer   19 the paper's editor   20 a glass factory

2 '... Mother's Day card ...'

66–67 **1** Angela's leg   the highest branches of the trees   the lock of my suitcase
your dog's leg   the bank's branch in Paris   the floor of your office
the leg of the table   my family's name   the town's atmosphere
our company's best sales manager   the police force's main problem
next week's timetable   last night's party   today's news

2 1 Helen's story; the story of the French revolution
2 the bed of the stream; the patient's bed
3 a/the policy of full employment; the company's policy
4 my favourite author's style; the style of the 1930s
5 the place of language education; women's place
6 the ideas of modern physics; my son's ideas
7 the club's rules; the rules of football
8 the committee's views; a/the view of the lake
9 the cat's head; the head of the queue
10 the arm of the chair; John's arm

3 'Fear? He doesn't know the meaning of the word.'
'Let's go. I've got somebody else's car parked outside.'
'Right, Mr Wilson. I have here the results of your tests.'

68–69 **1** 1 calm   2 calmly/clearly/slowly/softly/unhappily   3 cheaply   4 beautifully
5 terrible   6 softly   7 cheap   8 slow   9 calmly   10 beautiful   11 soft
12 clear   13 terribly   14 slowly   15 unhappy   16 clearly

2 1 amazingly   2 sure   3 real   4 truly   5 gently   6 amazing   7 wonderfully
8 gentle   9 slightly   10 really   11 kindly   12 badly   13 wonderful; awful
14 cleverly   15 surprisingly   16 unbelievably

70 **1** **adjectives:** cowardly; deadly; friendly; likely; lively; lonely; lovely; silly; ugly
both adjectives and adverbs: daily; weekly; monthly; yearly; early; fast; hard; late;
loud; well

2 2 daily/weekly/monthly/yearly/lively/lovely/silly
3 lively/lovely/silly/ugly/fast/loud
4 fast/loud
5 daily/weekly/monthly/yearly/early/late
6 cowardly/friendly/hard/lovely/silly
7 cowardly/friendly/hard/lively/lonely/lovely/silly/ugly
8 likely
9 lovely
10 friendly/lonely/lovely
11 early/fast/late
12 hard
13 deadly
14 deadly/fast/hard/lively/lonely/lovely/silly
15 lonely/hard/lovely
16 yearly/daily/friendly/weekly/monthly/early/late/loud

71 **1**
2 hot breezy weather
3 untidy red hair
4 The man was young and bearded.
5 The sea was cold and rough.
6 The church was old and ugly.

7 a quiet tense woman
8 yellow and grey sand
9 The badges were red and blue.
10 a narrow brown room

72 **1**
1 the blind   2 the young   3 the poor   4 the young; the old   5 the rich
6 the living   7 the poor; the rich   8 the dead; the living   9 the blind

73 **1**
1 a beautiful little Belgian city
2 a local jazz club
3 an excellent cold dinner
4 modern industrial buildings
5 a red silk evening dress
6 narrow colourless eyes
7 a flat gold frame
8 lovely old furniture

9 Swiss drawing ink
10 a short leather jacket
11 little brick squares
12 French ski boots
13 a blue woollen tie
14 grey cotton trousers
15 black nylon swimming trunks

74–75 **1**
(Examples of possible answers)
I am always in trouble.
My mother is never depressed.
Most people are usually friendly.

5
1 You are usually here ...
2 Her mum always cooks ...
3 We usually book ...
4 They probably think ...
5 You should always look ...
6 She is probably going to stay ...
7 Chocolate cakes are definitely the best.
8 I will probably be able ...
9 I have never had ...
10 We never saw sweets ...
11 I definitely remember ...
12 Do you usually read ...
13 I can usuallly manage ...

14 She has never done that before.
15 Something is definitely burning.
16 She has always been nervous.
17 I never feel cold ...
18 They were always against me.
19 We are definitely going to win.
20 February is usually the worst.
21 It is sometimes very difficult.
22 I always buy them ...
23 I have often tried ...
24 They are always fighting.
25 She often saw ...
26 You are probably right.

76 **1**
2 I'm only doing this ...
3 She even gets up ...
4 He even wears a suit ...
5 She only ate ...
6 I can only play ...

7 He can't even write ...
8 They even make you pay ...
9 I was only thinking ...
10 You can even ski ...

2
(Examples of possible answers)
I work every day, even on Sundays.   Only my mother really understands me.
They do everything together. They even brush their teeth together.
Hello! It's only me!   Even the cat thinks you're stupid.
She likes all animals, even rats.   Only the clock broke the silence.
Only his wife knew that he was ill.   Even his children hated him.
You can borrow it, but only for a few minutes.

77 **1**
1 I work best at night.
2 I paid the bill at once.
3 He always moves very slowly in the morning.
4 She speaks Japanese fluently.
5 I think we'd better open the parcel now.
6 She was crying quietly in her room.
7 We talked about it briefly at lunchtime.

8 I'm going to break the eggs carefully into the bowl.
9 Ann works at the village shop on Saturdays.
10 I can't explain my feelings clearly.
11 The team played brilliantly yesterday.
12 I always worked very hard at school.
13 She practises the piano here every evening.
14 I don't think she plays tennis very well.
15 He read every word slowly.
16 Put the butter in the fridge at once.

78 **1** 1 Are you still in the same job?
2 He's seventeen, but he's already married.
3 Has Susan arrived yet? (*or* ... already arrived?)
4 I've already finished!
5 9 a.m., and it's still dark!
6 4 p.m., and it's already dark!
7 Have you had breakfast yet? (*or* ... already had breakfast?)
8 Look – it's still raining.
9 Our old car still runs OK.
10 Is the rice cooked yet? (*or* ... already cooked?)
11 She's already gone to bed.
12 Is she still in that little flat?
13 Why are you still in bed? (*or* Why are you already ... ?)
14 I'm already bored with my new job.
15 It's not time to stop yet.
16 Have you written that letter yet? (*or* ... already written ... ?)

79 **1** **DIY** To make the comparative and superlative of one-syllable adjectives ending in -*e*,
you add -*r*, -*st*.
To make the comparative and superlative of other one-syllable adjectives,
you add -*er*, -*est*.
To make the comparative and superlative of two-syllable adjectives ending in -*y*,
you change *y* to *i* and add -*er*, -*est*.
To make the comparative and superlative of other two-syllable adjectives, you put *more*
and *most* in front.
To make the comparative and superlative of longer adjectives, you put *more* and *most*
in front.

2 **DIY** Before -*er* and -*est*, we double the last letter of adjectives that end in one vowel +
one consonant.

3 more/most boring cheaper/cheapest finer/finest fuller/fullest funnier/funniest
more/most handsome harder/hardest more/most honest more/most interesting
lazier/laziest lighter/lightest more/most nervous sadder/saddest safer/safest
sillier/silliest sorrier/sorriest more/most stupid more/most uncomfortable
more/most useful more/most violent wetter/wettest

80 **1** (*Examples of possible answers*)
2 It was the best. 3 She lived farther/further away than the others.
4 The cold got worse. 5 The worst. 6 Her older/elder sister; his older/elder brother;
her oldest/eldest sister. 7 Further tests. 8 The one that needs (the) least water.
9 The Blacks have more money than the Browns. The Browns have less money than
the Blacks. 10 The post office is farther/further away than the park.

81 **1** 1 faster 2 more beautifully 3 (the) hardest 4 earlier 5 the most sensitively
6 more peacefully 7 the latest 8 the most fluently

3 1 more slowly 2 faster 3 earlier 4 harder

82 **1** *(Examples of possible answers)*
The Great Pyramid is very much older than the Taj Mahal.
The Amazon is far longer than the Thames.
North America is a little larger than South America.
A dog is a bit bigger than a cat.
A computer is a lot faster than a typewriter.
Asia is even bigger than Africa.
A parrot sings no better than a cat.
Are you any more intelligent than your boss?

83 **1** *(Examples of possible answers)*
1 Is this box stronger than that one? Is this box the strongest you've got?
2 Alistair is taller than anyone else in the class. Alistair is the tallest in the class.
3 The state of Alaska is bigger than the other states in the US. The state of Alaska is the biggest in the US.
4 This wine is more expensive than that one. This wine is the most expensive in the world.
5 Al's party was better than Pat's party. Al's party was the best I've ever been to.

2 *(Examples of possible answers)*
Car Y is more expensive than car X.
Car Z is the most expensive of the three.
Car Y is more economical than car Z.
Car X is the most economical of all.
Car Y is safer than car X.
Car Z is the safest of the three.
Car X is the most comfortable of the three.
Car X is more comfortable than the other two cars.
Car X is much better off-road than car Y.
Car Z is the best of all off-road.
Car Z has more luggage space than car X.
Car Y has the most luggage space of the three.

84–85 **1** *(Examples of possible answers)*
1 faster and faster   2 taller and taller   3 hotter and hotter
4 more and more difficult/complicated *or* harder and harder   5 fatter and fatter
6 more and more depressed/unhappy   7 more and more expensive

2 *(Examples of possible answers)*
1 My mother's driving is getting more and more dangerous ...
2 ... he's getting better and better.
3 ... police officers are getting younger and younger.
4 My temper is getting worse and worse.
5 It's getting harder and harder to find time ...
6 Professional tennis is getting more and more boring.
7 Restaurants are getting more and more expensive.
8 Her holidays are getting longer and longer.

3 1 the faster ... the more ...   2 the longer ... the more ...   3 the older ... the darker ...
4 the more ... the angrier ...   5 the more ... the more ... the less ...
6 the more ... the less ...   7 the more ... the more ...   8 the warmer ... the more ...

4 1 The more ice cream he eats, the fatter he gets; and the fatter he gets, the more ice cream he eats.
2 The more he reads, the more he forgets; and the more he forgets, the more he reads.
3 The more she ignores him, the more he loves her; and the more he loves her, the more she ignores him.
4 The more shoes she buys, the more shoes she wants; and the more shoes she wants, the more shoes she buys.
5 The more money we spend, the more friends we have; and the more friends we have, the more money we spend.
6 The more I sleep, the more tired I am; and the more tired I am, the more I sleep.

86 **1** *(Examples of possible answers)*
2 in the Army   3 of the books I own   4 in the class   5 in Europe
6 in my family   7 of the four men   8 of the girls in her school   9 in the office
10 of the paintings in the gallery   11 in Rome   12 in the school

2 *(Examples of possible answers)*
1 Florence is the ...   2 Wolves are ...   3 I think Stoppard is the ...   4 Bill is the ...
5 The streets are ...   6 Working in the country is the ...   7 I feel

87 **1** 1 as; as   2 than   3 that   4 than   5 than   6 as   7 as   8 that   9 than
10 that   11 as   12 as

2 '... a better place than we found it!'

88–89 **1** *(Examples of possible answers)*
Jake didn't go to the same university as Susie.
Susie went to the same school as Jake.
Susie is not as tall as Jake.
Susie doesn't weigh as much as Jake.
Jake does/has the same job as Susie.
Jake isn't as old as Susie.
Susie was born in the same town as Jake.
Susie earns twice as much money as Jake.
Jake doesn't work for the same firm as Susie.
Susie doesn't have as many weeks' holiday as Jake.
Jake lives in the same street as Susie.
Susie has the same number of children as Jake.
Jake speaks French as well as Susie, but he doesn't speak German as well as her.
Jake doesn't read as much as Susie.

2 as black as night   as cold as ice   as flat as a pancake   as good as gold
as green as grass   as hard as iron   as old as the hills   as pretty as a picture
as quiet as the grave   as red as a beetroot   as thin as a rake   as warm as toast
as white as a sheet

90 **1** 1 as   2 like   3 as   4 as   5 like   6 like   7 as   8 like   9 like   10 As

2 2 as a secretary / union representative   3 as an office   4 like a person
5 As you know   6 as a union representative   7 like cardboard   8 as he writes
9 like her mother   10 as a dessert

91 **1** 1 so   2 such   3 so   4 such   5 such   6 so   7 so   8 such

2 *(Examples of possible answers)*
1 It was such cold weather ...   5 Their house is so nice ...
2 The weather was so hot ...   6 And they've got such a beautiful garden!
3 It was such a boring book ...   7 He has such a pleasant voice ...
4 The film was so good   8 I don't know why her voice is so loud.

3 *(Examples of possible answers)*
1 so dark   2 such bad   3 such a fast   4 so heavy   5 such a boring
6 so difficult/hard   7 such a nice   8 so tired   9 I wish my feet weren't so big.
10 I wish I hadn't got such a funny nose.

92 **1** 1 very fast   2 too fast   3 too hot   4 very hot
5 too tall   6 very tall   7 too expensive   8 very expensive
9 very small   10 too small   11 very slow   12 too slow

93 **1** 1 very much   2 very   3 very   4 very   5 very   6 very much   7 very
8 very much   9 very much   10 very much   11 very much   12 very
13 very much   14 very   15 very

94 **1** 1 is being   2 am   3 is being   4 are being   5 am   6 are being   7 was being
8 is

96–97 **1** I do agree with you.   I do need a job.
I do apologise for disturbing you.   Peter did enjoy your party.
I do feel ill/tired.   She does look ill/tired.
I do hate cooking / eggs and bacon.   You do talk a lot.
I do like cooking / eggs and bacon.   I do wonder if he's really happy.

2 'You don't love me.' 'I do love you.'
I may not be educated, but I do know something about life.
I'll be ready in a minute, but I do have to make a phone call.
I'm not sure she'll be there, but if you do see her give her my love.
It's a small house. Mind you, it does have a nice big kitchen.
My wife does the housework, but I do iron my own trousers.
Although she didn't say much, she did give me her phone number.
She doesn't really like sport. She does play a bit of tennis sometimes.
I made her go to the doctor's, and she did have a broken finger.
There's nobody at home. They did say eight o'clock, didn't they?

3 Scottish people don't speak Japanese, but they do speak English.
In England it doesn't snow a lot, but it does rain a lot.
Banks don't sell beer, but they do lend money.
Cats don't eat potatoes, but they do eat mice.
Napoleon didn't fight against China, but he did fight against England.

98–99 **1** **DIY**   1 do   2 make   3 do   4 do

3 ... to make decisions ...

4 2 doing   3 doing   4 making a photocopy   5 make his/the bed
6 made a mistake   7 make a cake   8 making a fire   9 do her hair
10 do 140 mph   11 done the washing up   12 to make a phone call

100–101 **1** 1 (You can) have a shower   2 ... have a swim   3 ... have dinner
4 ... have a game of cards   5 ... have a game of tennis   6 ... have a drink
7 ... have a rest   8 ... have tea   9 ... have a shave

2 (Examples of possible answers)
1 She's going to have a baby.   2 They're going to have a fight.
3 The patient is going to have an operation.
4 This person is going to have a nervous breakdown.
5 The person is going to have an accident.

102–103 **1** 1 I've got ...   2 Has your sister got ... / Does your sister have ...
3 I haven't got ... / I don't have ...   4 The school does not have ...
5 Did you have good teachers ...   6 She didn't have ...

2 (Examples of possible answers)
1 If you're bald, you haven't got any hair.
2 If you're penniless, you haven't got any money.
3 If you're childless, you haven't got any children.
4 If you're unemployed, you haven't got a job.
5 If you're toothless, you haven't got any teeth.
6 If you're lonely, you haven't got any friends.
7 If you're starving, you haven't got any food.
8 If you're an orphan, you haven't got any parents.
9 If you're unmarried, you haven't got a wife or husband.

3 1 Have you got; I've got; I've got; I haven't got   2 have you got
3 have got; It's got   4 I've got   5 have you got; I've got   6 Have I got; you've got
7 has got; he's got; he's got

4 (*Examples of possible answers*)
The man in the first advertisement has got a Porsche.
The woman in the second advertisement has got brown hair / blue eyes / a good sense
  of humour.
The woman in the third advertisement has got a nice smile / her own apartment.
The man in the fourth advertisement has got a suntan / a nice home / a yacht.

105

1 2 We have our knives sharpened ...
3 ... to have the roof repaired ...
4 ... have my jacket cleaned. ... have my raincoat reproofed.
5 ... have the car serviced ... have the oil changed.
6 ... had her jewellery valued ...
7 ... have your tennis racket re-strung
8 ... have the kitchen redecorated ...
9 ... have some more electric sockets put in

106–107

1 **DIY** 1 Infinitive without *to*. The exception is *ought*.   2 It doesn't have *-s*.
3 They are made without *do*.

2 1 play   2 to be   3 to do   4 go   5 finish   6 to get   7 make   8 pass

3 1 Can I stay here?   2 Must you go?   3 Will he understand?   4 Shall we drive?
5 Could she do it?   6 Would you like to?

4 1 to be able to   2 been able to   3 been allowed to   4 to have to   5 had to
6 be able to   7 have to   8 to have to   9 been able to

6 be able to

108–109

1 2 You must be crazy.   3 That can't be Janet ...   4 She must think I'm stupid.
5 I must look silly ...   6 ... they must make a lot of money.
7 He can't be a teacher ...   8 ... That must be an interesting job.
9 You can't be serious. You must be joking.   10 He must have another woman ...

2 (*Examples of possible answers*)
2 He must be in Scotland.
3 He may be Spanish.
4 She must be unhappy. / She can't be
  happy.
5 She might be in love. / She must be
  happy.
6 It may/might be a cat.
7 This person may be an artist.
8 She must be married.
9 It may be going to rain.
10 What can it be?

110–111

1 1 should   2 must   3 should   4 must   5 must   6 should   7 must   8 must
9 should   10 should

3 2 Should I move to London?
3 What should I call my/the baby?
4 Where should I put my/this bicycle?
5 When should I pay my tax bill?
6 Should I invite my mother?
7 How should I cook this a/the/this crab?
8 Should I go to the police?
9 Should I take a taxi?
10 Should I take a holiday?
11 How long should I wait?
12 What should I do at the weekend?

112

1 1 must   2 has to   3 must   4 must   5 has to   6 have (got) to   7 have (got) to
8 must   9 must   10 have to

113

1 1 must not   2 do not have to   3 must not   4 must not   5 do not have to
6 must not   7 don't have to   8 don't have to   9 mustn't   10 don't have to

2   (*Examples of possible answers*)
In rugby football, you must not pass the ball forwards.
In tennis, you do not need to hit the ball before it bounces.
In tennis, you must not hit the ball after its second bounce.
In chess, you must not touch a piece if you aren't going to move it.
In boxing, you must not hit your opponent below the belt.
In athletics, you must not start before the gun.
In hockey, you must not lift your stick above your shoulder.
In hockey, you do not need to hit the ball before it bounces.
In baseball, you must not throw the bat.
In football, you must not touch the ball with your hands.
In bridge, you must not look at other people's cards.

114–115   **1**   1 can   2 will be able to   3 can   4 can   5 will be able to   6 could
7 will be able to   8 can   9 could   10 will be able to   11 can   12 can
13 will be able to   14 could   15 can

2   1 could   2 managed to   3 managed to   4 couldn't   5 managed to
6 could; could   7 managed to   8 managed to   9 could   10 managed to

3   1 can smell   2 could see   3 can/could see   4 can hear   5 can taste
6 could feel; couldn't see   7 can see   8 can hear

116–117   **1**   2 Could I use your phone?
3 May I stop work early today?
4 You can take my bike if you want to.
5 Can children go into pubs?
6 You can't come into my room.
7 Could I speak to Jane, if she's there?
8 Can I have a beer?
9 Can students use this library?
10 Could I pay you tomorrow?

2   1 Can I take your coat?
2 Can/Could you start cooking supper now, please?
3 Can/Could you translate this for me?
4 I wonder if you could translate ... ? / Could you possibly translate ... ?
5 You could watch a video if ...
6 You can spend ... / Can you spend ... ? / Could you spend ... ?
7 I can feed the horses, ...
8 Could you possibly lend me £5? / I wonder if you could lend me £5.
9 Can/Could you tell me when it's time to go?
10 Could you (possibly) tell me ... / I wonder if you could tell me ...

3   'Miss Ellis, could you come in here and pass me my coffee?'

118–119   **1**   I'll wash up if you'll dry.
I'm tired. I think I'll go to bed now.
If you see Ann, would you tell her I got her letter?
She won't tell us what's wrong.
The cat won't eat.
The phone's ringing. I'll answer it.
This video won't play.
'Who's going to get the tickets?' 'I will.'
Will you deliver the furniture to this address, please?
Will you let me know when you're ready to leave?
Will you stop shouting?
Would you put the meat in the oven at 5.30?

2   (*Examples of possible answers*)
    1 I promise I'll write.
    2 I promise I won't smoke.
    3 I promise I'll go to church.
    4 I promise I won't stay out late.
    5 I promise I won't drink.
    6 I promise I'll study hard.

    7 I promise I'll go to lectures.
    8 I promise I won't fight.
    9 I promise I'll do exercises.
    10 I promise I'll get up early.
    11 I promise I'll wash my clothes.
    12 I promise I'll think of you.

120 **1**   1 will keep   2 would make   3 will play   4 will talk   5 will listen
        6 would take   7 will drive   8 will fall   9 will ring; will be   10 will tell

2   After you have bought something, you will find it somewhere else cheaper.
    If anything can go wrong, it will.
    If there are two good TV shows, they will both be on at the same time.
    If you explain so clearly that nobody can misunderstand, somebody will.
    If you throw something away, you'll need it the next day.
    No matter how much you do, you'll never do enough.
    The one who snores will fall asleep first.
    The other queue will always move faster.

121 **1**   (*Examples of possible answers*)
    3 Shall we stay in this country or go
       abroad?
    4 When shall we go?
    5 How long shall we go for?
    6 Shall we fly, go by train or drive?
    7 Shall we stay in a hotel or camp?

    8 Shall we stay in one place or travel
       around?
    9 Shall we take Granny?
    10 Shall we go with the Jacksons?
    11 What shall we do with the dogs?

122–123 **1**   2 could/might have killed
    3 would have phoned
    4 could/might/would have gone
    5 should have been
    6 should/could have put
    7 should/could have asked

    8 should have taken
    9 could/might have died
    10 could/should have hit
    11 might/should/could have told
    12 might/should/could have washed

2   1 may have gone   2 should/may have finished   3 can't have forgotten
    4 must have rained   5 must have been   6 may have been   7 can't have spent
    8 may have found   9 must have had   10 may/must have gone

3   1 can't have   2 may not have   3 must have   4 had to
    5 may not have / can't have   6 may not have

124–125 **1**   1 I can't sing.
    2 I would like to be able to travel more.
    3 He should work harder.

    4 Could you tell me the time?
    5 I had to work ...

2   1 might   2 may/might   3 can't   4 may   5 may not   6 can't   7 must
    8 should   9 have to   10 don't have to   11 can / will be able to
    12 will be able to   13 managed to   14 could / was able to   15 can   16 will stop
    17 may not   18 can't   19 had to do   20 must have left

4   'Can this be the same man ...?'
    '... I'll take them.'
    '... he might be Prime Minister ...'

    '... you could live for another twenty minutes.'
    '... it may not be a joke.'
    '... I wonder who it can be from.'

126 **1**   1 needn't laugh   2 needn't get   3 needn't write   4 needn't come
    5 needn't worry   6 needn't think   7 needn't ring   8 needn't take
    9 needn't phone/ring   10 needn't try

2 1 didn't need to water   2 needn't have cooked   3 needn't have done
4 needn't have bought   5 didn't need to fill up   6 needn't have worried
7 didn't need to go   8 didn't need to wait   9 needn't have studied

127 **1** 1 ... You'd better start ...
2 ... I'd better get ...
3 You'd better open ...
4 ... she'd better not forget ...
5 We'd better give ...
6 We'd better invite ...
7 I'd better do ...
8 You'd better not tell ...
9 ... You'd better have ...
10 You'd better not let ...

2 *(Examples of possible answers)*
1 You'd better see the doctor.
2 You'd better go to bed.
3 You'd better put a sweater on.
4 You'd better go for a walk.
5 You'd better take a day off.
6 You'd better tell me all about it.
7 You'd better learn some Chinese and Japanese.
8 You'd better take a sleeping pill.
9 You'd better start studying.
10 You'd better stop.
11 You'd better ring the police.

128 **1** 1 used to live   2 used to stand   3 used to look after   4 used to play
5 used to take   6 used to look at   7 used to go   8 used to buy   9 used to keep
10 used to have

2 *(Examples of possible answers)*
1 People used to travel by horse.
2 People used to cook with/on wood fires.
3 People didn't use to live so long.
4 People used to fight with spears.
5 People used to hunt with bows and arrows.
6 People used to believe in ghosts and devils.
7 People didn't use to be able to vote.
8 People used to think the earth was flat.
9 People used to have bigger families.
10 Children used to work.

129 **1** Aspirins are supposed to cure headaches.
Catholics are supposed to go to church on Sundays.
You were supposed to come and see me yesterday.
It's supposed to have instructions with it, but I can't find them.
Wasn't my computer magazine supposed to come today?
What am I supposed to do with all this chicken salad?
You're not supposed to go into the shower with shoes on.
You're not supposed to smoke in food shops.
You're supposed to be good at geography – where the hell are we?
I think you're supposed to pay at the cash desk on the way out.

2 2 It's supposed to be a cat.
3 It's supposed to be a plane.
4 It's supposed to be a horse.
5 It's supposed to be a bus.
6 It's supposed to be a tiger.
7 It's supposed to be the sun.
8 It's supposed to be a flower.

130–131 **1** Buy the cat food here. It'll be cheaper.
Don't give her your keys. She'll only lose them.
Get John to have a look at the TV. He'll fix it.
'He'll grow up one day.' 'I hope you're right.'
He'll need somebody to help him.
'How's June?' 'She'll be OK.'
I must get back to work, otherwise I'll get the sack.
If he doesn't stop drinking, he'll be dead in five years.
If we give a shout, she'll come and help.
If you put lemon in it, he'll drink it.
Knowing his luck, if he plays golf he'll get hit on the nose with a ball.

No good sending her a bill, is it? She'll just refuse to pay.
One day you'll be old, and then your kids will laugh at you.
She'll be fourteen on May 12th.
She'll forget about you.

2 3 will / will not get
4 will / will not be
5 will / will not be
6 will / will not disappear
7 will / will not be

8 Everybody / Not everybody will have ...
9 Everybody / Not everybody will have ...
10 will / will not be
11 will / will not eat

3 *(Example of possible answer)*
Tomorrow will be mainly dry, but there will be some rain in the north. There will be strong winds from the south-west later in the day. It will be quite warm in the south, but Scotland will be cold, and in the north of Scotland the rain will turn to snow during the afternoon.

132–133 **1** She is going to try to become a professional pianist.
But first, she is going to spend a year learning German.
Max is going to do maths and science for his final exams.
Then he is going to train as a pilot.
Jennifer's eight, and she doesn't know what she is going to do.
One day she says she is going to be a dancer.
And the next she says she is going to start her own business.
This summer, Jane is going to stay with her aunt in America.
Max is going to spend the summer learning to fly.
Their parents are going to spend two weeks walking in Scotland.
Then they are going to decorate the house.

2 *(Examples of possible answers)*
1 She is going to have a baby.
2 He is going to swim / to dive into the water.
3 She is going to knock a cup off the table.
4 He is going to get on the bus.
5 She is going to open the letter.

6 They are going to have dinner.
7 He is going to have some wine.
8 The cat is going to catch the bird.
9 The mugger is going to attack somebody.
10 The pianist is going to play.

134 **1** 1 She's playing tennis on Sunday morning.
2 She's having lunch with James at 12.30 on Wednesday.
3 She's flying to Amsterdam on Thursday.
4 She's meeting Mrs Parsons in the Oxford office.
5 She's going to the meeting with Mrs Parsons by train.
6 She's going to a funeral on Wednesday morning.
7 She's meeting the accountants at 4 p.m. on Monday.
8 She's going to the theatre on Friday evening.
9 She's spending Saturday at the races.
10 Matthew is coming to see her on Sunday afternoon.

135 **1** 1 is going to cost 2 will cost 3 is going to have 4 will have 5 I'm playing
6 He'll win. 7 She'll tell 8 isn't going to stop 9 will have
10 She's getting married 11 It's going to rain 12 it will snow

136 **1** 1 does 2 arrives 3 will write 4 are going 5 go 6 will stop 7 do 8 are
9 have 10 doesn't 11 will come 12 do 13 am playing 14 does
15 will post

137 **1** 1 when; grow up 2 if; rains 3 when; am 4 if; passes 5 if; don't find
6 if; say 7 if; doesn't want 8 when; comes

2 1 get 2 am 3 will find 4 will keep 5 stops 6 bring 7 will take
8 will make 9 will be 10 get

138 **1** *(Examples of possible answers)*
1 What time will you be getting up?
2 What will you be wearing?
3 How will you be travelling to work?
4 How soon will you be leaving?
5 Will you be taking the car?
6 Will you be having lunch out?
7 What time will you be coming back?
8 Where will you be sleeping?
9 How will you be paying?
10 When will you be going back home?

2 ... I'll be teaching you English literature ...

139 **1** I won't have finished the report by Monday, and it's needed for Monday morning.
In a couple of years the children will have left home and we'll be able to get a smaller house.
On our next wedding anniversary we will have been married for twenty-five years.
When I get home tonight I will have been driving for fourteen hours non-stop.
When I retire I will have been working for forty years.

2 *(Examples of possible answers)*
1 After ten days she will have written 100 pages; after a month she will have written 300 pages; after a year she will have written 3,650 pages; after ten years she will have written 36,500 pages.
2 She will have finished her first book in/after a month. A year from now she will have written twelve books.
3 She will have been writing for ten years.
4 She will have made £12 million.

140 **1** *(Examples of possible answers)*
After arriving at Star City Airport, the president is to inspect a guard of honour.
At 09.00, he is to have a working breakfast with President Jensen.
From 11.00 to 13.00, he is to tour Star City and meet the mayor and civic leaders.
At 13.00 he is to have lunch with Foreign Minister Svendsen and guests.
At 14.00 he is to visit inner city schools; then he is to open a new eye hospital.
At 16.00 he is to meet business leaders; then he is free until 20.00, when he is to attend a State Dinner as the guest of President and Mrs Jensen.

2 *(Examples of possible answers)*
You're to do your piano practice.
You're not to give chocolate to the cat.
You're to go to bed at nine o'clock.
You're to learn how to use the washing machine.
You're not to leave dirty socks on the floor.
You're not to leave empty crisp-packets lying around.
You're not to make hour-long phone calls.
You're to make your own bed.
You're not to open the door to strangers.
You're to write your Christmas thank-you letters.

141 **1** Carola and I hardly noticed each other that first evening. Two weeks later we would be married.
He was to regret that conversation for many years to come.
I was going to ring you yesterday, but I forgot.
She was leaving in two hours, and she still hadn't started packing.
So this was the school where I would spend the next five years. I didn't like it.
The letter that was to change my life arrived one Friday morning.

2 1 was going to say   2 was marrying   3 was going to be   4 were to lose
5 were to find   6 would return; would stand; would make

142–143 **1**   **DIY**   **simple present:** permanent; habit; always; usually
present progressive: temporary; just around now; just at this moment; these days but
not for very long

3 1 read; make   2 am making   3 do you speak   4 are doing   5 plays
6 is playing   7 is she playing   8 Does she play   9 plays   10 is playing
11 is cooking   12 shop; cooks   13 doesn't work   14 isn't working

4 '... He collects dust.'   'So how's everything going?'

144–145 **1**   A woman is sitting in a railway carriage when she notices that the man opposite her is
holding an orange in his hand and looking out of the window. Suddenly the man opens
the window, throws out the orange and closes the window again. 'Excuse me,' the
woman asks, 'but why did you do that?' The man takes another orange out of his bag
and starts opening the window. 'Because we are going through the mountains.
Oranges keep the elephants away.' 'But there are no elephants in these mountains,'
says the woman. 'You see?' says the man. 'It works.'

3 The police station.

6 *(Example of possible answer)*
You fill a saucepan with water and put it on the cooker. When it boils you put the egg
in. You leave it for four and a half minutes and then you take it out.

146 **1**   *(Examples of possible answers)*
Milk is getting much more expensive. Newspapers are getting more expensive. Haircuts
are getting cheaper.

2 *(Examples of possible answers)*

The world's population is growing.	The political situation is getting worse.
I'm getting older.	Children are getting taller.
My English is getting much better.	Cities are getting dirtier.
Prices are going up.	It is becoming more difficult to provide
The days are getting shorter.	medical care for everybody.
Pollution is getting worse.	Teenagers are getting more violent.
Roads are getting busier.	Unemployment is becoming very serious.
Trains are getting dirtier.	Sprinters are getting faster.
Cars are getting faster and more	Men are living longer.
comfortable.	Women are living longer too.
Air travel is getting cheaper.	Older people are becoming more isolated.
People are destroying the world's forests.	People's holidays are getting longer.
Wildlife is disappearing.	

3 '... How's your English getting on?'   'That funny noise is getting louder.'

147 **1**   **DIY**   1 By adding *-s*.   2 You add *-s*.   3 You change *-y* to *-ies*.   4 *s, x, ch, sh*
5 *do, go*

2 boxes; brushes; buys; completes; cries; defends; denies; destroys; excites; expects; fries;
guesses; looks; prays; reaches; receives; rushes; spends; wants; watches.

3 1 does; teaches   2 happens   3 takes; washes   4 gets; sings   5 hates
6 starts; does   7 loves; hates   8 makes   9 comes; waits

148 **1**   1 belongs
2 believe/realise/suppose
3 Do ... hate/like/love/prefer/remember/understand
4 owns

    5 hates/likes/needs/prefers/wants
    6 need/want
    7 believe/realise/suppose; like/love/need/remember/understand/want
    8 forget/remember
    9 believes/hates/likes/loves/needs/remembers/understands/wants; believe/hate/*etc.*
   10 matter
   11 prefer/want
   12 remember
   13 contains

2   1 am having 2 has 3 is appearing 4 appears 5 are you looking 6 looks
      7 see 8 am seeing 9 think 10 are you thinking 11 am feeling / feel 12 feel

149 **1** Dad is always teasing me about my clothes.
      He's always arguing or fighting.
      He's always giving people small presents.
      Her best friend is always dropping in to criticise the way she lives her life.
      I hate those cartoons where Tom is always chasing Jerry.
      Jamie is always having colds and chest problems.
      My wife's always buying new products.
      She's always criticising her family.
      She's always saying she wishes she was prettier.
      Someone is always giving a party in one of the houses.
      That old bitch is always making up stories about people.

     2 **DIY** Criticism.

150 **1** 1 don't eat 2 is coming 3 goes 4 play 5 's sitting 6 happens 7 drinks
        8 She's wearing 9 are you looking 10 'm staying 11 usually stay 12 runs
        13 are you doing 14 gets 15 fly

     2 1d; 2c; 3f; 4e; 5j; 6a; 7b; 8g; 9i; 10h

     3 1 think 2 know; mean 3 is always complaining 4 always start
        5 is melting; take; break 6 am thinking 7 believe; is changing 8 don't see
        9 are you looking 10 understand

151 **1** *(Examples of possible answers)*
      1 The Foreign Minister is dead.   7 All the plates, knives etc are clean.
      2 Lucy has got a new baby.   8 She has a new job with the BBC.
      3 Your coat is torn.   9 We still don't know where he is.
      4 My leg is broken.   10 It's quiet.
      5 He can't find his address book.   11 I don't remember your name.
      6 Is tea ready?   12 She speaks French.

     2 '... His temperature has gone down.'
       He's dead.

152–153 **1** 1 Polly and Simon have just got married.
        2 The firm has lost £30 million this year.
        3 United have won the cup again.
        4 My poor old father has gone into hospital again.
        5 Somebody has just crashed into our garden gate.
        6 Lucy has had a baby girl.
        7 A parachutist has just landed on the roof.
        8 Some people have bought the house next door.

2   Ana Gomez, of Peru, has set a new record for the marathon. She covered the 42 km in
          just over 2 hours and 16 minutes.
          Novelist Maria Santiago has married actor Tony Delaney. They met while working on
          the screenplay for the film *Sun in the Morning*.
          Peter has just offered me a new job! He said I was just the person he needed.
          Police have found missing schoolgirl Karen Allen. She was at a friend's house in
          Birmingham.
          The World Cup team have arrived home. Five thousand fans were at the airport.
          Three climbers have died in the Alps. They fell just before reaching the summit of Mont
          Blanc (4,807 m).
          Two prisoners have escaped from Caernarvon high security prison. They stole
          dustmen's uniforms and walked out through the main gate.

154–155 **1** **finished time:** a long time ago; before I was born; in 1991; just after I got up; last year;
          when I was nine
          unfinished time: in my life; lately; this year; today

2   1 haven't seen   2 've never seen   3 've done   4 left   5 did you get
          6 haven't finished   7 've often wondered   8 caught   9 read   10 Have you seen

3   1 were   2 haven't read   3 Have you visited   4 lived   5 didn't discover; knew
          6 have discovered   7 gave   8 have you been   9 have never enjoyed
          10 Did you hear

5   'Oh yes! I've met ...'   'When did you last feed ... ?'

156–157 **1** 1 Yes.   2 No.   3 No.   4 Yes.   5 Yes.   6 No.

2   2 ... She has had bad luck all her life.
          3 I wanted to be a doctor until I was fifteen.
          4 He has been unemployed ever since he left school.
          5 How long have you lived in this town?
          6 I didn't work very hard when I was at university.
          7 ... but he has been fine since then.
          8 I have had trouble sleeping all this week.
          9 I had trouble sleeping all last week.
          10 I have learnt a lot in this job.
          11 I did not learn much in that job.
          12 My boyfriend and I have known each other for ages.
          13 He lived in Durban for a year before he got married.
          14 I spent three days in hospital last month.

3   1 have played   2 has had   3 ran   4 have you drunk   5 came   6 wrote
          7 has written   8 cooked; have cooked   9 have made   10 have just lost

5   I've spent ...

158–159 **1** 1 has been raining   2 have been learning   3 has been playing
          4 have ... been living   5 has been walking   6 have been working
          7 has been crying   8 has been playing   9 Have ... been waiting *(cartoon B)*
          10 've been waiting *(cartoon A)*

2   Aren't you hungry?' 'No, I've been eating all day.'
          'Is it true that Philip's been arrested?' 'Yes, he's been stealing things from shops.'
          'Janet seems very cheerful.' 'She's been skiing with Roger for the last week.'
          'She's very dirty.' 'She's been cleaning the cellar.'
          'Why are my books all over the floor?' 'Helen's been looking at them.'
          'Why's your hair wet?' 'I've been swimming.'
          'You all look very miserable.' 'Yes, we've been telling each other our life stories.'

'You look tired.' 'I've been gardening all afternoon.'
'You're very late.' 'I've been talking to Henry, and he just goes on and on.'
'Your hair's all white.' 'Yes, I've been painting the ceiling.'

3 *(Examples of possible answers)*

   1 It's been raining.   4 They've been running.
   2 She's been playing tennis.   5 She's been writing letters.
   3 He's been playing the guitar.   6 He's/They've been fighting.

160   **1**   1 has been standing   2 has stood   3 has been gardening; has planted
        4 has gone   5 has been seeing   6 have you been waiting   7 have waited
        8 has farmed   9 has only been farming   10 have been learning   11 have learnt
        12 has done   13 have been doing   14 have cleaned   15 have been washing

161   **1**   **DIY**   *since* **+ starting point;** *for* **+ period.** (We use *since* if we say when something started; we use *for* if we say how long it has lasted.)

    3   1 for   2 since   3 for   4 for   5 since   6 for   7 for

    4   1 Jake has been running / has run a small business for five years.
        2 Andy has been living / has lived in Dublin for a year / since last year.
        3 Helen has been playing / has played the piano for two years.
        4 Rob has had a Mercedes for five years.
        5 Jan has been living / has lived with Pete since 1994.
        6 Sammy has been learning Turkish for four years.

162   **1**   1 has been (snowing); got up   4 has been; got
        2 have been; lost   5 went; haven't heard
        3 took up; has had   6 has been; had

    2   *(Examples of possible answers)*
    He looks much younger since he shaved off his beard.
    It's nearly three years since he had a job.
    It's only a week since I met her, but it seems like years.
    It's too long since we last had a proper talk.
    She's a lot happier since she stopped going out with Pete.
    Things are better since we got our own flat.

163   **1**   **DIY**   Rule 3 is true.

    2   1 came   2 didn't like   3 've been lying   4 've never been   5 's been raining
        6 didn't come   7 ('ve) paid   8 got   9 have left   10 's/has moved   11 died
        12 's been   13 was   14 's gone   15 've been   16 for   17 's always been
        18 's left   19 wasn't   20 haven't trusted   21 broke   22 said   23 was
        24 hasn't been   25 have taken

164–165   **1**   1 was having; went   2 was lying   3 were all talking
        4 was coming; was shopping   5 met; was travelling   6 was talking; walked; stole
        7 came; stopped   8 looked; saw; were flying   9 woke; was pouring
        10 broke; was playing   11 went; was; was crying   12 told; was having

    2   *(Examples of possible answers)*
    While she was watching TV the ceiling fell in.
    While he was talking to a friend somebody stole his wallet.
    He took her photo while she was playing tennis.

    3   1 were throwing   2 were dancing   3 was/were not dancing   4 was grinning
        5 was holding   6 came   7 ordered   8 asked

166–167   **1**   **DIY**   Rule 3 gives the best explanation.

2 1 was sorry; had not been   6 had invited; had not invited
2 came; had forgotten   7 found; had hidden
3 had seen; knew   8 had never heard
4 had not checked; broke   9 came; had been
5 had lent   10 had already started; arrived

3 1 went 2 had not been 3 arrived 4 spent 5 had had 6 saw
7 had shared 8 had lost 9 had not seen 10 called 11 looked 12 turned
13 realised 14 had 15 saw 16 went 17 explained 18 had got
19 was not 20 felt 21 had not passed 22 had said 23 had arrived
24 had 25 thought 26 had 27 got 28 began 29 had happened

4 After he had tried on six pairs of shoes he decided he liked the first ones best.
After Mary had done all the shopping she took a short walk round the park.
When I had washed and dried the last plate Paul came in and offered to help.
When Mark had looked through all the drawers in his room he started going through
the cupboards downstairs.
When he had finished eating lunch he went to the café in the square for a cup of coffee.

5 When/After I had written to my boyfriend, I watched television ...
When/After everybody had had a chance to say what they thought, we ...
When/After I had posted the letter I felt ...
After she had stopped trying to lose weight she looked ...
When/After he had bought presents for everyone in his family he bought ...

168–169 **2** **DIY** Simple past perfect: diagram B; past perfect progressive: diagram C.

3 1 had been repairing   2 had been working   3 had been lying   4 had been driving

4 2 Kate, because she had been (doing some) gardening.
3 Stephanie, because she had been playing tennis.
4 John, because he had been practising (his) karate.
5 Pam, because she had been (horse-)riding.
6 Philip, because he had been painting (the ceiling in his room).
7 Roger, because he had been swimming.

5 Mr Lucas said he had been watching TV, but actually he had been stealing cars.
Mrs Allen said she had been talking on the phone, but actually she had been making a
bomb.
Mr Nash said he had been washing clothes, but actually he had been forging £5 notes.
Alice said she had been playing cards, but actually she had been selling drugs.
Pete said he had been studying chemistry, but actually he had been fighting.
Aunt Jane said she had been writing letters, but actually she had been planning a bank
robbery.
Miss Fry said she had been washing her hair, but actually she had been out dancing
with her sister's boyfriend.
Rob said he had been painting his flat, but actually he had been playing roulette.

170 **1** 1 ... I've seen this film   7 ... all the family has been together ...
2 ... you've sung that song ...   8 ... I've eaten this year
3 ... I've felt happy   9 ... the first thing you've said to me ...
4 ... you've made ...   10 ... the first clothes I've bought
5 ... I've ever seen her cry   myself ...
6 ... you've drunk ...

2 It was the first time he had worn uniform.
It was the first time he had had to make his own bed.
It was the first time he had cleaned his own boots.
It was the first time he had fired a gun.
It was the first time he had walked more than a mile.

171 **1** 1 How many days did you intend to stay?
2 I was hoping you could lend me £10.
3 I was wondering if you had two single rooms.
4 Were you looking for anything special?
5 Could you give me a hand?
6 I'm looking forward to seeing you again.
7 I was thinking I would borrow your bike ...
8 We could ask Peter to help us.
9 I was wondering if I could ask you a small favour.
10 I thought it would be a good idea to invite Simon.

172–175 **1** 1 has crashed; hit; had put   2 turned; went; had forgotten
3 have been doing; have cleaned   4 was lying; rang
5 started; had not been/gone   6 have been playing   7 got; was watching
8 haven't seen   9 have you been learning   10 has changed; came
11 have you seen; 've seen   12 have never seen   13 got
14 have often wondered; got   15 Have you read   16 have just discovered
17 Did you hear   18 has been   19 was talking; started; broke   20 had done
21 has been standing   22 has stood   23 have spent / have been spending; got
24 was; studied   25 had finished; sat   26 met; had been working
27 have never learnt   28 Have you finished   29 lived; was   30 has had

2 1 got   2 got   3 was   4 were   5 got   6 had already started   7 fell
8 were sitting   9 hit   10 turned   11 was sitting   12 waited/was waiting
13 was carrying   14 asked   15 told   16 disappeared   17 opened   18 saw
19 had approached   20 saw   21 took   22 shot   23 has seen
24 (have) fought   25 has/had been   26 were   27 began   28 was

3 A Look, Mary, I must go; I started leaving my husband an hour ago.
B How long have you had this fear of heights, Mr Winthrop?
C You booked us a holiday abroad during the summer. Could you tell us, please,
where we went?
D I've found another bit of metal, Maureen.
E Good Lord, Fenton, I had no idea you had died.
F First time you've done this job, is it?
G Perhaps I could help you choose, sir – what, exactly, have you done?
H He has nothing to do. All his batteries have run down.

176–177 **1** were left: simple past   were stranded: simple past
had been ... locked in: past perfect   were given: simple past

2 1 is spoken   2 was built   3 will be opened   4 is being interviewed
5 was being followed   6 Have you been invited   7 had been stolen   8 are made
9 are asked   10 is being mended   11 was burnt down   12 has just been found

3 1 Hamlet was written by Shakespeare.
2 She has been arrested for shoplifting.
3 Your car is being repaired now.
4 Spanish is spoken in Chile.
5 Has Peter been asked?
6 This ring was made by my mother.
7 This car is driven by electricity.
8 You will be told where to go.
9 She was knocked down by a drunken
motorist.
10 Manchester were beaten 3 – 0 by
Liverpool yesterday.
11 Paper was invented by the Chinese.
12 Hops are needed to make beer.
13 Stamps aren't sold in bookshops.
14 Your application is still being
considered by the directors.

4 ... you're being replaced ...

178–179 **1** **DIY** It would be difficult to rewrite the text sensibly with active verbs.
The best rules are 2 and 3.

2 1b   2b   3a   4a   5b

3 1a; 2b; 3a; 4b; 5a; 6b; 7a; 8a; 9b

4 **DIY** 2 We were shocked that nobody was prepared to take him to hospital.
3 I was annoyed that Mary wanted to tell everybody what to do.
4 I wan't pleased that George rang me up at three in the morning to tell me he was in
love again.
5 I was confused by the fact that he looked completely different from the last time I had
met him.

A passive can make it easier to move a **very heavy subject** to the end of a sentence.

180 **1** 2 We were brought papers to sign.   7 We are taught French by Mrs Lee.
3 Henry was given a clock ...   8 I have been lent a car for a week.
4 The children were read stories.   9 We were promised a full explanation.
5 I am owed £5,000.   10 I was told a lot of lies by the secretary.
6 I have been offered a new job.

2 1 had been told   2 had been given   3 was shown   4 was given   5 was given
6 had never been taught   7 was sent   8 was offered   9 was promised
10 wasn't being paid

181 **1** *(Examples of possible answers)*
Bills are being prepared/paid.   Money is being changed/paid/taken.
Coffee is being made/ordered/prepared/   New guests are being welcomed.
served.   Reservations are being made/taken.
Drinks are being ordered/served.   Rooms are being cleaned/prepared.
Food is being ordered/prepared/served.   Tables are being laid.
Luggage is being brought down.

2 *(Examples of possible answers)*
The houseboats have been turned into floating restaurants.
A new car park has been built.
New schools have been built.
The opera house has been rebuilt.
The old fire station has been turned into a theatre.
A ring road has been built.
The station has been modernised.
Some streets have been widened.
The town centre has been turned into a pedestrian precinct.
A statue of you has been put up in the park.
The Super Cinema has been turned into a supermarket.
Your house has been turned into a museum.

182 **1** 1 It is thought that the government will fail.
2 Mr Evans was appointed secretary.
3 She was called a witch by the villagers.
4 It was believed that fresh air was bad for sick people.
5 There are said to be wolves in the mountains.
6 The man holding the hostages is thought to be heavily armed.
7 He is said to be in an agitated state.
8 She was considered strange (by everybody).
9 The rate of inflation is expected to rise.
10 He is said to be somewhere in Germany.

11 Harris was seen to leave the plane in Ontario.
12 She is thought to have died in a plane crash.
13 The earth was believed to be the centre of the universe.
14 There is thought to be oil under Windsor Castle.
15 I was made to give them details of my bank accounts.

183　**1**　1 Could you send the bill to me? 6 Read me the letter, will you?
2 I've bought you a present. 7 She teaches French to adults.
3 Leave some potatoes for me. 8 I took Mrs Samuels the report.
4 I lent £5 to Bill yesterday. 9 Would you get a beer for me?
5 Show your picture to Granny. 10 We owe the bank £20,000.

184–185　**1**　blow up – explode break up – disintegrate get up – rise give up – abandon
go away – leave go into – enter look for – seek put off – postpone send back –
return talk about – discuss think over – consider turn up – arrive

2　**DIY**　Rules 1, 4 and 6 are correct.

3　1 We talked about it. 2 I put it off. 3 Could you look after them?
4 We broke it off. 5 Can you clean it up? 6 She put it on. 7 I'm looking for it.
8 I wrote it down. 9 I sent it back. 10 I stood on it.

4　1 away 2 on paper 3 not working 4 quieter 5 into pieces
6 to various people 7 further 8 higher 9 working 10 louder

186–187　**1**　**DIY**　*get* + direct object: receive, obtain, fetch, buy ...
get + adjective: become
get + adverb particle/preposition: move, change position

2　get across – cross get better – improve get bigger – increase, grow
get off – alight from, leave (public transport) get on – board (public transport)
get out of – leave get over – recover from get smaller – decrease, shrink
get to – reach get up – rise (from bed)

3　1 getting better 2 got into 3 Get on; get off 4 Get out 5 get wet 6 get cold
7 get old 8 get really hungry 9 getting tired/sleepy 10 gets dark

4　'Shall we go swimming?' 'OK. I'll just go and get changed.'
'What time do the animals get fed?' 'Eight o'clock.'
Every time he goes walking in the country he gets lost.
His glasses got broken in the fight.
I was talking to her on the phone but we got cut off.
I'm going to get undressed and go to bed.
If you leave your bag there, it'll get stolen.
That child takes an hour to get dressed in the morning.
They're going to get married next April.

188　**1**　1 to be working 2 be repaired 3 to go 4 to have seen 5 be having
6 to listen 7 to be chosen 8 not to be 9 have told 10 to be interrupted

2　*(Examples of possible answers)*
2 She seems to be drinking. 6 She seems to be talking on the phone.
3 She must be driving. 7 She could be brushing her hair.
4 She may be playing tennis. 8 She may be reading.
5 She could be washing.

189 **1**
1 I'm glad to have met you.
2 I was sorry to have disturbed him.
3 I expect to have passed ...
4 You seem to have made ...
5 I'm happy to have had a chance ...
6 I was disappointed to have missed ...
7 She seems to have got lost.
8 She was pleased to have found ...

2
2 I would like to have seen his face when ...
3 He meant to have finished all his work ...
4 We were to have spent a week skiing.
5 It was to have been the happiest ...
6 She meant to have said goodbye ...
7 I would like to have lived ...
8 He was to have played ...

190 **1**
2 You should eat enough.
3 I might go sailing ...
4 She expects to get married ...
5 I agreed to help her.
6 We must make ...
7 He seems to be ill.
8 I wish I could change ...
9 I hope to come ...
10 You needn't apologise.
11 They have decided to open ...
12 I promise to pay you ...
13 I didn't manage to find ...
14 I would rather go ...
15 She refused to see ...
16 I've learnt to play chess.

191 **1** *(Examples of possible answers)*
'Ann really upset Granny.' 'I'm sure she didn't mean to.'
'Are you enjoying your new job?' 'Well, I'm starting to.'
'Can I see you home?' 'If you'd like to.'
'Can you mend this by Tuesday?' 'I'll try to, but I can't promise.'
'Did you get my coat from the cleaner's?' 'Sorry, I forgot to.'
'Do you collect stamps?' 'No, but I used to.'
'Do you think he knows what he's doing?' 'He seems to.'
'Do you want to come out with us tonight?' 'I'd like to, but I'm working late.'
'Does she think she'll win?' 'Yes, she expects to.'
'How would you and Sue like to spend the weekend with us?' 'We'd love to.'
'I think you ought to see the police about the people next door.' 'I intend to. They can't go on keeping the whole street awake every night.'
'Shall we go swimming?' 'I don't really want to – it's too cold.'
'Should we book seats in advance?' 'We don't need to – there's always plenty of room.'
We'd like to move to a bigger house but we can't afford to.

192 **1** *(Examples of possible answers)*
2 You go to a bookshop to buy books.   3 ... to see a film.   4 ... to see a play.
5 ... to swim.   6 ... to exercise.   7 ... to learn to drive.   8 ... to catch a train.
9 ... to catch a plane.   10 ... to book a holiday.   11 ... to pray.
12 ... to watch a football match.   13 ... to get money.   14 ... to buy stamps.
15 ... to have a meal.   16 ... to buy food.   17 ... to get petrol.
18 ... to buy a newspaper.

193 **1**
1 surprised   2 surprising   3 tiring   4 tired   5 disappointing   6 disappointed
7 excited   8 exciting   9 shocked   10 shocking   11 confusing   12 confused
13 annoyed   14 annoying

2 The visitors are boring (and the host is bored).

3
A botanist is interested in plants.
A cook is interested in food.
A doctor is interested in medicine.
An explorer is interested in travel.
A fashion designer is interested in clothes.
A geographer is interested in places.
A historian is interested in the past.
A linguist is interested in languages.
A mathematician is interested in numbers.
A zoologist is interested in animals.

194–195

1 1 Drinking   2 paying   3 hearing   4 lying   5 skiing; climbing   6 Learning
7 saying   8 Forgetting   9 Watching   10 Answering; typing

3 1 Do you mind me asking ... ?
2 I don't appreciate you shouting ...
3 I couldn't understand Pat wanting ...
4 What's the use of them asking ... ?
5 ... by Peter needing to see ...
6 I was astonished at you expecting ...
7 ... by Ann having to go ...
8 She can't stand me telling her ...

196

1 *(Examples of possible answers)*
Do you feel like helping me?
Do you have time to do anything else besides looking after the children?
He insisted on paying for everything.
He passed his exams in spite of not doing any work.
How about going out to a restaurant tonight?
I apologise for disturbing you.
I like walking as well as playing football.
I sometimes dream of having time to read all my books.
I'm fed up of/with selling things.
I'm not capable of understanding this – it's too difficult.
I'm tired of answering that child's questions.
She succeeded in convincing the police that she was not a burglar.
She talked about/of changing her job, but I don't think she will.
She's keen on cooking.
She's very good at swimming and dancing.
Thank you for telling me the truth.
We're excited about moving to Canada.
We're thinking of seeing George next week.
Why don't you come out with us instead of staying at home?
You can't live without eating.

197

1 2 By playing loud music.
3 By robbing a bank.
4 By oiling it.
5 By looking in a dictionary.
6 By taking an aspirin.
7 By using an extinguisher.
8 By switching on the ignition.

2 *(Examples of possible answers)*
A paperclip is for holding papers together.
Soap is for washing.
A saucepan is for cooking.
A pen is for writing.
Money is for buying things.
A knife is for cutting things.
A bag is for carrying things.
A hairbrush is for brushing hair.

198

1 **DIY** 1A   2C   3B

2 Aren't you used to walking this far?
Starting at half four's no problem – I'm used to getting up early.
I look forward to receiving your comments.
I look forward to seeing you again in six months' time.
I object to paying for it. It should be free.
I'll never get used to sleeping on the floor.
I'm not looking forward to going back to school.
I'm not sure where to turn. I'm not used to coming this way.
If you're used to having money, it's hard to be without it.
Sean's used to dealing with difficult kids.

199

1 **DIY** **verb + infinitive:** agree; dare; decide; expect; fail; happen; hope; manage; mean; offer; prepare; pretend; promise; refuse; seem; wish
verb + -*ing* form: avoid; can't help; deny; (can't) face; fancy; feel like; finish; give up; imagine; keep (on); mind; miss; postpone; practise; put off; risk; spend time; (can't) stand; suggest

2   1 liking   2 to stay   3 to hear   4 going   5 cooking   6 studying   7 smoking
8 being   9 to find   10 passing   11 seeing   12 to be   13 seeing   14 talking
15 to see   16 watching

200   **1**   1 You can go fishing   2 ... go riding   3 ... go sailing   4 ... go shopping
5 ... go skating   6 ... go swimming   7 ... go skiing

201   **1**   1 The shoes need cleaning.   5 The chicken needs cooking.
2 The window needs mending.   6 The car needs servicing.
3 The racket needs re-stringing.   7 The wall needs painting.
4 The bed needs making.   8 The man's hair needs cutting.

202–203   **1**   *(Examples of possible answers)*   Her son wants her to buy him some new
Her boss wants her to work harder.   clothes.
Her daughter wants her to buy her a car.   The butcher wants her to pay his bill.
Her husband wants her to cook supper.   The dog wants her to take him for a walk.
Her mother wants her to leave her   The government wants her to pay taxes.
   husband.   The vicar wants her to go to church.

2   1 They didn't allow us to look at the   6 Did you mean me to pay?
   house.   7 The captain ordered the men to attack.
2 I asked Jake to be more careful.   8 I reminded Sue to buy coffee.
3 She encouraged me to try the exam.   9 She taught me to cook.
4 I expect him to come soon.   10 I don't want her to tell anybody.
5 I left him to solve the problem.

4   'I'm not asking you to serve me ...'

5   1 Her parents let her stay up late.
2 Her parents made her do the washing up.
3 Her parents let her read what she liked.
4 Her parents made her iron her own clothes.
5 Her parents made her do her homework.
6 Her parents let her drink beer.
7 Her parents made her clean up her room.
8 Her parents made her go to church.
9 Her parents let her have parties.
10 Her parents let her choose her own school.

204–205   **1**   **DIY**   Things people did: *remember ...ing*. Things people have/had to do: *remember* +
infinitive.

2   **DIY**   Change: *go on* + infinitive. Continuation: *go on ...ing*.

3   **DIY**   Infinitive after object; *-ing* form if there is no object.

4   **DIY**   Activity stops: *-ing* form. Reason for stopping: infinitive.

5   **DIY**   Only infinitive after *would like, would prefer* etc.

6   **DIY**   Both structures for things that are difficult; *try ...ing* for experiments.

7   **DIY**   Action going on: object + *-ing* form. Completed action: object + infinitive
without *to*.

8   1 meeting   2 to post   3 not visiting   4 to talk   5 learning   6 to make
7 visiting   8 watching / to watch   9 to spend   10 to come   11 reading
12 to repair / repairing   13 waiting   14 break   15 crawling   16 to get
17 working   18 to tell

206   **1**   **DIY**   The five which cannot are *fine, intelligent, lazy, unusual, well*.

2 *(Examples of possible answers)*
I'm bad at getting up early.
I'm bored with seeing the same faces every day.
I'm capable of going for a long time without sleep.
I'm excited about seeing my family next weekend.
I'm fed up with (*or* of) studying.
I'm fond of dancing.
I'm good at repairing cars.
I'm guilty of breaking the speed limit.
I'm tired of listening to the children.

207

1 **DIY** **Followed by infinitive:** decision, need, plan, time, wish
Followed by preposition + ...ing: difficulty, hope, idea, thought

2 1 to go 2 in reading 3 of arriving 4 of leaving 5 to tell 6 to spend
7 of losing 8 to go 9 to meet

3 Has he got any hope of passing the exam?
He made a decision to start a new life.
Does your fear of flying stop you travelling?
Lucy has difficulty in keeping her temper.
She hated the thought of dying without seeing the world.
She was a fool to buy that car.
There's no need to get angry.
They have a plan to start a business.
Time to get up!

208–209

1 1 There's no need for the meeting to start before eight.
2 It's time for the postman to come.
3 It's unusual for him to be late.
4 I'm anxious for the children to go to a good school.
5 It's a bad idea for John to go to Australia.
6 It would be a mistake for Sue to change her job just now.
7 Is it possible for Paul to come to the meeting?
8 It's important for the car to have regular services.
9 It's normal for him to stay up late on Saturdays.
10 I'd be happy for you to take a holiday.

2 1 It's important for there to be public libraries.
2 It's vital for there to be a good public transport system.
3 It's important for there to be plenty of open spaces.
4 It's essential for there to be enough car parks.

3 *(Examples of possible answers)*
English is easy to understand.
Chinese is hard to learn.
Small children are interesting to watch.
Silver is hard to clean.

Boiled eggs are good to eat.
Lobster is hard to eat.
Some modern music is boring to listen to.

210–211

1 Was the train very crowded, dear?

2 *(Examples of possible answers)*
1 Where is the small village?
2 Where do the three families live?
3 How many children have Alice and George got?
4 Who has got a baby daughter?
5 What does George do?
6 What do Joe and Sue do?
7 What does Alice take care of?
8 Where does Joe work?
9 What does Joe design?
10 What does Pam do? / What is Pam's job?
11 How many of the children go to school in the village?
12 How do the other children go to school?
13 Where is the secondary school?
14 How far away is it?

3 *(Examples of possible answers)*
1 Who does the cooking?
2 Who does the housework?
3 Who does the repairs?
4 Who takes care of the garden?
5 What is their biggest worry?
6 What needs replacing?
7 What needs repairing?

212 **1**
1 'What's your flat like?'
2 'How's your mother?'
3 'How's work going?'
4 'How's business?'
5 'What's Anne's boyfriend like?'
6 'How's school?'

2 *(Examples of possible answers)*
1 What size 2 What colour 3 What sort of 4 What make 5 What time
6 What time 7 What sort of 8 What size 9 What make of 10 Where ever
11 Who ever 12 What ever

213 **1**
2 Austrians don't speak Japanese.
3 Roses aren't green.
4 Cats can't fly.
5 Shakespeare wasn't French.
6 Fridges don't run on petrol.
7 The sun doesn't go round the earth.
8 Telescopes don't make things smaller.
9 There aren't seventeen players in a rugby team.
10 Bananas don't grow in Scotland.

214–215 **1**
1 Aren't you cold?
2 Why aren't you eating?
3 Don't you speak French?
4 Aren't the shops closed?
5 Hasn't the postman come?
6 Isn't your mother at home?

2
2 Don't you speak German?
3 Isn't that Pamela ... ?
4 Didn't you study ... ?
5 Isn't this your coat?
6 Isn't your father a doctor?
7 Wasn't Tony going to come ... ?
8 Won't you be in Edinburgh next week?
9 Aren't you making a mistake?
10 Wouldn't it be better to stop now?

3
2 Didn't she pass the exam?
3 Haven't you paid for your ticket?
4 Didn't you lock the door?
5 Can't you understand English? ...
6 Don't you like my cooking?
7 Didn't you get the letter I sent?
8 Didn't you enjoy the film?
9 Aren't you and John going to get married?
10 Don't you want any more potatoes?

4
2 No, I don't. 3 No, I can't. 4 Yes, it is. 5 Yes, I have. 6 Yes, she was.
7 No, I'm not. 8 No, I didn't.

216 **1**
1 not 2 not 3 no 4 not 5 no 6 not 7 not 8 Not 9 no 10 not/no

217 **1**
1 I don't think you're right.
2 I don't believe you've met my sister.
3 I don't suppose you know where Ruth is.
4 I don't imagine we'll arrive before midnight.
5 I don't think they know what they're doing.
6 I don't think I made myself clear.
7 I don't suppose you remembered to bring my book back.
8 I don't believe I've got enough money.

2 1 He doesn't seem to be well.
   2 I don't expect to be home late.
   3 I never want to climb another mountain.
   4 It doesn't seem to be raining.
   5 I don't expect to pass the exam.
   6 He never wants to get married.

218–219

1 1 Don't use 2 Add 3 Mix 4 oil 5 put in 6 Shape 7 bake

3 1 Always add salt ...
   2 Always check the tyres ...
   3 Never cook chicken ...
   4 Never wait more ...
   5 Always unplug ...
   6 Always count your change ...
   7 Never/Always put off ...
   8 Never/Always say ...
   9 Always/Never pay ...
   10 Never apologise ...

4 *(Examples of possible answers)*
   1 Don't be (so) greedy.
   2 Do be careful.
   3 Don't be angry.
   4 Do be back by midnight.
   5 Don't be frightened.
   6 Don't be (so) stupid.
   7 Do be on time.
   8 Don't be (so) rude.
   9 Don't be (so) jealous.

220

1 *(Examples of possible answers)*
   3 Let's play tennis. 4 Let's go for a walk. 5 Let's not play cards.
   6 Let's play chess. 7 Let's go to Paris. 8 Let's go and see a film.
   9 Let's not go dancing. 10 Let's go skiing. 11 Let's do the washing up.
   12 Let's go to a restaurant.

221

1 **DIY** The subject and verb come at the end of the exclamation.

2 2 How interesting!
   3 What a nuisance!
   4 What big eyes you've got, grandmother!
   5 How disgusting!
   6 How noisy those children are!
   7 How well he cooks!
   8 How wrong we were!
   9 What a lot of nonsense he talks!
   10 What funny clothes she wears!
   11 How badly she plays!
   12 What a fool I was!

3 2 Isn't that interesting!
   3 Isn't that a nuisance!
   4 Haven't you got big eyes, grandmother!
   5 Isn't that disgusting!
   6 Aren't those children noisy!
   7 Doesn't he cook well!
   8 Weren't we wrong!
   9 Doesn't he talk a lot of nonsense!
   10 Doesn't she wear funny clothes!
   11 Doesn't she play badly!
   12 Wasn't I a fool!

222–223

1 1 There is 2 There were 3 there was 4 there will be 5 There's
   6 Are there 7 There have been 8 There are not 9 There's been 10 there isn't

2 1 There's 2 It's 3 It's 4 There's 5 It's 6 There's 7 There's 8 It's
   9 There's 10 It's

3 According to the forecast, there's likely to be more snow tonight.
I can't see how to open the door. There must be a keyhole somewhere.
I'm looking forward to the party. There are sure to be some nice people there.
OK, children, now I don't want there to be any noise while I'm on the phone.
That must be Jeff. There can't be two people who look like that.
There are too many people looking for too few jobs in this country.
There aren't any tickets now, but there may be some tomorrow.
There's no need to hurry. We've got plenty of time.
There's no point in going out if you've got a headache – you won't enjoy it.
There's something the matter with the car – it won't start.
'What did the doctor say?' 'He says there's nothing wrong with me.'
'Why have we stopped?' 'There seems to be something lying in the road.'

224 **1**   1 My wife's on holiday.   2 I couldn't ...   3 Have you seen Joe?   4 Be careful ...
5 There's nobody ...   6 I don't think so.   7 The train's late again.
8 Do you know ... ?   9 Have you got ... ?   10 I've lost ...

2   1 Changed my job.   2 Doesn't know ...   3 Cost you £10.   4 Careful of ...
5 No time ...   6 Bus is coming.   7 Speak English?   8 Haven't been there.
9 Thinks he's clever.   10 Got a light?

225 **1**   1 ... but I can tomorrow.   6 ... Yes, it is.
2 ... and Sue has too.   7 ... but I can.
3 ... Yes, I would (have).   8 ... and Celia doesn't either.
4 ... It certainly does.   9 ... but I do.
5 ... I have.

2   *(Examples of possible answers)*
1 think the whole thing is too absurd /   5 come round
   think so   6 ready to take offence
2 thought that/so   7 ready to take offence
3 think that/so   8 want to quarrel
4 come round   9 want to say another thing about it

226 **1**   1 aren't I   2 aren't we   3 are they   4 am I   5 were they   6 is she   7 isn't it
8 isn't he   9 can't he   10 mustn't it   11 won't it   12 don't they   13 will they
14 isn't there   15 hasn't she   16 does she   17 haven't they   18 wasn't I

227 **1**   1 they   2 are you   3 is there   4 does it   5 they   6 did she   7 haven't they
8 is there   9 did you

2   Do have some more tea, won't you?   Pass me the newspaper, could/will/
Don't drive too fast, will you?   would you?
Let's start again, shall we?   You couldn't tell me the time, could you?

228 **1**   *(Examples of possible answers)*
1 Yes, I am. / No, I'm not.   6 Yes, I have. / No, I haven't.
2 Yes, I do. / No, I don't.   7 No, I can't. / Yes, I can.
3 It certainly is.   8 He certainly does.
4 I won't.   9 Yes, she did.
5 I will.   10 I will.

2   *(Example of possible answer)*
'It was a lovely wedding.'
'Was it?'
'Yes. Though I didn't think much of Maggie's dress.'
'Didn't you?'
'No, that colour doesn't suit her at all.'
'Doesn't it?'
'No, it doesn't. Anyway, I don't really go for church weddings.'
'Don't you?'
'No. And the service went on for ages.'
'Did it really?'
'Yes. And I was sitting right at the back, so I couldn't hear the vicar.'
'Couldn't you?'
'No. The music was nice, though.'
'Was it?'
'Yes. They played that hymn about sheep. Lovely. I must say I didn't enjoy the
   reception much.'
'Didn't you?'
'No. The food wasn't very good.'

'Oh, dear. Wasn't it?'
'No. And the bride's father made such a stupid speech.'
'Did he, dear?'
'Yes. And I got one of my headaches.'
'Did you? I am sorry.'
'Yes. Champagne always gives me a headache.'
'Does it?'
'Yes, it really does. And I was sitting next to that Mrs Foster from down the road. I can't
    stand that woman.'
'Can't you?'
'No, she's always criticising.'
'Is she really?'
'Yes. Anyway, I must go.'
'Oh, must you?'
'Yes. Nice to talk to you. It really was a lovely wedding.'

229   **1**   *(These are the sentences that the people said, but other answers are possible.)*
          1 I think so   2 I'm afraid so   3 I suppose so   4 I think so   5 I hope so
          6 I think so   7 I think so   8 I'm afraid so   9 I hope so   10 I suppose so

          2   1 I'm afraid not   2 I don't think so   3 I hope not   4 I suppose not
          5 I'm afraid not   6 I hope not   7 I suppose not   8 I don't think so

230–231   **1**   1 so is   2 Neither/Nor have   3 neither/nor can   4 So do   5 So did
          6 neither/nor do   7 so was   8 neither/nor will   9 So do   10 Neither/Nor was

          3   *(Examples of possible answers)*
          The cat is black, and so is the handbag.   The parrot isn't green, and neither is the
          The car doesn't cost much, and nor does   butterfly.
              the motorbike.   The shoes are white, and so is the fish.
          The car is green, and so is the frog.

232–233   **1**   2 It annoys me to hear her talk like that.   6 It makes me tired to watch him.
          3 It takes four hours to get ...   7 It upsets me to hear her complaining.
          4 It's silly to get upset ...   8 It's hard to say no to people.
          5 It's nice to get up in the morning, but
              it's nicer to stay in bed.

          2   2 It's a good thing that she's got some money saved.
          3 It doesn't bother me that he's got long hair.
          4 It worried her that John never talked to her.
          5 It is essential that she should be told immediately.
          6 It was strange that he didn't remember my name.
          7 It's a pity that he can't come.
          8 It is important that the children should get to bed early.
          9 It is not true that wolves attack people.
          10 It shocked me that she stole money.

          3   *(Examples of possible answers)*
          It doesn't interest me what you think.
          It looks as if we're going to have trouble with Ann again.
          It seems that he forgot to buy the tickets.
          It will be a pity if we have to ask her to leave.
          It's exciting when a baby starts talking.
          It's important that everybody should have a chance to speak.
          It's probable that we'll be a little late.
          It's surprising how many unhappy marriages there are.

5 He made it difficult to like him.
His bad leg made it a problem to walk.
I thought it strange that she hadn't
    written.

He made it clear what he wanted.
I find it interesting to hear her stories.

234–235 **1** 1 It was the baby that/who put marmalade ...
It was marmalade that the baby put ...
It was Dad's trousers that the baby put marmalade on ...
It was this morning that the baby put ...
2 It was Maria that/who gave ...
It was her old bicycle that Maria gave ...
It was Pat that Maria gave her old bicycle to ...
It was last week that Maria gave ...
3 It was Carl that/who broke ...
It was the kitchen window that Carl broke ...
It was a ladder that Carl broke the kitchen window with today.
It was today that ...
4 It was Mark that/who met Cathy ...
It was Cathy that Mark met ...
It was in Germany that Mark met ...
It was in 1992 that Mark met ...

2 2 It's not you I love, it's Peter.
3 It's not Carol that's/who's the boss, it's Sandra.
4 It's not the music I hate, it's the words.
5 It wasn't my glasses I lost, it was my keys.
6 It isn't Bob that's/who's getting married, it's Clive.
7 It wasn't Judy I saw, it was Jill.
8 It's not maths he's studying, it's physics.
9 It's not Max that's/who's crazy, it's you.
10 It's not a nail you need, it's a screw.

3 2 What I need is a drink.
3 What I like is her sense of humour.
4 What I hate is his jealousy.
5 What keeps me fit is cycling.
6 What makes the job interesting is the travelling.
7 All I want is five minutes' rest.
8 What I found was something very strange.
9 What stopped us was the weather.
10 What I don't understand is why she stays with him.

236 **1** **DIY**   all; at; by; this; under; with

2 Although he was very bad-tempered, he had lots of friends.
Always brush your teeth after you have a meal.
Always wash your hands before you have a meal.
As Liz told you, her mother left for Berlin last Friday.
Because I knew her family, I did what I could for her.
Talk to me like that again and I'll hit you.
Don't do that again or I'll hit you.
He had a terrible temper, but everybody liked him.
Liz explained to you that her mother went back home last week.
I was sorry for her, so I tried to help her.
If you do that again, you'll be sorry.
There'll be trouble unless you stop that.

237 **1** 1 After I've finished work, I'll come round to your place.

2 When the weather gets better, let's have a weekend in the country.

3 Before you go back to Canada, you ought to see Paula.

4 Although I didn't understand everything, I enjoyed the lecture.

6 Until Sean phones, we won't know what's happening.

7 As we're going out tonight, I'm going to buy some new jeans.

8 While they were asleep, somebody broke into the house.

9 Since he met Julie, he hasn't looked at another woman.

12 Because he was deaf, he didn't understand the policeman.

The order cannot be changed in 5, 10, or 11.

2 1 did   2 spoke   3 went   4 gave up   5 felt   6 left

238–239 **1** 1 as long as / provided   2 until   3 so that   4 while   5 as if / as though
6 until   7 as if / as though   8 as long as / provided   9 so that   10 While

2 He went to Switzerland so that he could learn French.

I don't mind you singing as long as you do it quietly.

We moved the piano so that there would be room for the Christmas tree.

We took some blankets so that we would be warm enough.

We'll come back this afternoon as long as that's OK with you.

We'll play tennis as long as it doesn't rain.

3 2 While she's very clever, she's got no common sense at all.

3 While I know how you feel, I think you're making a mistake.

4 While the job's well paid, it's deadly boring.

5 While I'm interested in economics, I wouldn't want to work in a bank.

6 While the hotel was nice, it was a long way from the beach.

4 1 She looks as if she's going swimming.   5 She looks as if she's had bad news.

2 He looks as if he's lost something.   6 He looks as if he's seen a ghost.

3 She looks as if she's been painting.   7 It looks as if it's going to rain.

4 He looks as if he's got a cold.   8 He looks as if he's had good news.

240 **1** 1 before   2 while   3 After   4 when   5 since   6 before   7 after   8 since
9 while   10 when/while

2 Don't go swimming immediately after eating.

Have a rest every hour or so when driving long distances.

He has been terribly depressed since failing the exam.

I had a word with Janet before talking to Eric.

I often solve problems in my head while running.

She always gets nervous before going on stage.

Since coming back from America we haven't even had time to unpack.

A few days after returning from holiday he began to feel ill.

241 **1** 1 Having left school at twelve, he had ...   7 A lorry broke down in High Street,

2 It tastes delicious fried in butter ...   causing a ...

3 Walking over to her desk, she picked ...   8 Not wanting to frighten her, I phoned ...

4 The water came into the houses,   9 Sent first class, it should ...
flooding the ...   10 At 3 a.m. Simon came in, waking

5 Knowing his tastes, I took ...   everybody ...

6 Putting on his coat, he went out.

2 1 thinking   2 staring   3 getting   4 sacrificing   5 thrown   6 dreaming

242   **1**   1   He repairs both cars and motorbikes.
2   He speaks neither English nor French.
3   I neither like nor dislike her.
4   I both admire (him) and distrust him.
5   Both Paul and Sally are on holiday.
6   Neither the secretary nor the accountant had the file.
7   The play was both funny and shocking.
8   He collects both paintings and jewellery.
9   You're neither right nor wrong.
10   She neither looked at me nor said anything.

243   **1**   Did you know there were mice in   I thought you'd get lost.
     the cellar?   I was surprised she wasn't angry with me.
He suggested we might like to go skiing   I'm glad we've had this talk.
     with him.   It's funny he didn't say hello to you.
I believe this is your coat.   Tell me you love me.
I expect you've seen this already.   Were you surprised I phoned you?
I heard you'd got a new job.   You knew I wouldn't forget your birthday.

     2   1   provided that   2   so   3   Now   4   such ... that   5   so that   6   provided
     7   Now that

244–245   **1**   1   will find; go   2   have; will write   3   Will you stay; takes   4   will be; recognises
     5   will go; go   6   will give; finds   7   will ask; want   8   will find; are
     9   win; will have   10   arrive; will phone

     2   1   would be able; thought   6   would tell; thought
     2   would always; was; knew   7   would be; could; liked
     3   would never do; went   8   would not give; asked
     4   would be; had; wanted   9   would mean; spent
     5   would hit; talked

     3   1   was; had not helped; needed   4   had done; needed
     2   has been; lasted   5   talks; is thinking
     3   have usually liked; worked

246   **2**   **DIY**   2 is the best explanation.

     3   You're; today; Oh, thanks; You are; OK; you (sit); I'll (get) you; (There)'s;
     Yes (there) is; there; I don't (want); (It)'s; I'll (sit); here; you can't; these;
     are (taken); etc.

247   **1**   **DIY**   **a**   neither has to be changed   **c**   the first 'this' has to be changed
     b   the second 'this' has to be changed   **d**   both have to be changed

     2   last week – the week before   next week – the next week/the week after
     now – then/that day/right away   this – that/the/last   this morning – that morning
     today – that day   tomorrow – the next day   tonight – that night
     yesterday – the day before

     3   2   that evening   3   there   4   the week before   5   the   6   right away/then
     7   that morning   8   that night   9   the day before   10   that day

248–249   **1**   **DIY**

DIRECT SPEECH	INDIRECT SPEECH
simple present	simple past
present progressive	past progressive
present perfect	past perfect
simple past	past perfect
will ...	*would ...*

2 1 was   2 played   3 could   4 were leaving   5 hadn't brushed   6 had had
7 had left   8 wouldn't say   9 would know   10 had been opened

3 1 fancied   2 had never met   3 had   4 wanted   5 was   6 did   7 was doing
8 could not   9 moved / was moving   10 thought   11 wanted   12 could
13 would call   14 wanted   15 thought   16 was falling   17 was lying
18 had   19 didn't matter   20 were   21 was going   22 were   23 had left

250 **1** 2 I asked what the dark-haired child's name is/was.
3 Are you deaf? I said I'm/I was utterly fed up.
4 I told you it's/it was raining.
5 I said you'll/you'd get your money.
6 This article … said the weather is/was changing.
7 Al told me the repairs will/would cost £5,000.
8 I asked if Jane is/was coming to see us.
9 Pat told me that you're/you were going to the north.
10 I bet … that you won't/wouldn't pass your exam.
11 See – I told you he hasn't/hadn't got much sense of humour.
12 Sue … said they're/they were getting married next week.

251 **1** 1 I asked what Peter's address was.
2 … when the new manager was coming.
3 … how she knew my name.
4 … why all the windows were open.
5 … how many books he wanted.
6 … where they kept the money.
7 … what time the meeting was.
8 … when the last train left.
9 … how the photocopier worked.
10 … how often Ann went shopping.

2 1 I wondered if they liked me.
2 … if/whether I would be ready in time.
3 … if/whether there was any food in the house.
4 … whether/if service was included or not.
5 … if/whether I could pay by cheque.
6 … if/whether my hair looked funny.
7 … if/whether the postman had been.
8 … if/whether they spoke English.
9 … if/whether I was doing the right thing.
10 … whether/if the meeting was on Tuesday or Wednesday.

252 **1** 2 She offered to cook supper.
3 He advised me to leave early.
4 She asked me to close the door.
5 She promised to stop smoking.
6 He offered to do the shopping.
7 She advised me to tell the police.
8 I told her to wait outside.
9 He agreed to pay half.
10 She told me to park round the corner.
11 I asked him how to find the house.
12 She told me when to phone.
13 I told him what to say.
14 We offered to pay for the tickets.

253 **1** **DIY**   1 After **tell**, we normally say **who** is spoken to. We do not put 'to' before the object.
2 After **say**, we don't have to say **who** is spoken to. If we do, we put 'to' before the object.
3 **Tell** means 'inform' or 'instruct'. It can't introduce questions.
4 **Say** can't normally be used before an infinitive.

2 1 said   2 Tell   3 told   4 say   5 tell   6 told   7 say   8 tell   9 said   10 Say

254 **1** 1 I knew (that) I had seen him once before in London.
2 The professor said (that) Shakespeare didn't speak French.
3 When I got there, I found out (that) he had died two years before.
4 It said on this TV programme that three thousand years ago there were tigers in England.
5 It said on this morning's news that somebody had thrown a bomb at the Prime Minister.
6 I read in a magazine that the ancient Romans suffered from lead poisoning.

2 1 She asked me if I would like a drink.
2 I said (that) I couldn't help it.
3 They thought (that) they should be home about six.
4 The forecast said (that) it might rain.
5 Everybody said (that) she must be joking.
6 I explained that I hadn't seen the notice.

255 **1** 1 She thought (that) he was ill.
2 He said (that) he would be back the next day.
3 She said (that) she didn't like the music.
4 She asked me where the bus station was.
5 I asked him if/whether he had finished.
6 I felt (that) nobody loved me.
7 He asked her whether/if she wanted tea or coffee.
8 She offered to clean the flat.
9 I asked when the car was going to be ready.
10 I wondered what I was doing there.
11 He proved that the earth is/was not flat.
12 I knew (that) those figures couldn't be right.
13 She thought (that) her cat understood everything she said.
14 I asked what the boss wanted.
15 I wondered if/whether Mary had phoned back.
16 I wondered if/whether dinosaurs laid eggs.
17 He advised me to see the doctor.
18 She asked him if/whether he would like a drink.

2 '... I thought they were yours.'
'... no doubt you're wondering why I sent for you.'

256–257 **1** If anybody asks you what you're doing, say you're with me.
How can you make decisions if you don't know what's going on?
If I buy three kilos, that'll do for a few weeks.
If I don't get up till nine, I never get anything done.
If I can't fix the video, I'll take it back to the shop.
I'll go with you if you like.
The shops are easy to get to if you park near the station.
We don't have to go out if you're not feeling up to it.
If you're ready before eight, we can catch the early train.
You have to practise if you want to learn a musical instrument.

2 1 if 2 when 3 when 4 if 5 if 6 when 7 if 8 when 9 when 10 if

3 1 say; will scream 2 will be; manages 3 come; will cook 4 will need; go
5 will miss; move 6 wash; will dry 7 will be; doesn't come 8 get; will phone
9 look; will find 10 will be; gets

5 Pete.

258–259 **1** 1 would look; had
2 would be; didn't see
3 would be; didn't get
4 knew; would go
5 would you do; won
6 would be; used
7 were not; would show
8 had; would make
9 loved; would buy
10 would help; asked
11 was/were not; would tidy
12 had; would show
13 had; would send
14 would you go; needed
15 Would you mind; went
16 came; would you have
17 would be; spent
18 would not do; did not have

2 *(Examples of possible answers)*
2 If I had a big house, I would invite lots of people.
3 If I had a yacht, I would go round the world.
4 If I had plenty of money, I would buy a horse.
5 If I didn't have a job, I'd be happier.
6 If I had more time, I'd study biology.

4 1 could/might play 2 might feel 3 might go 4 could/might get
5 could/might understand 6 might taste

260 **1** 1 comes 2 find 3 lived 4 arrived 5 We'll 6 would 7 would 8 will
9 will 10 stop

2 *(The most probable answers)*
1 live 2 lived 3 were 4 wake 5 declared 6 have 7 gave 8 thought
9 is 10 is 11 banned 12 have

261 **1** If I were a rabbit, I'd live in a hole.
If I were forty years younger, I'd go dancing all night.
If I were Moroccan, I'd speak Arabic.
If I were the manager, I'd give everybody ten weeks' holiday.
If it weren't so cold, I'd go for a walk.
If it were Sunday, I wouldn't be working.
If my nose were shorter, I'd be quite pretty.
If people were more sensible, there wouldn't be any wars.
If she were better-tempered, life in the office would be easier.

262–263 **1** 1 had known; would have invited
2 would have gone; hadn't been
3 had said; wouldn't have cooked
4 would have won; had played
5 hadn't cut; would have finished
6 hadn't invented; would have done
7 hadn't spent; wouldn't have been
8 wouldn't have got; had remembered
9 hadn't been; wouldn't have become
10 had had; would have sold
11 hadn't spent; would have had
12 wouldn't have caught; had taken
13 would have won; had run
14 would have got; had booked
15 would have been; had asked
16 had been; would have been

2 1 If he hadn't worked so hard, he wouldn't have passed his exams.
If he hadn't passed his exams, he wouldn't have gone to university.
If he hadn't gone to university, he wouldn't have studied languages.
If he hadn't studied languages, he wouldn't have learnt Chinese.
If he hadn't learnt Chinese, he wouldn't have gone to China.
If he hadn't gone to China, he wouldn't have gone climbing in Tibet.
If he hadn't gone climbing in Tibet, he wouldn't have tried to climb Everest.
If he hadn't tried to climb Everest, he wouldn't have disappeared ...
2 If he hadn't bought a bicycle, he wouldn't have gone for a ride in the country.
If he hadn't gone for a ride in the country, he wouldn't have fallen off.
If he hadn't fallen off, he wouldn't have woken up in hospital.
If he hadn't woken up in hospital, he wouldn't have met a beautiful nurse.
If he hadn't met the beautiful nurse, he wouldn't have written a bestselling novel
about her.
If he hadn't written the bestselling novel, he wouldn't have got rich.
If he hadn't got rich, he wouldn't have married the nurse and had three charming
children.
If he hadn't married the nurse and had the three children, he wouldn't have lived
happily ever after.

3 If Mary's mother hadn't gone out that evening, Mary wouldn't have cooked for
   herself.
   If she hadn't cooked for herself, she wouldn't have got interested in cooking.
   If she hadn't got interested in cooking, she wouldn't have opened a very successful
     restaurant.
   If she hadn't opened the restaurant, she wouldn't have had the Prime Minister as a
     customer.
   If she hadn't had the PM as a customer, he wouldn't have ordered mussels.
   If he hadn't ordered mussels, the mussels wouldn't have poisoned him.
   If the mussels hadn't poisoned him, he wouldn't have died.
   If he hadn't died, Mary wouldn't have gone to prison for life.

264 **1** He'll get thrown out of school unless he starts working.
      I always watch TV in the evenings unless I go out.
      Let's have dinner out – unless you're too tired.
      I'll see you at ten unless I phone to say I can't come.
      I'll tell you a good joke – unless you've heard it before.
      Things will go on getting worse unless there's a change of government.
      We're going to have a picnic unless it rains.
      You can have the last sausage unless the children want it.
      You can't open the door unless you know the code.

    2 3 You can have the car tonight unless Harriet needs it.
       5 I'm going to dig the garden this afternoon unless it rains.

265 **1** She's packing a German phrase book in case the hotel staff don't speak English.
      She's packing a pack of cards in case she meets people who play bridge.
      She's packing a racket in case there is a tennis court.
      She's packing a thick sweater in case the weather is cold.
      She's packing a swimsuit in case the hotel has a heated pool.
      She's packing aspirins in case the sun gives her a headache.
      She's packing binoculars in case she wants to go bird-watching.
      She's packing her address book in case she decides to send postcards.
      She's packing some books in case she has time to read.
      She's packing walking boots in case she wants to go walking.

    2 1 in case 2 if 3 if 4 in case 5 in case 6 if 7 if 8 in case

266–267 **1** 'It's time to clean the car.' 'I'd rather not clean it today.'
       'It's time to cook supper.' 'I'd rather have something cold.'
       'It's time to get a new fridge.' 'I'd rather go on using the old one ...'
       'It's time to get your hair cut.' 'I'd rather keep it long.'
       'It's time to go home.' 'I'd rather stay here for a bit longer.'
       'It's time to invite the Harrises.' 'I'd rather invite the Johnsons.'
       'It's time to plan our trip to Scotland.' 'I'd rather go to Wales.'
       'It's time to see the dentist.' 'I'd rather see her next year.'
       'It's time to start work on the garden.' 'I'd rather start next week.'

    2 2 It's time she got her hair cut.   7 It's time he grew up.
       3 It's time we had a holiday.   8 It's time we painted the kitchen.
       4 It's time you cut the grass.   9 It's time he got/bought a new car.
       5 It's time you washed that sweater.   10 It's time that team won a match.
       6 It's time you stopped smoking.

    3 2 No, I'd rather we talked tomorrow.   7 I'd rather you asked him.
       3 I'd rather you came at ten.   8 I'd rather he stayed in.
       4 I'd rather you didn't.   9 I'd rather they brought their own.
       5 I'd rather she worked with Maggie. 10 I'd rather they did something about
       6 I'd rather you cooked tonight.   the homeless.

268–269 **1**   2 I wish I spoke Russian.
  3 I wish I had a car.
  4 I wish I was/were hard-working.
  5 I wish I was/were good at sport.
  6 I wish I liked dancing.

  7 I wish it didn't rain all the time.
  8 I wish she didn't work on Sundays.
  9 I wish I could eat eggs.
  10 I wish the radio worked.

2   2 I wish it would snow.
  3 I wish the phone wouldn't keep
      ringing.
  4 I wish the baby would stop crying.
  5 I wish the kettle would boil.

  6 I wish the traffic lights would go green.
  7 I wish your mother would write.
  8 I wish Pat would find a job.
  9 I wish the exam results would come.
  10 I wish spring would come.

4   I wish I'd chosen a different career.
  I wish I'd done more travelling when I
      had the chance.
  I wish I'd gone to a better school.
  I wish I'd gone to bed earlier last night.
  I wish I hadn't got married when I was
      eighteen.

  I wish I hadn't told him the truth.
  I wish I'd saved money when I was
      earning a good salary.
  I wish I'd studied harder at university.
  I wish I'd taken better care of my teeth.

270–271 **1**   *(Examples of possible answers)*
  Do you know a shop which sells good coffee?
  I know somebody who could mend that chair.
  I want some plates which can go in the microwave.
  I was at school with the man who is driving that taxi.
  I'd like to speak to the person who deals with exports.
  She's got friendly with a boy who lives next door.
  The police haven't found the man who stole my car.
  There's some cheese in the fridge which needs to be eaten.
  We've got some light bulbs which last for years.
  This is the switch which isn't working.

3   1 The people who live in Greece speak Greek.
  2 The language that people speak in Hungary is called Hungarian.
  3 The language that people speak in China is called Chinese.
  4 The people who live in Italy speak Italian.
  5 The people who live in Turkey speak Turkish.
  6 The language that people speak in Algeria is called Arabic.
  7 The language that (some) people speak in Scotland is called Scots Gaelic.
  8 The people who live in Holland speak Dutch.
  9 The language that (some) people speak in Ireland is called Irish.
  10 The people who live in Portugal speak Portuguese.
  11 The language that (some) people speak in Wales is called Welsh.
  12 The language that people speak in Japan is called Japanese.

5   All the poetry that he wrote was destroyed in a fire.
  At school I learnt nothing that was useful to me.
  I've told you everything that happened.
  Nothing that she said made any difference.
  It's the best western film that was ever made.
  The most useful thing that you can do is leave now.
  This is the only hire car that I could get.
  You can have everything that you want.

272–273 **1**   **DIY**   The relative pronoun can be left out in sentences 1, 2 and 6.
  Rule 4 is correct.

2   1 S   2 O   3 S   4 O   5 O   6 S   7 O   8 S   9 O   10 O

3 2 Our doctor is a person I really respect.
4 I've lost that nice ring Bill gave me.
5 It's a book everybody talks about and nobody reads.
7 That's the man I wanted to see.
9 He keeps telling you things you already know.
10 They never thanked me for the money I sent them.

4 1 Here's the paper you asked me to get you.
2 We went to see the film you recommended, but we didn't think much of it.
3 The car my sister bought last month has broken down four times already.
4 The actor you didn't recognise on television last night was Kiefer Sutherland.
5 Only a very few of the friends Jane had at school went on to university.
6 The operation my father had for his heart problem was only a partial success.
7 The essay Mark wrote while we were on holiday has won a prize in the school competition.
8 Some of the friends my daughter brings home look as though they never wash.

274 **1** Did you read about what happened to poor Harry?
He just teaches you what you already know.
What I want to know is where's my car gone?
The dog can have what I don't eat.
The holiday wasn't at all what I expected.
They hadn't got what she asked for.
You misunderstood – that isn't what I meant.
What you said made me very happy.

275 **1** *(Examples of possible answers)*
2 A good parent is one whose children are happy.
3 A good gardener is one whose plants are healthy.
4 A good doctor is one whose patients get better.
5 A good writer is one whose books are successful.
6 A good teacher is one whose students learn things.
7 A good tourist guide is one whose tourists see interesting places.
8 A good cook is one whose food tastes nice.

2 1 Anton, whose brother Fritz helps him run the sports shop, lives with Marika, whose sister Anneliese also helps out in the sports shop.
2 Anneliese has a younger brother Max, whose wife Paula works in the restaurant run by Anton's other brother Toni, whose girlfriend Heidrun is an instructor at the ski school.
3 The person in charge of the ski school at the moment is Klaus, whose wife Monika works part-time for the baker down the road, Karsten, whose daughter Liesl runs the pizzeria.
4 Monika also helps in the bar, the 'Happy Skier', which is run by Erwin, whose uncle Erich runs a hotel, in partnership with Klaus's brother Paul, whose wife Christiane was national ice-dancing champion in her younger days.

276–277 **1** **DIY** The ones in the 'a' sentences.

2 **DIY** 1 The 'b' sentences.
2 To show that they are not an essential part of the sentences – they can be separated.
3 Identifying clauses (the ones in the 'a' sentences).
4 Identifying clauses.
5 In a formal style.

3 1 No change possible.
2 People that don't answer letters
   annoy me.
3 What happened to the oranges
   I bought yesterday?
4 No change possible.
5 No change possible.
6 No change possible.
7 I like a film that has ...
8 No change possible.
9 Do you remember those people we
   met in Corfu?
10 No change possible.
11 No change possible.
12 No change possible.

4 1 which 2 what 3 what 4 which 5 what 6 which 7 which 8 what
9 which 10 which

278 **1** 1 Who's that good-looking man talking to Alison?
2 Luggage left unattended will be taken away by police.
3 Left-handed children forced to write with their right hands often develop
   psychological problems.
4 The nurse looking after my aunt is very kind to her.
5 All the rubbish floating in the sea is a real danger to health.
6 Ham made in the traditional way costs more, but tastes better.
7 Women tourists wearing trousers are not allowed in the temple.
8 James thought that the man with his girlfriend was her brother.
9 The man bitten by my neighbour's dog was her husband's boss.

2 1 I keep having a dream in which there's a woman standing with her back to me.
2 James said he heard a shot fired in the street.
3 Are those your trousers hanging over the balcony?
4 They live in a beautiful old house built 300 years ago.
5 The Navajo are famous for beautiful jewellery made of silver and turquoise.
6 Passengers standing on Platform 2 are asked to keep behind the yellow line.
7 Pauline has a very strange old painting of a woman holding a small dog.

279 **1** 1 which 2 what 3 that 4 what 5 that 6 which 7 which 8 that
9 what 10 that

2 1 who 2 – 3 that 4 that *(informal) or* who 5 which 6 – 7 who 8 –
9 that 10 which

3 'I'll discuss it with you,' she said, in a voice that could have been used ...
A politician is a statesman who approaches every question ...
Any man who hates dogs and babies can't be all bad.
Anyone who has been to an English public school will feel ...
Consultants are people who borrow your watch ...
No man can lose what he never had.
Nothing that is worth knowing can be taught.

280–281 **1** **DIY** 2

2 1 The earrings which/that he gave her for Christmas ...
2 The fax which/that he got that morning ...
3 The sofa which/that we bought last year ...
4 The people whom/that he had hoped to introduce Lee to ...
5 The flat which/that the terrorists hid the guns in ...
6 The song which/that she could not remember the name of ...

3 1 The rosebush.
2 The tall men are the nephews; Duncan and Jack are the uncles.
3 The man my mother was working for.
4 No.
5 (People from) the newspaper.
6 Police.

4   1 A man I met ...   2 The dress ...   3 The little flat ...   4 A very ordinary-looking
woman ...   5 Some Polish people ...

282–283 **1**   1 Whoever   2 whatever   3 whatever/whichever   4 wherever   5 whenever
6 However   7 whoever   8 However/Whenever   9 whoever   10 Whenever

2   1 Send it to whoever pays the bills.
2 Whatever is in that box is making ...
3 People always want more, however rich they are.
4 However you travel, it'll take ...
5 Whatever you say, I don't think ...
6 Whichever room you use, make sure ...
7 Whatever problems you have, you can always come ...
8 Whoever phoned just now was very polite.
9 Whenever I see you I feel nervous.
10 Whatever you do, I'll love you.

3   1 No matter what   2 No matter where   3 No matter how   4 No matter what
5 No matter when   6 No matter how

4   Whether he's lying or telling the truth, it's a wonderful story.
Whether we tell her now or later, she's not going to be pleased.
Whether you're a beginner or an expert, you'll learn something ...
Whether you ski downhill or cross-country, the equipment costs a lot.
Whether you like her or dislike her, you have to admire her.

284 **1**   1 –   2 at   3 –   4 at   5 on   6 into   7 on   8 of   9 –   10 into   11 in
12 –   13 of   14 in   15 in   16 to   17 –   18 for   19 after   20 to   21 –
22 to   23 for   24 of   25 for   26 of   27 for   28 in   29 into   30 of
31 by   32 In   33 in   34 in   35 in   36 on

2   **DIY**

> **Rule**
> at + clock time
> in + part of a day
> on + part of a particular day
> on + particular day
> at + weekend, public holiday
> in + longer period

3   4 on

4   1 at   2 on   3 in   4 in   5 on   6 in   7 –   8 – (or at)   9 at   10 –   11 –
12 on

285 **1**   **DIY**   *At* and *in* are used for **position**.
To is used for **movement**.

2   laugh; look; point; shoot; smile; wave
Shouting at and *throwing at* are aggressive.

3   1 in   2 to   3 at   4 at/in   5 to   6 to   7 at   8 to   9 at   10 to   11 at
12 to   13 to   14 in

286 **1**   **DIY**   *By* is used: 3 to say that **something will happen at or before** a certain
moment.
Until is used: 1 to say that **a situation will continue up to** a certain moment.

2   1 until   2 by   3 by   4 until   5 by   6 by   7 Until   8 by   9 by   10 until

287 **1** (*for* and *during*) **DIY** *For* tells you **how long**. *During* tells you **when**.

2 1 during 2 for; during 3 during 4 for 5 during 6 for

1 (*opposite* and *in front of*) **DIY** The **bus stop** is *opposite* the house; the **car** is *in front of* the house.

2 1 opposite 2 In front of 3 in front of 4 opposite 5 in front of 6 opposite

288 **1** **DIY** We say *among* a group, crowd or mass of things that are not seen separately.
We say *between* two or more clearly separate people or things.
We say *between* things on two sides.

2 1 between 2 between 3 between 4 among

3 1 between 2 among 3 between 4 among 5 among 6 between
7 among 8 between 9 between 10 among

289 **1** 1 'What are you thinking about?'   6 'What did she hit him with?'
2 'Who did you buy it from?'   7 'Who does your father work for?'
3 'Who did she send it to?'   8 'Who did you make it for?'
4 'What will you carry it in?'   9 'What's the book about?'
5 'What can I eat it with?'   10 'Who were you talking to?'

2 (*Examples of possible answers*)
1 'What are you waiting for?'   6 'What are you looking at?'
2 'What are you worried about?'   7 'What are you looking for?'
3 'What were you talking about?'   8 'What are you interested in?'
4 'Who were you speaking to?'   9 'Who are you writing to?'
5 'Who do you work for?'   10 'What are you thinking about?'

3 (*Examples of possible answers*)
What is she waiting for?   Who did you have lunch with?
What were you listening to?   Who did you buy that car from?
Who do you usually play tennis with?   Who is Anne in love with?
What country do you come from?   What did you change your job for?
Who is that letter from?   What are you studying English for?
Who did you get it from?

290–291 **1** A cup is something that you drink out of.
A picture is something that you can look at.
A tap is something that water comes out of.
A toy is something that a child plays with.
A vase is something that you put flowers in.
A window is something that you can look through.

2 1 things that you bite with (B)   6 a thing that you hang clothes on (D)
2 something that you sleep in (C)   7 liquid that you wash dishes with (H)
3 something that you put things on (E)   8 something that you can start a fire
4 something that you put valuables in (G)   with (A)
5 a thing that you clean your teeth with (F)

4 3 somebody (that) I have great respect for   5 the problem (that) I was worried about
4 the girl (that) I was writing to   6 a car (that) I paid too much for

5 John is the man (that) Bill plays chess with / Sally is married to.
Anne is the woman (that) Ron plays chess with / Peter is married to / Bill works with.
Alice is the woman (that) Peter plays chess with / Bill is married to / Sally works with.
Mary is the woman (that) Sally plays chess with / Ron works with.
Sue is the woman (that) Ron is married to / Peter works with.

Bill is the man (that) John plays chess with / Alice is married to / Anne works with.
Ron is the man (that) Anne plays chess with / Sue is married to / Mary works with.
Peter is the man (that) Alice plays chess with / Anne is married to / Sue works with.
Sally is the woman (that) Mary plays chess with / John is married to / Alice works with.

292   **1**   1 operated on   2 talked/spoken about   3 spoken/talked to   4 slept in
5 sat on/in   6 paid for   7 heard of/from   8 played with *or* spoken/talked to
9 looked at *or* spoken/talked to

    2   *(Examples of possible answers)*
Who was America/Australia/penicillin/electricity discovered by?
Who was the novel *Anna Karenina* / *Hamlet* / *Happy Birthday to You* written by?
Who was radio/television invented by?
Who was the film *The Birds* directed by?
Who was the Eiffel Tower / the Taj Mahal built by?
Who was the Mona Lisa painted by?

293   **1**   1 She's nice to talk to.   6 The river was difficult to swim across.
2 He's difficult to live with.   7 Her village is hard to get to.
3 My brother's impossible to argue with.   8 He's very easy to get on with.
4 Those old trains aren't very pleasant   9 Water-colours are difficult to paint with.
   to travel in.   10 She's interesting to work with.
5 Ice isn't easy to drive on.

    2   *(Examples of possible answers)*
A broken cup is hard to drink out of.
A broken fork is difficult to eat with.
A cushion is comfortable to sit on.
A small hard chair is uncomfortable to sit on.
A warm bath is nice to lie in.
Baby animals are nice to play with.
Classical music is interesting to listen to.
Family problems can be difficult to talk about.
Lectures are often hard to listen to.
People who travel a lot can be interesting to talk to.

    3   *(Examples of possible answers)*
A very small spoon is hard to eat with.
Shoes that are too small are uncomfortable to walk in.
A hard bed is uncomfortable to lie on.
A noisy hotel room is difficult to sleep in.
A broken pencil is hard to write with.

294–295   **1**   1 a hundred   2 one thousand, four hundred and fifty pounds   3 a thousand
4 three thousand, one hundred and forty-four   5 one dollar (and) eighty-five (cents)
6 one thousand pounds

    2   1 hundred   2 million   3 hundred   4 millions of   5 Thousands of   6 dozen

    3   second; third; fourth; fifth; sixth; seventh; eighth; ninth; tenth; twelfth; sixteenth;
twentieth; twenty-first; thirtieth; hundredth; thousandth

    4   1 10 April 1996
2 17 September 1911
3 16 June 1979
4 the sixteenth of May / May the sixteenth, nineteen seventy
5 the twelfth of March / March the twelfth, nineteen ninety-three
6 the fourteenth of January / January the fourteenth, nineteen eighty-six

296–298

1
1 I'm tired.
2 She's French.
3 She's forgotten.
4 They've finished.
5 I thought you'd left.
6 We'll tell you tomorrow.
7 I wish he'd stop.
8 How's your mother?
9 Nobody's perfect.
10 My car's broken down.
11 You needn't worry.
12 I can't swim.
13 The door won't close.
14 It doesn't matter.
15 I haven't forgotten.
16 I'm not sorry.
17 Why aren't you in bed?
18 Don't you like this?

2
1 ... where she's staying.
4 ... No, I haven't.
5 It isn't true. / It's not true.
8 I don't believe they're fresh.
9 ... if you can't come.
10 ... No, I can't ...
Contraction not possible in 2, 3, 6 and 7.

3
1 there's 2 you've 3 he's 4 can't 5 he'd 6 I'll 7 that's 8 we've

298–302

1
nouns: uncountable soup, petrol, wood; **singular countable** suggestion, suit, book, brother, problem; **plural countable** potatoes, buildings, people, rules
adjectives: ordinary small, cold, stupid, high, new, dry; **comparative** more interesting, older, younger; **superlative** best, cheapest, worst
determiners: articles a, the; **possessives** my, his, our; **demonstratives** this, those, these; **quantifiers** (a) few, some, many, no

2
other personal pronouns: me, he, him, her, we, they, them
other possessive pronouns: his, hers, ours, theirs
other reflexive pronouns: yourself, himself, herself, ourselves, yourselves, themselves

3
lost, rains, open, tastes, won, got

4
1 future simple (*aux.* will)
2 present progressive (*aux.* is)
3 past perfect (*aux.* had)
4 simple present
5 simple past
6 future progressive (*aux.* will be)
7 past progressive (*aux.* was)
8 future perfect (*aux.* will have)
9 present perfect (*aux.* has)
10 simple past (*aux.* did)

5
conditional would ... stop   **-ing form** smoking   **infinitive** stop
perfect infinitive have started   **past participle** ordered, started
imperative shut (up), leave   **active verb** smoke, would ... stop, could, talk, say, shut (up), leave, don't ... think, 'll stop, suppose; should ... have started
passive verb 'm ordered

6
prepositions: at, with, by, for, in
adverbs: usually, yesterday, suddenly, terribly, loud
Out is an adverb particle.

7
1 **subject** Jake   **direct object** songs
2 **subject** I   **direct object** my address   **indirect object** Monica
3 **subject** you   **direct object** the time   **indirect object** me
4 **subject** you   **direct object** what sort of books
5 **subject** you   **direct object** a postcard, time   **indirect object** me

8
1 pretty 2 tired 3 a student 4 sorry

9
conjunctions: 1 while 2 if 3 where 4 when 5 before 6 although
subordinate clauses: 1 while I'm trying ... 2 if you stay ... 3 where you were staying 4 When I get back 5 Before you went out 6 Although it was snowing
interrogative main clauses: 3, 5 **affirmative main clauses:** 1, 4
negative main clauses: 2, 6

Index